The Lives and Legends of Jacques Lacan

THE LIVES AND LEGENDS OF
JACQUES LACAN

Catherine Clément
Translated by Arthur Goldhammer

New York   Columbia University Press   1983

Columbia University Press is grateful to the French Ministry of Culture for
its assistance in the preparation of this translation.

Library of Congress Cataloging in Publication Data

Clément, Catherine, 1939–
The lives and legends of Jacques Lacan.

Bibliography: p.
Includes index.
1. Lacan, Jacques, 1901–   —Addresses, essays,
lectures.   2. Psychoanalysts—France—Biography.
3. Psychoanalysis—Addresses, essays, lectures.
I. Title.
BF175.C5613   1983   150.19′0924   82-4283
ISBN 0-231-05568-4

Columbia University Press
New York   Guildford, Surrey

CONTENTS

TRANSLATOR'S INTRODUCTION

In French this book is written in a brisk, colloquial style. Incomplete sentences of the sort common in everyday conversation abound, as do allusions to events familiar to Frenchmen, or at any rate to Parisians attuned to the vicissitudes of intellectual and political life. I have tried to retain the colloquial flavor, as far as English permits. I have also tried to explain, succinctly, allusions that might be lost on the reader unfamiliar with French politics and intellectual fashions. I felt, too, that it was necessary, even at the risk of seeming leaden and humorless, to explain the many French puns and word-plays that come up in the course of the discussion.

This brings me to a further problem of translation. The work of Jacques Lacan is fairly well known in this country, and some of it has been translated into English, most notably the selection from *Ecrits,* translated by Alan Sheridan and published by Norton. Normally, where such a standard translation exists, I would use it in rendering citations from Lacan's work into English. Here, however, while drawing heavily on Mr. Sheridan's excellent work, I have preferred to give my own translations of many passages. For the reader interested in comparing my translations with the existing ones, I have given page references to the original French edition of *Ecrits* as well as to the Norton translation whenever possible.

Readers of Lacan in English translation will know that it is customary to leave certain terms untranslated: *jouissance, méconnaissance, objet-petit-a,* and so forth. It is my understanding that Lacan wished this convention to be observed. I have gone along with this practice, though not without misgivings, except in the case of *jouissance*. Ms. Clément uses the word in one place to refer to orgasm, in another to refer to religious ecstasy. Lacan was not the first to link the two; Bernini's statue of Saint Theresa translates the metaphor into stone. Nevertheless, to obscure the fact that the French word has two distinct connotations would only mystify the English reader, and I have dotted the i's where I thought it necessary to do so.

The Lives and Legends of Jacques Lacan

You think I came to play with you, but in fact I came to turn the game upside down. You think I'm cheating because you think I'm in the game—you don't see that I'm not. You thought you had me and I jumped you, but I didn't do it on purpose. I'm always getting away from you, but I don't do it on purpose. You don't look for me where I am when I'm there, and you don't watch where I'm going. I win hands down every time, and if I lose it's only for a little change of pace. Like a flame crazy about itself, I creep and then I leap and then I subside into ashes, from which I shall rise again when I please. I die knowing that I shall live again. And yet in dying I bleed; but you don't see the blood; and when I was bleeding you didn't see it.

Montherlant,
Le Génie et les fumisteries du Divin

LISTEN, WOODCUTTER,
STAY YOUR SAW A WHILE

In 1899, Freud, who was about to publish *The Interpretation of Dreams* and knew that it would become the fundamental work of psychoanalysis, decided to date the book 1900, anticipating by a few months the advent of the new century, our own. In the following year Jacques Lacan was born in France. He is thus almost as old as the century. [Lacan died in October 1981, shortly after this book was first published in French—trans.]

One day, at the age of seventy-nine, he decided to dissolve his school of psychoanalysis, which he prided himself on having founded. This aging figure had become the center of a fierce intrigue, notable for the distress it caused his disciples. He was by now one of the most illustrious of French psychoanalysts. Behind him was a solid body of work and teaching; he had made a name for himself. He was loved by some, hated by others. But his disciples were worried: what would become of them once the master was gone? In their agitated enthusiasm they became conservative idolators of Lacan's theory, jealous to defend his minutest utterance, as if the poor man did not have the right to make any statement that was not pure gold. In muffled tones they deplored the onset of old age, signs of whose ravages were beginning to appear. Until one day the old man shook them all off with one furious shudder, scattering the swarm of hangers-on that buzzed around him as one might chase away flies. The general public took a lively interest in the affair, though most people knew very little about Lacan, beyond his name, and understood nothing of a theory whose secrecy was jealously protected in the most traditional way, by shrouding it in esoteric language. Perhaps they sensed in some vague way that what was going on was a life and death struggle, a battle for survival.

And in a way it was just that. Lacan was fighting for his life. He shed his old skin as he had done on many previous occasions. But he held on to what was essential: his glory, whose luster he would not allow to be diminished by those who called him "old." And his work, which was being dispensed piecemeal by those who repeated his dicta badly and too often, who had been heaping discredit on his teachings for some time. I felt like saying to all of them, to all who had been sneering at the old man, what Ronsard said long ago to the woodcutter in the forest of Gastine:

> Those are not trees you're cutting down:
> Don't you see the blood trickling
> From the nymphs who lived beneath the bark?

A thinker cannot be put to death. He survives his idolators. Not because he is the master and they are the disciples—no, not that. What could possibly be more deadly than all those disciples dedicated to immortalizing Lacan, who repeatedly told them that he was not their master and wanted no part of their adoration? A thinker cannot be put to death if he has really done his job of thinking. No matter how his life comes to an end, whether by old age, accident, suicide, madness, or crime, his thought will have lived and will go on living. In spite of his disciples, in spite of itself.

Lives and Legends of Jacques Lacan: my intention was to write a sacrilegious work, to write of Lacan as if his old age were no longer an issue, to go beyond the life and death of the man and treat him as I always experienced him, as a shaman, a sorcerer possessed by a poetic inspiration—which he was at least as much as he was the unbending founder of a new psychoanalytic theory (there can be no doubt that he was this too). I hoped to anticipate history, writing, not without affection, in a style that would run the gamut of tenses from past to future. I wanted to speak of Lacan in the past—the simple past as it is sometimes called; in the pluperfect—more than perfect; in the imperfect, so aptly named; and in the future anterior, which fulfills destiny while leaving open the possibility of the future. Lacan the shaman flirted with immortality: there are intimations of immortality in his thought, one of the most powerful and misunderstood intellectual achievements of our time. Lately, the misunderstanding of that achievement has been compounded by the fact that Lacan's thought, now fashionable, has been reduced to jargon, turned into a parody of itself.

Lives and Legends of Jacques Lacan—let me end this introduction with the last line of Ronsard's poem, which also deserves a place in the story of Lacan:

The substance remains and the form is lost.

CHAPTER 1

LOVE'S PLEASURES

. . . last but a moment, or the fascination of the Seminar; Lacan the Christian versus Freud the Jew; the style of a poet and the attraction of a shaman; the iron skeleton.

Spring 1980

In the spring of 1980 the magazine *Actuel* published an issue devoted to the adventures of Jacques Lacan, psychoanalyst.

My daughter read it and loved it.

There, on the cover of the magazine, was a fellow wearing a blue and white striped blazer, his arm poised in anger, ready to smash a stack of dishes. Glaring furiously, he had a demented look, with his mouth wide open. "The Adventures of Jacques Lacan, Psychoanalyst" came complete with cartoon drawings—very nice old-fashioned cartoons in a sensational style—depicting the same fellow counting bank notes, rolling on the ground, breaking more dishes, always with his mouth open. The fellow, of course, was supposed to be Lacan.

In the photographs he came across mostly as a pretty good sort. Dignified, with thick hair and a look as blank as a wall, his mouth is generally closed—and yet he was a man who really loved to talk. Behind him in many of the pictures is the eternal blackboard covered with circles, lines, mathematical symbols. These rare photographs resemble Lacan the way old family portraits resemble the dear departed relative, that is to say, scarcely at all. They are frozen, reverential, beautiful. He did not like photographs.

My daughter, as I was saying, ate it up. She knew Lacan by way of a sort of family mythology, through her parents' talk about him. Was he a family friend? Not exactly—more a name that came up often around the dinner table. My daughter is now fifteen. Nothing upsets her; she is as impassive as Lacan in the photographs. Time marches on, for her, for me, for other people.

We were slow to recover from the defeat of the left [after May 1968—trans.] and never recovered from its disintegration [an allusion to the breakup of the Socialist-Communist alliance in 1978—trans.]. The world was slipping through our fingers. Burials followed one another in rapid succession. First came the death of Marx, it seems a long time ago. Pious hands continued to lay poisonous wreaths on his tomb, however, and these continued to bring forth new blossoms. Freud too was in his death throes. Ideas were rotting like flowers left too long in the vase. A few big names from the halcyon days of yore remained alive: Lévi-Strauss, Dumézil, Lacan. Barthes died at the height of his glory. Pierre Goldman and Nikos Poulantzas also died. Lacan was getting old.

He had just turned eighty when the first out-and-out attack on him appeared. It scored a tremendous success. Previous criticism had been limited to a few vague strictures from within the psychoanalytic milieu, circulated in mimeographed form, plus a few very serious and very sad articles by colleagues who disagreed with him. People knew these battles were raging, but nobody paid any attention. It had all been going on for so long. Lacan seemed to be aging very gently, still surrounded by old enmities that kept him warm and comfortably ensconced in his seminar, which continued without incident.

This first critical sally, a pamphlet entitled "L'Effet 'Yau de Poêle," treated Lacan as if he were a young man, attacking him with a ferocious vigor usually reserved for thinkers in the prime of life. The author, though in fact a rather mild fellow, had always detested Lacan.[1] He was an editor of *Les Temps modernes* [the magazine founded by Sartre after World War II—trans.] and part of Sartre's entourage. Sartre too was getting on in years but his audience was growing as his body declined. He was blind and could no longer write and scarcely even walk, but his glory had never been greater, as the reaction to his death made clear. His young friend started the ball rolling with his attack on Lacan: the time had come.

This in itself would not have been worthy of the cover of *Actuel* if the whole matter had not quickly become topical, a burning issue of the day. Lacan, an old and rather dignified man largely forgotten outside his own field, was suddenly a name on everyone's tongue. One fine day in January he let it be known that he was dissolving his school of psychoanalysis.[2] Of course Freud had done the same thing in his day, but at least Freud went about it in the proper manner. It was Freud's custom to send the members of his association a short but courteous letter suggesting that they not come back if their heart was no longer in it. Lacan did the same, but in his own inimitable style: he published an open letter in which, as was his custom, he affectionately insulted his flock. He said it straight out: "I am speaking without the least hope—of making myself understood especially." Those who no longer pleased him, and whom he no longer pleased, he sent packing, not without a wry humor. "I don't need many people," he wrote. "And there are people I don't need." He ended by pulling out all the stops: "I'm leaving them up the creek so they can show me what they can do, besides hang on my neck and turn my teaching, every bit of which is so carefully weighed, to water."[3] So much for the Ecole freudienne de Paris. The uproar was enormous.

And a strange thing happened: the commotion made its way into the media, though there was no lack of other news. The Soviet Union had just invaded Afghanistan, the Iranian revolution was turning sour, and President Carter was committing blunder after blunder just months before the American elections. But in France everyone was bored stiff. Amid the tedium of Communist attacks on the Socialists, internal dissension in all the parties, and clarion calls from dissidents on both sides, what soon came to be known as the "Lacan affair" filled a void. It became a major item. Lacanian psychoanalysts were flabbergasted. Their school had been dissolved, they didn't exist any longer, but at last they were being talked about. Sporting knowing smiles and repeating bad puns, they went hat in hand looking for a vacant newspaper column where they might place "their" article. Lacan had asked them to write to him personally to apply for admission to the new school that no one doubted he would soon start. So they wrote. But not merely to Jacques Lacan, rue de Lille. They wrote publicly. They wanted to participate in the ascendancy of their Master, and if he had written to the newspapers (which hastened to publish his letter), why shouldn't they? So they went to the press with their epistles, with their startling new revelations, convinced that they were going to shed new light on this murky affair. In speaking about Lacan the papers were really speaking about them. Their moment of glory had come. Of course the papers were only interested in Lacan. And Lacan said virtually nothing, refused all interviews, made no public appearances, and released only tiny fragments from previously delivered lectures. In so doing he kept faith not only with himself but also with all the clowns turning somersaults around him—indeed, he kept faith with them more than they kept faith with themselves.

A few days after his original letter, in an announcement to the members of his dissolved school, Lacan put it this way: "It's the whirlwind I'm counting on."[4] He got it in spades. It was overwhelming. And he made no secret of the fact that he was tired— of being overwhelmed. That he was suffocated by love, like a child so stuffed with food by its mother that it becomes anorexic to the verge of starvation as a way of demonstrating to its mother that it wants to be hungry. Nearly eighty, Lacan hungered after being hungry. He had had enough of his disciples' treacly love, enough of disciples who, because he was getting old, were beginning, unwittingly perhaps, to mummify him, to bury him alive. Their respectful affection and their adulation he dismissed as "glue"—in French, *"la colle,"* close to l'Ecole, the school.

This is how he put it: "The Other is missing. That strikes me as funny too. I'm holding on, though, which dazzles you, but that's not why I'm doing it. . . . If I ever do leave you, tell yourselves that it's in order to be Other at last (*afin-d'être Autre enfin*)." [5]

For it was his role in life to be the fixed beacon, the reference point, and he had had enough of being everyone's Other. So he left—like de Gaulle. In that same year, the tenth anniversary of the General's death, there was a nostalgic and chauvinistic melody in the air that evoked his spirit. Lacan did the same thing in his analyst's domain: in slipping away he revived the theater of Baden-Baden or Colombey-les-Deux-Eglises. But the plot quickly thickened. After the initial shock some exclaimed "At last!"—as though all along they had expected nothing else—and enthusiastically followed their master in his next venture, the founding of the new group La Cause freudienne. Others were of no mind to allow themselves to be dissolved like so much soap powder. They brought suit under the Law of Associations of 1901, on the grounds that the members of a collective enterprise have something to say about the end of that enterprise—they were fighting a duel to save their honor. But Lacan formed a group to take charge of the dissolution of his school and let the more dynamic members go about it as they wished: they called the internal newsletter established for the purpose "Delenda"—*Delenda est Carthago, delenda est l'Ecole freudienne.* Rome and Lacan—the same battle.

Never have there been people so determined to deny their own existence. The subterranean disputes that had undermined the

Lacanian groups and motivated Lacan's decision raged on, but on new ground. Those who loved Lacan and wanted to dissolve the school fought with those no longer willing to suffer his authority: the stakes were a man, a name, a symbol. Everyone claimed to speak in Lacan's name. Everyone claimed to possess the truth of the moment: to dissolve or not to dissolve. A judgment was handed down. The lawyers won a compromise: The School would be dissolved, but only after due process, legally. A meeting was necessary. They were all there, lined up in rows in the chemistry department lecture hall, Lacan among them.

He walked as people of his age do walk, in brief, halting steps. He stared into space as he had always done. He looked as he always did, a little pale perhaps. His secretary walked alongside him as always. Nothing seemed to have changed. He had become an old man, indifferent and serene. The same man of whom the speakers on the platform spoke, presided over by a representative of the court, whose named seemed to have been chosen by fate: Attorney Zecri.

"I don't get it," my daughter interrupted.

"Zecri—Les Z'Ecrits de Jacques Lacan [Lacan's Writings, *Les Ecrits,* were published in French in 1966, in English in 1977; in French pronunciation liaison is made between the *s* of the definite article and the following noun if it begins with a vowel, so *Les Ecrits* and the name Zecri are assonant—trans.].

My daughter thought this was ridiculous. She didn't laugh. I had aged. So had Lacan: that was what was unacceptable. On the platform those disciples who refused to accept the unacceptable plaited the eternal laurel wreath that had always been his. Occasionally a speaker would address himself to Lacan, looking over in his direction, but Lacan did not so much as blink an eye. He was bored, everyone was bored, I was bored. The funeral ceremony finally drew to an end. One by one the Lacanians climbed the platform to cast a vote for or against the dissolution of their School.[6] I recognized almost all of them: my whole youth passed before me. That cardboard urn contained not only the ballots cast by the members of the dead School but also the ashes of "Lacan." He knew it. I don't think he gave a damn.

The Seminarists

In the sixties, the halcyon days of *Salut les copains,* Brigitte Bardot, and the early Fifth Republic, the small group of philosophy students of the Ecole normale supérieure to which I belonged began to hear reports of a magical figure. These rumors nettled us: the person in question was neither a *normalien* nor a philosopher nor an *agrégé* [that is, he had not taken the difficult *agrégation* examination, a prerequisite for appointment to the highest positions in the French educational system—trans.] nor a professor. But he was talked about. His writings passed from hand to hand and were disseminated everywhere. He was unlike anything we were familiar with: ours was a classical education, Plato-Spinoza-Descartes, and we had few resources with which to break out of its narrow confines. To be sure, for the sacrosanct *agrégation* we had to read Freud and Hegel, about whom Jean Hyppolite lectured to us with lisping enthusiasm. Freud contradicted the essence of the philosophical spirit: the dressing gown of classical reason was tattered. We were already beginning to suffocate with our humanities. But when it came to reading Lacan we were as impenetrable as a wall—we heaped insults on the man. And this, believe it or not, happened in Paris in the heyday of the "sixties."

In the great vaulted hall of the Hôpital Sainte-Anne, where we went to see the circus sideshow of madmen on display and where the psychiatrists responsible for "bringing out" their symptoms lined the psychotics up in preparation, we eyed a rather small man, who was speaking to the rest. He didn't say much, speaking slowly and in a rather soft voice before an audience of terrified young psychiatrists. From time to time Lacan raked them over the coals. They would start out stiff with stage fright and then suddenly the boom would be lowered. Department heads who terrorized their own subordinates with contemptuous authority quaked in their boots when they had to speak in front of Lacan. In 1964 Lacan moved to the Ecole normale supérieure; behind the move was a long story whose details we learned only much later. With Lacan near at hand we enjoyed the spectacle even more. Despite the practical jokes, hooting, and stink bombs with which the science students greeted his appearance, Lacan held his seminar every Wednesday. It wasn't long before he was filling the lecture hall. You had to get there quite early: an hour in advance was barely sufficient to get a seat. We listened to Lacan, we future professors, as though he offered a powerful antidote to the professorial word that it was our vocation to preach. May 1968 was not far off, but from where we stood nobody had the slightest inkling of what was to come. In form Lacan's teaching was entirely in keeping with the purest traditions of the French university, in whose crown it will remain one of the brightest jewels. But we had the exquisite sensation of tasting the forbidden fruit of a rhetoric that attacked our teachers precisely where our teachers bored us, with their classicism, their humanism, and their endless repetition. Even if we didn't always understand him, at least this fellow was saying something new, something romantic, something ascetic, something difficult. And this story too, believe it or not, took place in Paris.

The hall quickly filled to overflowing. Besides the psychoanalysts and the *normaliens,* curious at first and quickly conquered, there were actors and writers. With each new term new faces were added to the crowd. And with each new term Philippe Sollers [editor of the review *Tel Quel*—trans.] returned with his entourage, in which faces also changed at about the same pace: Sollers was already past master of what he himself later came to call the "permanent dissolution" of his group. Technological progress changed things a bit: now there were tape recorders and the room bristled with wires in which we happily tangled our feet. Near Lacan, his secretary, admirably impassive, stood watch, and a stenographer recorded the lectures on a stenographic machine as Lacan spoke. As if all this apparatus were not enough, people also took notes: some occasionally, others determined not to miss a thing, noting down every word, leaning over toward their neighbors if by chance a word or syllable escaped them. No politician ever had such minute attention paid to his every utterance. It sometimes took Lacan as long as an hour to warm up.

Seldom did we leave the auditorium without some aphorism capable of stimulating an almost indescribable state of meditative euphoria, which lasted for a good long while afterward. Little by little, hour by hour, week by week, there was woven in us an implacable mesh of language, unconscious but effective, that had the property of rendering all other modes of thought obsolete. Lacan's speech was slow, halting, marked by fleeting passages of brilliance, trenchant statements uttered in a low voice, word play that revealed a cutting sense of humor. His mind was curious and obsessed with myths. All this produced a frightful obscurity. We thought about what he had said but even more about the enigma of what he might have meant. In the end we forgot Lacan's thought and thought Lacan. We passed him on as the Greek rhetoricians probably passed on their teaching: bit by bit, by means of endless citation. True enough, this left no room for anything else. Anyone who did not immediately walk away in disgust was caught. This is how a dogma is born.

No doubt there was something monstrous about this, but this is the way the seminar worked, and the seminar was Lacan's major work. For he wrote little and published almost nothing: his thesis in medicine, a few articles for reviews and encyclopedias— that's about it. The rest—the *Ecrits,* despite the contradictory title, the *Seminars, Télévision*—is all taken from the spoken word. The message was delivered, transcribed, rewritten, either by himself or by his son-in-law, Jacques-Alain Miller, who was later criticized for his relationship to Lacan, often in rather vulgar terms. It was part of Lacan's strange fate not to have found any genuine interlocutors in his maturity. By Lacan's own admission

Miller was the primary one, and the son-in-law several times received written proof of his official recognition from Lacan.[7] That
didn't win him any friends either: Lacanians are like other people, envious, gossipy, and petty. All the more so, because for the
most part they remained astonishingly passive: Lacan conquered
his audiences but struck them dumb. His anxiety shrouded itself
too much in ceremony; his utterances were too prophetic. Imagine trying to talk to Moses on Mount Sinai.

Sometimes we were bored, terribly bored. It is the teacher's
lot, uttering his wisdom into a void that is all ears, to provoke
boredom. The best of his listeners knew how to recognize the
moment when inspiration was about to explode. It was a marvelous spectacle: if only one side of Lacan's genius were to endure, it would undoubtedly be his genius with the spoken word.
Sentences flew like arrows toward their prey. After a long arc of
periods they would suddenly tear open a bleeding wound. Sometimes they would turn somersaults of esoteric allusion before
homing in on their target. Lacan spoke as the hawk flies, circling
about an idea before grabbing it in a lightning swoop. Sometimes too he would fall silent. He seemed to hesitate. It was obvious that he did his thinking in public. And the pains he took
to prepare his "lectures" did not lessen the degree to which his
language was improvised.

As with any inspired preacher, some days nothing worked.
The magic evaporated like snow in the heat of the sun. There
was nothing there but a small man, who spoke in a rather soft
voice, and slowly.

In Andalusia bullfighting is an inspired art. Andalusian torea-
dors are not like other Spanish bullfighters, classical, courageous,
serious, or dramatic. To perform as their art requires, they need
a kind of magic. And no one but the bullfighter himself can supply that need.

One of them, Curro Romero, draws fanatical crowds of Span-
iards to his exhibitions. They await each new flick of the cape,
each new pass, which in an instant can have the entire crowd on

its feet shouting interminable olés! But in order for that to happen the *duende* must take a hand—the duende, or demon, which is nothing less than inspiration itself. The duende can be frightened off by a bull that comes in the wrong way, by an inopportune cloud, by a black cat crossing the road, or by nothing at all. Without the duende the stout toreador with the flat, dull face looks like a helpless clod. No one holds it against him. Everybody knows it isn't his fault. His duende has been gone for several years now. The fans wait unconcerned: there's always next year. This year in Seville the duende has returned: our man is off to a fresh start, he'll be able to keep his genius going for quite some time to come. In this idea of the duende there is something very much like an intimation of immortality: the inspired bullfighter has all the time in the world—more than a lifetime.

In Lacan's seminar too there was an intimation of immortality. Lacan too had all the time in the world. The idea of dissolving his school and starting a new one was dictated by inspiration. The uninspired will say, "To build is bad enough, but to plant at his age . . ." But this kind of whispering is of no concern to Lacan. He has all the time in the world.

"Mother, you poor thing, you were in love with him," my daughter says.

Yes, I loved him. Like most of my generation I was in love with an idea. Such fascination with an idea is irritating to those who do not share it. In comparison to one spellbound, the critical intelligence is like a prospective mother-in-law regarding the cad who is about to steal away her daughter: understanding nothing of the passion involved, the critic, asserting rights of ownership, cold-bloodedly dissects the affair. And in this case the critics were right: the whole Lacan phenomenon was a truly Parisian affair, a fashion, a folly, a kind of snobbery. They were right, except on one point: the reason for this collective passion, so much like love, remained inaccessible to all outside observers, even those who knew best what they were talking about. Lacan sometimes seemed to have a hard time putting up with this per-

manent adulation. At the end of each year he raised the possibility of ending the seminar: would it go on? But come fall he was
always there, ready to begin again. We were all relieved but at
the same time put upon: we would have to begin all over again.

Sure, it was love. When you're always on time for every appointment, when nothing can make you miss one, when you
leave disappointed sometimes but always enamoured, what else
can it be? I'm well aware that this sort of thing is no longer "in."
People call it "dogmatism." And it's true: love of this sort gives
rise to self-betrayal, intransigence, the end of intellectual independence. But it can also give rise to another kind of thought, a
thought that is at war with itself and that in the most favorable
of circumstances destroys its object. There remains a "hard core"
attached to the loved object—the object that originally elicited
love. And that hard core of my original love for Lacan is something I still carry with me, even if I have shed the husks, skins,
and shells that used to surround it.

But this love went the way of all the others. One day you
don't show up for an appointment—something else seems more
important. You feel guilty. It takes a long time to come to the
moment of final separation. Decade after decade, disciples left
Lacan and then began to hate him. Their attitude toward Lacan
is like that of ex-Communists toward the Party, and the reasons
are similar: the once-dominant figure has to be killed. As for
myself, my feeling of indebtedness in both cases is too great to
permit me to go to such lengths: I know where the myths are,
and where they were. I am grateful that they existed.

For it is an absolute rule that one never thinks alone. To think
with Lacan—to "think Lacan"—was no worse than to "think
Mao." It is scarcely surprising that those who rushed to follow
Mao were the same ones who used to trot along after Lacan. The
inner laws were the same. I don't think we have anything to be
ashamed of. This is the way minds are formed, and no mind ever
gives birth to itself. Whether it is nourished by a teacher, an author read and reread a hundred times over, an actor, or Lacan,

the story is the same. To have been formed by Lacan was no worse than to believe, as we are now advised by a mistaken ideology, that we can shape our own minds unaided. As though we were adults. In any body of thought there is an adolescent figure, never entirely effaced. And what if being adult simply meant no more thinking? Lacan's disciples all retained the fervor, the rage, the ebullient irritation, and the unbearable prejudices of adolescence. They were as fanatic as the fans of a pop star. But they did not grow old: Lacan preserved their youthfulness.

In May 1968, the master himself encountered serious personal difficulties. Vincennes did not spare Lacan, who was challenged and jeered as he systematized his attacks on the University without changing the form of his seminar one iota.[8] After May had come and gone, Lacan remained. But the revolutionary virus had infected the minds of his loyal following. He had impassively withstood the assaults of the "students," who in any case did not allow anyone but themselves to speak; but things did not go as smoothly within his own School. By degrees a shifting opposition to Lacan formed within the School, an opposition at first fleeting but later organized on an increasingly permanent footing. Some dared to make use of other texts and other ideas, despite repeated warnings to toe the line. There were dissidents. Felix Guattari gleefully explored Italy with Basaglia's help and North and South America with Bateson's. Françoise Dolto no longer made a secret of her Christian inspiration.[9] There were some who followed the evolution of Jacques Derrida, despite the interdiction.[10] And there were women with whom Lacan quarreled: Luce Irigaray and Michèle Montrelay, to name just two. He did not always treat the rebels well. There were internal battles. People were banished from the seminar. Some were held up to ridicule, intermittently at first, later in a more sustained manner.

One day the rumors began to change. Rumors had always circulated: *Actuel*'s special issue on Lacan was full of them. The journalist in charge of the investigation for the article planned to write a very accurate story about the very illustrious Doctor Lacan, not necessarily taking every piece of gossip about him at face value.[11] As a biographer, this reporter was full of good intentions. But everywhere he turned he had doors slammed in his face, as he himself recounts. No one would, or could, tell him anything specific, except for some bits and pieces out of *Who's Who* together with a few old articles that disclosed no secrets but only what was by this time public knowledge. There was nothing to go on but gossip. What was Lacan like when he was angry? What about Lacan as a seducer? What about the gold riding crop he was supposed to have sent to Jeanne Moreau? Lacan inside out, Lacan outside in. Lacan as charlatan: a crowd of patients milling about in his round waiting room, waiting quietly for hours for a session that lasted only a few minutes. Lacan and his secretary. According to one—accurate—rumor, an English colleague who came to visit was surprised, when Lacan came out to greet him, to be met with a cry of "Gloria," enigmatic to say the least. The English fellow was so surprised that he answered, mindlessly, "Gloria tibi, domine." Gloria was the first name of Lacan's secretary: the only religious incantation involved was in the mind of Lacan's hapless English colleague. A legend grew up around Lacan, as though he were a movie star, or an actress in the demimonde of the Gay Nineties. That was the way he acted when he entered the full lecture hall: nervous, treading carefully, he didn't look at anyone for fear of meeting too many glances, filled with either hatred or love.

But in January 1980 a different message made the rounds. Rumor had it that Lacan was dying. That he was suffering from a disease that affected his intellectual faculties. People were convinced that an appointment had been made with a neurologist, even that Lacan was about to be hospitalized, locked up. A sublime rumor, it announced that Lacan had been touched in the head. That he would end his days demented: somehow that was in keeping with the logic of his story, the story of a lengendary hero. For the legend included more than just grudges against Lacan and jokes about him. It obviously had to have its heroic battlefields, its great deeds, its secret exploits. But the legend never captured Lacan's real heroism: he is a reserved person. No one knew this story, told by someone close to him. During World War II Lacan's wife Sylvia committed an indiscretion: she declared herself to be Jewish at the behest of the "French" government. Lacan went to the Gestapo determined not to leave without his wife's dossier. He got it. And the daughter who was born to him he named Judith. Deliberately. The whole story was a secret. And his heroism still is: it was a private, bourgeois heroism. He never sought the attention of the media. He gave few interviews and appeared on television only once, for a program devoted to scientific research, in which he spoke directly to the camera. The director was Benoît Jacquot, who was shooting a very austere, very nice little film, very much in the style of Lacan's obstinate heroism.[12] Lacan made absolutely no concessions to his audience: it was sublime if you were disposed to like him, ridiculous if you didn't try to understand this poor old man with the outdated necktie, the very image of the big-shot doctor except that he talked like a poet.

He was a hero in the fifties when he set out to do battle against American-style psychoanalysis, which had invaded the Old World along with the liberation and the first oranges. He was a hero in the way he did battle, defensive at first, and later, when he no longer had a choice, offensive, pitted against the psychoanalytic establishment, which made him a permanent outcast with no hope of ever being taken back into the fold. Indeed he was forced to be a hero from the moment when, in 1953, he became a prize to be fought over by two camps: the medical establishment on the one side, and those in favor of opening psychoanalysis to nonphysicians on the other side, the mandarins versus the angry young men. He sometimes spoke as though he were the prince of Homburg of psychoanalysis: the hero who dreams of victory and of laurel wreaths but who is cast into prison for disobeying orders, despite his bravery. The positive side of the Lacan legend is as fascinating as the negative: the anger and the snide remarks are the counterpart of the hero's pride and courageous choices. The prince of Homburg is inseparable from the dear old clown with his too fancy suits and his knotted lace in lieu of necktie. I remember seeing him not ten years ago set himself a private test: at the foot of his apartment staircase, he took a deep breath— remember the man was seventy years old at the time—and like Tintin [a boy detective in French comic books] in short pants ran skipping up the stairs, just to prove that he could. Athlete and fancy-rag man, that was Lacan. Motherlant, in describing Gallo the bullfighter, the "bald god," who used to amuse himself by fighting badly to give his fans a fright and dazzle them all the more in the end, spoke of Genius and the pranks of the gods. And he mentioned the clown.

> At this point in the conversation, in which the artist, a sublime clown, was steadily engaged with Mr. Loyal, in the center of the audience cockatoos of whom Mr. Loyal was, so to speak, the designated representative, Mr. Loyal tore his clothing: "He blasphemed!" And then, foaming at the mouth, he gave the Clown a kick in the behind. But this kick sent the Clown, like the one at Banville, "up into the stars." The orchestra stopped playing. The lights came down. From the loges, from somewhere, there came a laugh, receding into the distance, and a deceptive voice saying, "Look for me." [13]

But heroism can become tiresome. One day I stopped going to the seminar: that familiar voice was no longer speaking to me. I gazed upon the spectacle as though I had never seen it before. Sollers was still hanging on. The audience, some of whom had aged quietly, seemed like children waiting for a puppet show to begin. Nothing in this great Parisian get-up could move me any more. I felt ridiculous being there. My love was dead. There were still the texts. But "it was all over."

About love nobody ever spoke better than Lacan. He talked about it between the lines, between words, in talking about other things, in talking about nothing at all. Sometimes he dwelt on it at length. But usually it was like an albatross swooping over the surface of his words, beating its wings in a fleeting allusion. Love was a permanent presence, ever so lightly touched upon as he lingered lazily, lengthily over the dead ends of desire, the desperations of fantasy, and the impossibility of "sexual intercourse." In Lacan's system, which is less inflexible and less fully worked out than some people think, love will no doubt remain one of the few escapes, perhaps the only one. Love was a door which, unlike the others, was not closed. A door left ajar. He frequently cited Rimbaud's poem, *A une raison:*

> Ta tête se tourne
> Un nouvel amour
> Ta tête se détourne
> Un nouvel amour . . .

(You turn one way, a new love, you turn the other, a new love). One day my head turned the other way.

But when the pamphlet attacking him came out, I refused to join the chorus. François George, the author of *L'Effet 'yau de poêle,* wrote to me then: "I am happy to see he's found himself a champion. I've always been hostile to him, but lately when I see people turning against the lion now that he's old, after licking the bottoms of his paws when he was in his glory, it fills me with contempt." This very gentle young man was also a man of decency. When the Lacan Affair erupted a few months later, I was outraged. Everything was grist for the mill: his ties, his butterfly knot, his glasses, his escapades, his sessions—everything but his ideas. As if he had never been anything but a splendid clown, a guru *de luxe* for Parisian intellectuals. "Magnificent, pathetic Harlequin": the words, shouted at Lacan, were those of Louis Althusser, who had come to make a splash at one of the meetings of the "Delenda" group.[14]

Now that rumor has Lacan dead and all the hubbub has finally died down of its own accord, perhaps it will be possible to talk about what he actually said. Forget the butterfly knot, the expensive tastes, and the masks. And above all forget the School, which hides him like a smoke screen.

$$B.A. = BA$$

My daughter put aside *Actuel* to take up *Télévision*, since this is the shortest of Lacan's books and has a cover, depicting a Roman woman with outstretched wings, that she likes. She came away from it looking grim. After a few words she stopped and said, "I can't understand a thing."

Télévision begins with these words: "I always tell the truth: not the whole truth, because the whole truth is something one never comes to the end of." And inscribed in the margin of the narrow page without title or introduction like an enigmatic bit of graffiti was one of Lacan's logical formulas: S ($\emptyset$).

"What's that?" my daughter wanted to know.

Forget about that. We'll get to it later, the second time around. For any Lacanian this would have been one of the first elements of the code. Like a beacon of sorts? If you like. But look at the sentence itself. "I always tell the truth . . ."

"He doesn't mince words, your Lacan!" she said.

No, he never did. But watch how he corrects himself. "Not the whole truth." Because you can't tell the whole truth.

"Why? Because you lie? Because you forget?" she said.

Because in order to say everything, you'd need more time, more words. And that's exactly what he says in the next sentence. "To tell the whole truth is impossible, materially: the words are lacking."

"You can't tell everything," she said.

You see, that wasn't hard. And what about the funny symbol? All you have to know to read it is what the capital letters stand for. S stands for two things: the signifier or the subject—I didn't have time to finish my sentence.

"The subject of the verb?"

If you like. The subject of all verbs: that which speaks, which thinks, the one on whom the unconscious plays tricks. When you use the wrong word, when you say a word other than the one you meant to say, it's not really you who is speaking. You are spoken. The subject is at once you and not-you. You're just a conduit for that which has decided to escape from within at all costs. A mistake like that is called a "lapsus," from the Latin word meaning to "slip" or "fall." The word falls like a piece of meat that slips from your mouth, like a mouthful of milk that flows over your lips when you drink a little too quickly. You don't get it right, you miss the target. Freud said that the lapsus was an "omitted act": like missing a step, falling on the side-walk, or forgetting your scarf. These things happen through you: you don't think about them, they're stupid mistakes. Stupid mis- takes on which all of psychoanalysis is built. And the subject is neither "I" nor "you" nor "he." It is the meeting place of the unconscious.

"But Lacan starts off by saying 'I,' doesn't he?"

All his life he bet on telling the truth but not the whole truth. Because the whole truth is something you never come to the end of, and "I" was not "him." He didn't come to the end of the truth either—that goes without saying. But he did, by dint of hard work and careful statement, tell a little more of the truth than other people did. The only ones who thought he told the whole truth were the bewildered note-takers, the eager re-corders, and the fans who placed him at the head of a cult. They didn't listen closely.

"And you said S stands for something else too?"

When you speak, a sound escapes from your lips. And when you write, a shape is traced on the paper. The sound and the shape are parts of the language, its substance. Putting together many sounds or many shapes yields a kind of supple thread of sounds or shapes that make up sentences. And when it's all done it "means something": simply put, it speaks. The signifier is the most elementary component of language: your cause, just as the lapsus was your cause a moment ago. It represents you. Even if you keep quiet, it causes you to exist, you, your words and your name.

"And what about the O? Why is there a line through it? Is it a mistake?" (The business of the signifier bored her.)

You might explain the slashed O like this: A philosophical proofreader, a compositor of genius made a mistake. O is the Other. You for me, me for you, anybody for anybody else, and also the first who made you as you define yourself: with your first name, your given name, your identity.

"You mean God?"

Nobody said anything about God. That made her laugh. But all right, if you like, God. And if not God then your father, whose name you bear. And if not just him, then his father too, and the whole generation that is making you talk today. You depend on the Other—Lacan uses a capital O to make clear that it's not just the fellow you're talking to in the street. You depend on an idea of man, or of God, or of the State, or of a dictator, or of order. Whatever it is, it sets up a kind of dam in you. Going to school, for instance, any school, is a way of building a dam. The dam existed before you were born; it will exist for your own children.

You might call it—culture. In every sense of the word: not only the culture they teach in school but also the culture that anthropologists talk about when they try to describe the rules by which others live, people who don't live the way we do. They don't eat the way we do; they don't sleep on pillows; they don't bury their dead but burn them, or let them rot and stick feathers on the bones when there's nothing else left, or they eat them. All these things are learned: a child's education is nothing other than the learning of those rules that make you French or American or whatever—wash your hair, come to dinner on time, brush your teeth, get dressed—and not a Nambikwara, for whom the rules are "roll in the sand, don't wash, pick the lice off me, and go make love with your little cousin." Your culture hampers you: that's what it's for—like a dam. It too is the Other. Your father, in bequeathing you his name, gave you your culture as a gift along with it.

"And the line (*barre*) through the O is supposed to represent the dam (*barrage*)?"

No, it's just the opposite. It stands for the completely crazy idea that you might be able to get rid of the Other, cut the moorings, and do whatever you please. And to say whatever you please as well. But to think you can really do it is an illusion. The slashed O doesn't work: it's an unattainable limit. But all the same it would be some pleasure to be able to say and do everything all at the same time.

I told her a story. I almost didn't say anything. I had to talk about the master signifier, the phallus, and about pleasure, and I had to explain a few equations. . . . But she left before I was finished. She was right. So now I'm stuck again with my own illusions. Reminded of S, the subject that I am, hemmed in on all sides by the need to explain a system whose principle is not clarity but penumbra. Reminded of my illusions about the nature of teaching. The same illusions in which Lacan became entangled.

Just before leaving, my daughter said that all these slashes, parentheses, constraints, and ideas of dependence weren't much fun. And she immersed herself in the complete works of Woody Allen.

The Obscure Clarity of Christianity

Psychoanalysts are never much fun. Is this because they are more conscious than others of being repositories of the culture, which they are partly responsible, symbolically, for transmitting? Lacan, though, knew how to say some funny things about our painful limitations. The jarring discord between the need for dis-

cipline and the exuberance of style—a discord Lacan used mas-
terfully—was for him the source of tragedy. More torn than
Freud, whose passion for construction he lacked, Lacan believed
in the necessity of discord. Failure, strife, and conflict in human
life—these were his subjects. There is nothing surprising, therefore, in the fact that he himself became a scapegoat, excluded
from the flock—harking back to the original function of the sacrificed goat, from which according to Greek myth Athenian
tragedy was born. Scapegoat, tragic symbol, contested prize: Lacan allowed himself to be fought over, more than Freud, who
kept a dour watch over his legacy. There was in Freud a single-
minded stubbornness that comes through in spite of himself,
even when conflict erupts and the movement is riven by schisms.
Freud had the temperament of the founder of a discipline. He
had both to rally adherents to the cause and to keep them in line
after they became disciples. He had to be both mother hen and
father with the whip. Come what may he was driven to create,
from the ground up, an institution whose purpose was to develop a science that had scarcely yet been born. In Lacan there
was a streak of mimicry that could make one think of the dead
father, the great figure of Freud to which he wished to return.
But Lacan also hated groups, with all their stickiness. He allowed
himself to be disseminated, copied, interpreted. From time to
time, however, he experienced the desire to make himself whole
again. He would then expel the most outrageous of his Bacchantes—the ones who ripped him to shreds with teeth bared
beneath broad smiles, who loved him too well and hated him
too sincerely—and recover his intact self. His theory was safe and
his name pure. But before long others would come to fight over
"Lacan." The most recent of these battles is typical of the lot:
they tore him to shreds, they fought over him, and then he came
and dissolved the School and once again became "Lacan." A few
months later he allowed all comers to enter the new school then
being organized, and once again other people began speaking in

his name, invoking his authority, defending him against attack—
in short, people started carving him up all over again.

Still, Lacan took from Freud his drive to found an institution
in his own name. He was the inheritor of the dream that Freud
recounted one day to his friend Fliess: that a marble plaque would
some day mark the spot where he made his discoveries. On the
plaque would be inscribed: "Here, on July 24, 1895, the secret of
dreams was revealed to Dr. Sigmund Freud." A dream of immortality. Like the founding father Lacan erected a monument
to himself. He derived no narcissistic gratification from his celebrity. Neither Freud nor Lacan cared a jot for the petty pleasures
of notoriety: their fantasies were wilder. They dreamt of being
remembered centuries hence, of having their names become syn-
onymous with their age. Lacan's most secure, most immediate
triumph is this: he succeeded in establishing his name.

Lacan also took from Freud his desire to establish a system of
knowledge. But he took risks and sawed off the very limb of the
tree of knowledge on which he, as a psychoanalyst, was se-
curely seated. He criticized everything: the linguistics he made
use of, the ethnology that had given him so much, the psychology that had always horrified him. He sat in the midst of a desert,
like a stylite on his pillar, always proud, prestigious, and alone.
The only nourishment the hermit took with him into the desert
was mathematics. Graphs, equations, knots, (Klein) bottles,
structures, (Möbius) strips—all transformed into an illegible
scrawl on the blackboard. He made mistakes, just like anyone
else. His theory, though, seemed armor-clad, bristling with symbols, protected by logic. Everything was just "like Freud"—in
the sense that a patched-up used car is "like new." Freud—the
papa—also elaborated complex models. Freud also used the science of his day—it was not this part of his work that earned him
immortality. In this respect, at least, Lacan may resemble him:
the mathematical portion of his thought is not the most immortal
part.

But the spectacle of his followers—the "Lacanians"—makes one suspicious. Always involved in the latest mathematical fad, they play with spheres, dabble with topological spaces, cut up paper strips—and think they're making theory. And the terribly obsessive way in which they play with these little toys seems to fill them with profound sadness. As for Lacan himself, it is by no means certain that his mind was not more playful than the minds of his disciples. It is by no means certain that all those graphs, tori, and annuli have not left Lacan's thought full of holes, naked, blank spots, imaginary oceans on which the master sails his paper boats. Grown-up children play with strings, and the game is very serious indeed. But it's still a game.

Strings: Lacan frequently made a great show of them, as though to defend himself. To defend himself against his own poetic language, so deeply a part of himself and by far more personal than all the mathematical baggage. The strings and knots were stamped with the "rigor" of topology. At first, the graphs had a pedagogical function—to make people understand—but soon they took over. Lacan's story was the story of a poet who wanted to be a mathematician too, of an actor who also wanted to be a gymnast, of a psychoanalyst who never ceased to be a philosopher, of a sorcerer who rejected his own potions. He was an old-fashioned hero who wanted at all costs to be up to date.

I like the other Lacan better. The one who let himself be carried away, who made mistakes at the blackboard, who got steamed up and let his sentences roll one on top of another, not caring how much they ran away with him. The other Lacan, prophetic and blundering, enchanted me. Yet I too played with strips of paper. Even so, Lacan the sorcerer seduced me all the more. Love for him grew out of the way he made phrases, took them back, and then shattered them in a gale of laughter, like a mole undermining every certitude—restless, anxious, he was constantly on the move, like the balance wheel of a watch, incapable of standing still. And Lacan spoke my language—French.

Both Freud and Lacan fathered theories in the womb of language, in their mother tongues. Each of them had a seductive style, but their charms were different. Freud's were those of the pain of Jewish existence combined with Austrian Germanness; the Mosaic quest combined with familial *gemütlichkeit;* mystic exile, "next year in Jerusalem," and matzoh-ball soup; boiled chicken, "pickle fleisch," and evening walks on the Prater. The lace doilies that Martha placed on the tables coupled with memories of the Dead Father. Even though he refused to practice the religion of his fathers, in Freud I recognize myself as a Jew.

In Lacan I recognize myself as a Frenchwoman. Not for "nationalistic" reasons but for reasons of culture: a culture that is far more than language but a whole way of life, a landscape. Instead of the family there is the solitude of the philosopher, alone at night as the candle burns low in the first glimmerings of dawn, or in the midst of a noisy crowd on the place de Grève. Instead of matzoh-ball soup there is a gourmet dish, carefully arranged and decorated, or there is the bread of the host and the pitcher of holy water. Instead of Moses and Jerusalem there is the Jansenist cross, there is Port-Royal, there is the bare cell of the monastery. The row of trees is not, as in the paintings of Velazquez, a curtain in front of the horizon but rather a charming accent marking the end of a field or the bank of a river in a country where open space never extends very far. Lacan may have succeeded in establishing, through his work, the first plausible image of the French psychoanalyst. He is French to the very tip of his tongue, down to his erudite and antiquated way of citing a text in Latin, Greek, or any other language—without translation. It was for this quality that in 1939 he received plaudits, along with a shower of rebukes, from none other than Edouard Pichon, psychoanalyst, grammarian, and distinguished activist in the Action Française [a political group of the extreme right— trans.] in those dark days when Maurras was riding high, the Popular Front was everywhere being denounced, and France was rushing headlong toward disaster. Commenting on an article on the "family" recently published by Lacan,[15] Pichon raked him gently over the coals, speaking as an elder colleague who hopes that his advice will be heeded by an angry young man who has gone a bit too far. Here is what he said: "It seems to me that Monsieur Lacan has not chosen the appropriate adornment for his intelligence, which is French by virtue of blood, upbringing, and training." An ambiguous homage: if Pichon reproaches Lacan for not "calling tradition by its name" and using too many foreign terms, both English and German, he does so because in his eyes Lacan is the perfect French psychoanalyst, "one of the most brilliant minds in the younger generation of French psychiatrists." French for three reasons sanctioned by Maurras: by virtue of blood, breeding, and social class. All stated openly. And yet, in loosing his arrows, Pichon was extolling Lacan's use of language, of which as a grammarian Pichon knew the ins and outs. And I myself know intimately that Lacan speaks my language, speaks it splendidly. As steeped as he is in foreign scholarship, as bristling with exotic terminology, he remains quintessentially French.

French, and Christian—a scion of the traditional bourgeoisie. Not the "two hundred families" [which according to legend rule France—trans.] but that part of the bourgeoisie on which the unchanging political complexion of France has been based, a stratum that owns some property, that attaches a great deal of importance to culture, and that has traditionally produced doctors, lawyers, and other professionals. Lacan's language is not "Jewish": it doesn't catch the ear or stumble, it never hesitates. In Lacan's work one never finds glaring absences of the sort prevalent in texts informed by the Chassidic tradition,[16] and there are none of those confusing, repetitious formulas in which Freud shrouded his discoveries. In the elegance of Jacques-Marie Lacan can be seen, from the beginning, the mark of the dominant religion of his people—anyone who writes cannot help being marked by religion in some degree. Later on, in speaking of his enemies, he is proud of being a martyr, of being a dignitary of the Church ready to abide by its commandments. In the heart of his writing there is no sign that he fears persecution, which affects him not in language but elsewhere. If there are gaps in his speech, they are placed deliberately. If he stutters and stammers, it is not because he has succumbed to the infirmity that sometimes afflicted the prophets of Israel but because he is in complete control of his word play. Lacan has the pride of style: in that too he is French. In him there is not the least bit of the émigré.

Whether or not he was an atheist is of little importance. Among his disciples are Marxists, Catholic priests, Protestants, and Jews. As an apostle he castigated them all. When he spoke to his disciples he treated them at times with the severity of the apostle Paul, at times with the charity of Jesus on the mount. His flock, he was fond of saying, was divided between the "stupid" and the "rabble." He claimed of course to prefer the rabble. But he sometimes uttered the word "stupidity" with such tenderness that, despite himself, he showed that he bestowed his love on the poor in spirit. Blessed are the poor in spirit, for the kingdom of heaven belongs to them. He did not like stupidity, but as a propagandist he cherished it. Naked loyalty was worth something. And when he spoke of Freud he could not help transforming him into an inspired figure, something of a Greek. And something of a Christian too, insofar as Christianity was able to absorb the mythology of Greece through syncretism and the Roman Empire. "Who could be so naïve," he said, "as to suppose that Freud was nothing more than a proper Viennese bourgeois, who dumbfounded his visitor André Breton by not making himself the object of the Maenads' obsession? . . . Who better than he, confessing his dreams, knew how to spin the thread along which slides the ring that binds us to existence? And as that ring passed from hand in the game of concealing human passion, who better than he knew how to expose its brief luster and make it gleam? Who grumbled as much as this quiet doctor against the monopolization of pleasure by those who heaped the burden of need on the shoulders of others?" [17] In Freud Lacan looked for a prophet; he spoke, for his part, as a proselyte. In the famous letter dissolving his School, he himself said, "Je père-sévère" ("I, severe father," but also "I persevere").[18]

And he did persevere. "Thou art Peter, and on this rock I shall build my church." This sentence was often addressed by Lacan to one person or another, pregnant with cathectic connotation: one Peter after another received the call to build along with Lacan the Ecole freudienne. Perhaps his egregious predilection for puns came from his profoundly Christian spirit.

In the beginning the puns were just what they are for anyone: a sudden explosion to provoke laughter and relax the audience, allowing for a breathing space in the lecture and not unlike the snapping noises made by storytellers when they want to awaken listeners who have fallen asleep. People laughed. But that's just it: psychoanalysis never laughs without asking why. Freud explained the nature of the joke: it is the expression of the repressed. Lacan, by renewing the function of language in its relation to the unconscious, made every nuance of meaning manifest, where Freud had merely described with precision. The slightest duplicity in the meaning of a word served as a pretext for Lacan to demonstrate to his seminar audience how the analyst works: to interpret is to play on words. To interpret is to hear *père-sévère* instead of persevere, or, to take an English example, to catch the double-entendre when Hamlet asks Rosencrantz and Guildenstern if they live about Fortune's "waist or in the middle of her favor," and Guildenstern replies, "Faith, her privates we."[19] In the beginning puns also served as examples. People laughed and then they understood. They quieted down and they thought about the meaning of the joke.

But a day came when the puns became an end in themselves. Completely unfettered and still good for making people laugh, they had a different ring from before. In the later years of his seminar Lacan uttered nothing but puns. The punning became a carnival, a fad, a dazzling display of fireworks. Rockets went off in every direction. And the meaning evaporated.

Lacan always fought against the inflation of meaning and un-

derstanding. He said, rightly, that the unconscious has no meaning. The unconscious is not directed toward a goal. It plays and
then it settles down. Lacan therefore detested philosophies of
meaning and he hacked their presuppositions to pieces. So much
so that by dint of efforts not to say anything "sensible" he came
to the point where he just "said." He opened his mouth and the
words danced playfully. They no longer meant anything, no
longer "wanted" to mean anything. No one knew which way
was up. It was all just foolishness. Playfulness. Lacan became a
colossus of language: devilishly clever and malicious, he chopped
his sentences into bits, and each little snippet was immediately
engulfed by the next. Crucified on a cross of puns, thought succumbed.

The astonishing thing is that his disciples—always the same,
the stupid ones along with the rabble—went along with the act.
And even tried to copy it, without having any of Lacan's genius,
without sharing his poetic phrasing or sense of punctuation, which
even at his worst moments never abandoned him. The result
provides material appropriate to a history of strange aberrations.
Witness this little masterpiece, signed Danièle Arnoux: "The spirit
(joke) Lacan breathed into his School, it—dare I say—breathed
into him, the imperative, Speak! It, which believed itself to be
one, lost, speak, of being found" [a rough rendering into English
of the highly peculiar and quite untranslatable French cited in the
original—trans.].[20] And so on.

This is not very far from Lacan. A hair's breadth away. A
century away. Only the rhetorical polish is missing. The liberties
that one person may allow himself to take, provided he is a poet,
are ridiculous if imitated by anyone else. But Lacan's disciples
didn't mind making themselves ridiculous by imitating his word
play, just as they followed him in his mathematical divagations
on knots, circles, Klein bottles, and Möbius strips. Just as they
aped his myriad references to Chinese, to Aristotle, to Plato, and
to Hegel. The puns lost their essence, just as mathematics had
done. Nothing explosive remained. They became a deadly habit,

a monstrous tic. For Lacan created monsters in the proper sense of the word: creatures turned away from their true function. Creatures of style. The monster—that surprising mix of two species—is also something that one puts on display in a laboratory, a carnival sideshow, or a medical-school amphitheater. Very little distinguishes the monster from the mutant of science fiction. And very little distinguishes the monster from the excluded individual: the hysteric was considered monstrous, and before her the witch. To call Lacan's creatures monsters is to link his work to the tradition of alchemy, witchcraft, and militant madness. The pun became a monster of the Lacanian style.

Lacanians are often monsters, Golems of this social alchemist, automata inspired by a spirit not their own.

But not all of them. Some faces returned year after year. On one side were the veterans, the real troopers, the truly faithful followers. Resembling one another, they followed their own path, pursued their research, and spoke a language of their own. Only the fact that their hair turned a little whiter each year indicated that time was passing. Among them were Françoise Dolto, Serge Leclaire, Lucien Israël, Octave and Maud Mannoni, Paul and Gennie Lemoine, to name a few of the best known.

The other faces changed from time to time. They imitated the habits of the master in different ways, depending on when they arrived on the scene. And then they continued their odyssey elsewhere, sometimes looking a bit haggard for having lost their "Other." Some never recovered. These were the monsters, astonishingly similar from generation to generation: infinitely serious, infinitely mimetic, they inhabited a hermetically sealed universe. To be sure, those who kept faith with themselves rather than with Lacan were "normal." But who knows whether or not the really faithful disciples were not in fact these monsters reduced to childish dependence on the master's word and thought?

When the dissolution came, some of the "monsters" were in favor of disbanding on the spot, as the master wished. It seems never to have occurred to them that it might have been them that Lacan had in mind when he said he was sick and tired. They found a scapegoat in the person of Françoise Dolto, who defended as best she could a position that was at least logical. To be loyal to Lacan, she argued, was to leave him free to make his own decision but not to renounce him. Therefore his resignation should be accepted, but the school should not be dissolved. "Down with the she-ass," they shouted: *Delenda est* Françoise Dolto. The alchemist was asking that the crystal that he himself had produced be dissolved. The sorcerer was smashing his toys, his wax dolls. His private religion no longer satisfied him. Monstrous and splendid: everything was turned upside down. Monstrous and fascinating. Witchcraft was involved.

Witchcraft and instruction. The multifarious fables, be they pagan, Greek, or Roman, or, more secretly, Christian, the endless puns, the citations in Chinese—all were facets of a single prism: Lacan's style. A style that was incomprehensible, difficult, esoteric, and obscure. Clear and obscure at the same time, he always occupied what he called the "middle ground of speech" [the *midire,* "midspeak," a pun on "half-speaking," *mi-dire,* and slander, *médire*—trans.]. Lacan's *chiaroscuro* style belongs to a French tradition that is not new: it can be traced back to Maurice Scève, to Mallarmé—poetic precursors. The essence of Lacan's work is in his style. Even if his medium was the spoken word, his work was also that of a writer.

The Deficiency of Culture

"Style is the man . . . to whom one is speaking," Lacan announced at the beginning of *Ecrits,* a collection of texts the earliest of which dates from 1930. This was his way of suggesting that there is no such thing as autonomous writing and that the constraints on writing come as much from the person for whom the work is destined as from the producer. This tragic misunderstanding (*malentendu*), which establishes the essential function of style, is the source of all Lacan's teaching. Style produces under-standing of evil (*mal-entendu*): all psychoanalytic practice is based on the ability to hear something other than what the patient says, on the capacity to hear, within the conscious message enunciated by the speaker, the patterns produced by the unconscious. The problem, then, is to premeditate the misunderstanding. Interpre-tation amounts to deliberately deceiving oneself. I say "Barbara," and he or she hears "Berber." He or she will be right to hear "barbarian" if my Father is a Kabyle (i.e., an Algerian Berber) and my mother a Breton. And so, by way of the songstress "Barbara," I recover my repressed barbarity (*barbarie*).[21]

Suppose a style of therapy is based on misunderstanding: How can it be taught? Lacan constantly tried to work this dissonance into his style, perfecting that style at the same time. "Any return to Freud that gives substance to a doctrine worthy of his name can only come about by taking the path that leads to where the most hidden truth is revealed in the revolutions of culture. That path is the only training that we can claim to offer those who follow us. It is called: a style."[22]

So? A style, it follows, influences the revolutions of culture. A commonplace: any writer with a genuine style of his own changes the language and therefore changes a part of the culture. But what about the psychoanalyst? His social function has nothing in com-mon with that of the writer. Instead, perhaps, he listens—with that "third ear" that Theodore Reik talks about—to that neces-sary misunderstanding, the shared material of language. And if he listens to it in his cockeyed way, shifting phonemes about from place to place, his relation to language is a fleeting one, not likely to endure after the patient is cured. In this sentence of La-can's, the psychoanalyst counts for less than the teacher.

Teacher of what? Psychoanalysts have never gotten beyond this naïve question, rehashed time and time again ever since Freud. What can a psychoanalyst teach his colleagues? Nothing. That is, "normally" nothing, for psychoanalytic practice can only be learned on another analyst's couch.

Suppose you want to be a psychoanalyst. If you're in France, your first thought will naturally be, "There must be a school for that." Perish the thought. So you go look for one. You go to see the professors at the university. If they're honest fellows, they'll tell you that here and there you can find a course on Freud or on the unconscious or about psychoanalysis. But then, looking embarrassed, they'll drop a hint that taking one of these courses is not the way to become a psychoanalyst. How do you go about it, then? Well, you have to undergo psychoanalysis yourself. Disaster: you'd thought of everything but that. Nine out of ten applicants for psychoanalytic instruction make tracks when they hear the bad news. They were looking for a school in order to avoid the couch. The tenth embarks upon his quest for the Holy Grail. He will look all around and even inside himself for the courage to "go." And go he will. For four or five years he'll chat away on his little couch, and if at the end of that time he still wants to be a psychoanalyst he will then, but only then, begin his formal schooling.

What is more, his schooling will be of no use to him in learning the practice of psychoanalysis, since this is something he will already have learned as a patient on another analyst's couch. The purpose of the school is quite different. In the first place, it ends the analyst's isolation, which is important. Second, it enables him to discuss his peculiar occupation with others already experienced in its practice as well as with those who aspire to practice: the analyst keeps up to date by seeing where everybody else runs into trouble and starts mumbling. Finally, the school enables the analyst to make contact with the "university": not the real university, but a sort of alternative one in which he can sign up for "seminars." The word is a nice one; it long ago came into vogue as a replacement for the "lecture," a relic of a bygone era. Make no mistake, though: lecture courses may have gone by the boards, but seminars, in which professor and student presumably have an equal part, have also changed over the years. Courses have turned into debates between teachers and students, whereas seminars, following a precisely opposite path, have in many cases, become one-man shows. Our friends the psychoanalysts showed themselves particularly adept at assuming the magisterial role that formerly belonged to the professor.

So our apprentice psychoanalyst—still chatting away on his couch but by now a little more knowledgeable about the rules of the game—signs up for his seminars. At the same time, thanks to a complicated process involving contacts, influence, and rites of initiation, he snags his first client. This first analysis will be conducted, if the apprentice is serious, under "supervision." In other words, the apprentice will go to another analyst and tell him what is happening with his patient. Well and good. So far the transmission of psychoanalytic knowledge has followed a pattern entirely different from the familiar pattern of education in the French system of nationally-supervised public schools and universities, in which all knowledge is codified in books and imparted according to prescribed rules, so that if necessary education could go on in the absence of a teacher. By contrast, analytic training is more like the education of an African witch doctor or any other sorcerer: the young are initiated by their elders. To put it in more academic terms, psychoanalysis is one of the few disciplines in which theory and practice are taught simultaneously—not to say "on the job." All the while our apprentice, trembling in his office, is learning how to listen without saying a word. He is learning what words to say on occasion. He is learning how to avoid becoming petrified with fear when a patient becomes aggressive toward him. And he is learning how not to become too absorbed in what the patient calls forth from the analyst's own personal history. Apart from that, he attends his seminar. And not just Lacan's seminar, which is only one among many.

What will our intrepid young man or woman learn at his seminar? History. The history of the young discipline founded by Freud no more than eighty years ago. And he will read Freud. And reread Freud. And read the others. Perhaps he will also learn a bit of the vocabulary of psychiatry, the nearest neighbor—and bitterest enemy—of psychoanalysis. He will read a great deal. Broadly speaking, he will cultivate himself. And that's where Lacan comes in. I haven't forgotten him. He was waiting for us just around the bend.

In Freud's day psychoanalysts also cultivated themselves. They yearned for community. They took an interest in Greek mythology. They commented on the future of the world. They explored the newly-blazed trails of ethnology. They were all exciting people: read *Imago,* the journal of applied psychoanalysis, and you will find signs of an extraordinary culture and genuine research efforts. Then came the Second World War. In France psychoanalysis did not yet amount to much. The initial penetration had produced some results, but not much was happening. In the United States, on the other hand, things were going rather well. The international psychoanalytic community, swelled by émigrés fleeing the Nazis, spoke a language that was partly German, partly American. The "Ich" and the "Self" consorted happily, and culture was left far behind. And yet the émigré analysts were also worthy people. The problem was that everything was swallowed up in the American compost, reducing the past to nothing.

Lacan's whole story can be summed up in terms of a cultural deficiency. Europe was invaded by American cigarettes and by a culture derived from the Marshall Plan. And pushed by Americans, the flabbiest psychology made a powerful comeback.

Lacan, for his part, cited not only Hegel but also Molière and Victor Hugo. He cited poets: it seemed like a dream. He had acquired these bad habits before the war. He wrote poems and articles in *Le Minotaure* alongside the ethnologist Michel Leiris, the writer Paul Eluard, and the folklorist Georges-Henri Rivière. He saw a great deal of the surrealists. In short, he was "literary," despite his very classical training as a psychiatrist.

The story might have ended there: the medical world is full of highly cultivated practitioners, like Jean Delay, a psychiatrist who wrote about Gide and who in his old age became a historian of the seventeenth century.[23] This was not Lacan's story, however.

He began teaching. In that he was not alone, but he was the only one to talk about language. This complicated matters. To the cultural tradition of psychoanalysis as Freud conceived it—a great deal of mythology, a little history, above all no politics, a dash of literature, a soupçon of painting, and a bit of elevated mysticism thrown in for good measure—Lacan added linguistics, so-called "foreign" languages, mathematics, logic, and philosophy. Listening to Lacan required either enormous knowledge or enormous amounts of documentation; his disciples read like crazy. He can be reproached for many things, but not for having lowered the cultural level of his flock.

The subject of language immediately brought up the idea of letters. He used to say, logically enough, that the psychoanalyst must be "literate." By this he meant not merely someone who is "widely read" but quite simply a person who understands the meaning of letters—letters of the alphabet, a, b, c, the smallest structural elements of our language, or, as Lacan put it, "the essentially localized structure of the signifier." [24]

There it is again: the signifier, virtually the symbol of Lacan's thought. Yet Lacan was not the originator of the term. The idea of the signifier came from Ferdinand de Saussure, who held a seminar of his own from 1906 to 1911. His lectures too were collected by his disciples and published in what came to be known as the *Cours de linguistique générale:* it was a high time for theoretical bibles out of which whole disciplines later grew.

The signifier is the very substance of language: the letter, the mark, the comma, the period, the phoneme. The signified is that to which the signifier refers. Suppose I say, "as dumb as the ground." The ground signifies stupidity—except that when I say "as dumb as the ground," I bring certain overtones of the word "ground" into play: the ground is no longer merely that on which I plant my feet but something flat and inert, suggesting some of the qualities of stupidity.

To open his listeners' ears to the cunning of the signifier and the signified, Lacan spoke not of the ground but of lavatory doors.

On one door the word "Gentlemen" is written, on the other the word "Ladies." Otherwise the two doors are identical. Lacan told a story about two small children on a train stopped in a station, looking out the window at the lavatory doors on the station platform. Each laid claim to one of the doors. "Look," said the brother, "We're at Ladies!" "You imbecile," his sister replied, "Don't you see we're at Gentlemen?"[25] Each child sees its own object: the door designating the sex of the other. This Dissension (the capital D is authenticated in *Ecrits*) Lacan sees as the beginning of an epic. "Ladies and Gentlemen will for these two children always represent two different countries toward which their souls will each of them fly on divergent wings, and with which it will be all the more impossible to come to terms since in truth they are the same, and therefore neither will be able to concede the superiority of the one without impugning the glory of the other."[26] Here, in a few excessively stylized lines, we have the war between the sexes and the cultural division of men and women based on "the laws of urinary segregation." And here we have a fine portrait of the psychoanalyst: working with the most trivial material, he hearkens to the nobility of legend and the force of myth. Like the ethnologist, the psychoanalyst knows that there is no difference between the noble and the ignoble: read Lévi-Strauss's *Mythologies* and you will learn how the world is created out of a grandmother's urine and the suffocating farts with which she poisons the demiurgic hero. And when the historians set to work on the "historical psychology" of ancient Greece in the hope of stripping away the grandiose and modest cloak the nineteenth century had thrown over her body, they discovered parings, waste, dribbling milk, and noxious odors. To be cultivated is to become aware of the obverse of culture, which centuries of textbook literature have carefully hidden from view.

As I was saying, the signifier is the smallest element of language. It is governed by two laws: ultimately, each signifier is distinguished from the rest by a differential element, and signifiers combine with one another according to a closed set of rules. No signifier can exist in isolation. Each signifier connects to its nearest neighbor, and its nearest neighbor in turn connects to another, and so on, until we come to the next higher unit, the word or sentence. Moreover, the signified cannot be assigned to any one signifier. Rather, it slides from one to another, and this sliding or shifting is what we call "meaning." One more step and we will join Lacan in the private preserve of rhetoric: the science of figures of speech. Rhetoric is the art of style; there we shall discover the heart of Lacan's teaching.

In fact we have already taken the step in speaking of the simile "as dumb as the ground" or discussing the example of Ladies and Gentlemen. But consider now one further example, superbly developed by Lacan: the tree (*arbre*). [Lacan begins by imagining this word broken down into what he calls "the dual spectrum of its vowels and its consonants." The dominant vowel sound is "ah," as in *platane,* the French word for the plane tree, so common in France. The dominant consonant sounds are "r" and "b," which suggest to Lacan the French word *robre,* or robur tree (the British oak).—trans.]

Even when the word "tree" is broken down into the dual spectrum of its vowels and consonants, it still evokes, with the plane tree and the robur, the connotations of strength and majesty that it takes on within our flora. Drawing on the many symbolic uses of the word "tree" in the Hebrew Bible, it erects on a barren hill the shadow of the cross. Or again, pared down, it reduces to a mere capital Y, the sign of dichotomy, which would have nothing to do with trees at all were it not for the family trees that adorn aristocratic genealogies. Then there is the "circulatory tree," the "tree of life of the cerebellum," the tree of Saturn, and the tree of Diana; there are the crystals formed in a tree struck by lightning. Is it your image, O Tree, that traces our destiny for us in the tortoise-shell cracked by the fire? Or are you really the lightning bolt that rends the black infinity of night to reveal the slow change of being in the Εν πάντα of language . . .[27]

Here we have Lacan in his full rhetorical splendor. Playfully taking the letters of the French word for tree to suggest trees that grow in France. Playing on Christianity and the tree of the cross. Playing on the anatomy that he learned while studying medicine in order to become a psychiatrist, and on chemistry, and on associations of images inspired by Roger Caillois. Recalling the tortoise, and mimicry in the animal kingdom. And ending finally, after invoking the Greek term for essence and the Whole, with a verse of poetry. All that in a tree: he makes the shifting of the signified come alive before our eyes. Word for word, he calls it. It demands to be read in simultaneous translation. In rhetoric this figure is known as metonymy. Similar to metonymy is metaphor: no longer word for word, but rather one word for another. Not the tree of the cross but the tree in place of the cross: the part for the whole, the wood of the tree for the body it supports, and the meaning it implies. I told you that Lacan's teaching was a matter of style. A question of his ability to play all the strings of culture as though it were an immense harp capable of giving off resonant harmonies.

Actor and Martyr

From very early on, then, Lacan's style was admirable, difficult perhaps in its extreme refinement but always perfect. And yet there were moments when he was merely a rhetorician. Before the war Lacan enjoyed a period of creativity. He made new observations and established a system of new concepts. This work was completed fairly early: if one reads what he wrote in the thirties, one finds in latent form all the main points of the theory that he would later develop to the full. Then came a time when his creativity ceased. Rather than forge new concepts, he translated old ones into a variety of languages: the work of a rhetorician. The signifier is not a Lacanian concept. Metaphor and metonymy are not concepts forged by Lacan. And even the "matheme," one of his latest discoveries, derives from mathematical logic. No, Lacan was not the inventor of a system. He was far more a skillful rhetorician capable of translating the terminology of psychoanalysis into a language other than "Freud."

Rhetoric, moreover, overwhelmed him to the point where it hindered his conceptual imagination. By 1964 he had said all he had to say. And 1964 was the year he got himself expelled from the International Psychoanalytic Association. Having been subjected to severe censure, it took him more than ten years to establish his own School. But from that moment Jacques-Marie Lacan began his transformation into "Lacan." It was not long before he was able to speak of himself in the third person. And the more he lived as a "leader," the more polished his rhetoric became. From rhetoric he moved on to pure celebration, to compulsive word play—a logical trajectory. Language got the better of him. Saint Lacan, actor and martyr.

We do not find in Lacan any signs of an intimate sense of persecution such as Freud betrays in some of his writings, but we do find, most palpably, a martyr's crown. It was a crown that Lacan wore ostentatiously, about which he speechified and wailed while his disciples loudly beat their breasts. There was a special issue of *Ornicar?* [the Lacanian journal, whose title comes from the last three words in the textbook list of French conjunctions, *mais ou et donc or ni car*—trans.] entitled "L'Excommunication." [28] Lacan as Galileo, Lacan as Giordano Bruno, Lacan as Saint Blandina. The psychoanalysts of France and the United States were cast as the lions, Lacan as the martyr. As a rhetorician he could do no other. For the other psychoanalysts, the members of learned societies that chewed over Freud's texts, did not have his passion to pass the torch. Lacan was the first to look for a valid way of passing the torch of a kind of learning that was all but impossible to teach. The trap snapped shut.

Lacan continued to track the truth. The truth that can never be told whole. The word "truth" comes up again and again. When

he first used it, the word had little currency among analysts. Freud
scarcely mentions it. There was a great deal of talk about "reality," which has little to do with truth. Our Lacan set himself the
task of speaking in the name of truth. Not of truth, but in its
place. He set himself the task of elaborating the discourse of truth,
a *prosopopoeia,* the personification of a concept. Plato put into the
mouth of Socrates a *prosopopoeia* on the Laws, in which they defended themselves as laws. Lacan gave voice to the truth, just as
Bossuet before him gave voice to death. "So I am for you an
enigma, she who disappears as soon as she appears, you men
who try so hard to conceal me beneath the tawdry finery of your
conventions. . . . I, truth, will speak."²⁹ That was the beginning. The end drifted off into terrible puns, on the borderline
between creation and senile doddering: "Enter the lists when I
call, and shout at my voice. There you are, already lost. I con-
tradict myself, I challenge you, I take cover: you say I'm defending myself" [here, merely translating the sense of the words ob-
scures the point of the utterance, in French an ambiguous run of
assonant associations: "je me démens, je vous défie, je me défile:
vous dîtes que je me défends"—trans.].³⁰ Later on, he returns to
the same series of assonances in speaking of the signifier: the
challenge (*défi*), the contradiction (*démenti*), suggestive of what
Freud called denial (in French: *dénégation*); and defense, a classical
portmanteau word in the lexicon of the compleat garden-variety
psychoanalyst. Which brings us back to our apprentice psychoanalyst: the reader may be wondering what became of him.

He hasn't the foggiest idea what's going on. He came to hear
a little Freud and learn some of that Germanic jargon that is supposed to turn our would-be analyst into a fountainhead of science. Instead, he hears talk of metaphors, for the first time since
leaving high school. He hears talk of Bossuet, whom he's never
read. He hears talk of linguistics, about which he knows nothing.
And this fellow up in front of the room claims to be the truth in
person. But Truth is not naked, she has no mirror in her hand,
her eyes are open, and it's a tired little man who's speaking in

her place. If the magic is working, the young psychoanalyst enters into a new world. He embarks on an apprenticeship in his own culture. The same culture he studied in the *lycée,* except that now he comes to it of his own free will. With delight he goes back to school. He recycles himself. And it cannot be denied that he is really learning something. But whether or not what he is learning is really psychoanalysis is another question. The only guarantee Lacan offers seems tenuous in the extreme: he is a psychoanalyst himself.

A tenuous guarantee indeed. As he himself said repeatedly, shouting from every rooftop that no one could presume to offer such a guarantee without risk, unless he was the one and only psychoanalyst, *the* "shrink" in person. And to defend himself—but the trap was still shut—he called this wholly illusory guarantee the "subject-supposed-to-know." The one who embodies all of psychoanalysis in his person, the one who is supposed to know. It must be said that he does nothing to ease the task of the apprentice. He cites Greek without translating it and so the clever fellows end up thinking him learned; and he is. By playing in the comedy of language, he wins the saint's crown of martyrdom. Sartre has given a good explanation of this particular kind of passion in *Saint Genêt, Comédien et martyr.*

Saint Genêt—the real Saint Genêt [i.e., Genesius—trans.]—was an actor in the days when Roman emperors liked to feed Christians to the lions. He was an actor and quite pagan—until the day he had to play the role of a Christian before the emperor. Grace touched him on that occasion, and he converted. He experienced the greatest difficulties in convincing the emperor that he was no longer playing his part: actors are always hailed as geniuses of the theater. The only thing he could do was to play his role "for real" and act out his martyrdom unto death, to prove that he was no longer acting. The second Saint Genêt—Jean Genet, the writer—became a thief and a homosexual when a voice took him by surprise and told him, "You shall be a thief." And he became one. Lacan may have experienced the same passion: "I, the truth, am speaking." This was merely a *prosopopoeia*. But in the eyes of others it became a first-person truth. You shall be Lacan. And he became Lacan.

The discourse of truth concluded with a very dangerous definition of the psychoanalyst. The psychoanalyst compared himself to Actaeon, who was guilty of having surprised the chaste goddess Artemis in her bath, stark naked. Taken aback, the goddess transformed him into a deer on the spot, and his dogs then devoured him. A fine subject for painting. "Actaeon, too guilty to hunt the goddess, the prey that traps, O huntsman, the shadow that you become, let the pack pass without hastening your step. Diana will recognize the dogs, for what they are." [31] There are several allusions here for our apprentice psychiatrist to make out: one to Mallarmé's *L'Après-midi d'un faune* [whose last line is "je vais voir l'ombre que tu devins," I go to see the shadow you became—trans.]. And another to a famous remark made by a Dominican inquisitor. [The story is told that, during the Albigensian crusade, siege was laid to a heretic stronghold. When the town was taken, the commander of the Inquisition's troops asked the inquisitor which of the inhabitants of the city were to be put to the sword, since some Christians had been held within the walls by the Cathari. "Kill them all," the Inquisitor replied. "God will recognize his own." In French, the last phrase is "Dieu reconnaîtra les siens." At Lacan's hands, this became, in the passage cited above, "Diane . . . reconnaîtra les chiens."—trans.] Once our apprentice has deciphered these allusions, he will understand that he is being asked to expose himself to the snarling hounds. Pagan passion; Christian passion—"take and eat, this is my body," the latent message of a man who never ceased defending himself. This is the reason for the reactions of outraged integrity, for the "subject-supposed-to know," who, precisely because he is supposed to know, knows no more than anyone else. And "if it ever happens that I go away, tell yourselves that it is in order to be Other at last." Finally to be Other. But it was too much for him; once again he would be misappropriated.

The apprentice perseveres. The Ecole freudienne had its Saint Veronicas, who wiped the Holy Face with clean linen and cried for joy at each step of the way. There were Josephs of Arimathea to lend the tomb, the room, and the cash. Holy women and Saint John, jack-of-all-trades. The Roman soldier, the last convert. And the last-minute disciples ready to divide up the Golden Fleece. It would take the apprentice a long time to understand that it could not help being a missed appointment.

Lacan said so himself, in dissolving his School: it had become a place of mistaken encounters. "Like the famous lovers' rendez-vous at the costume ball. When they lowered their masks, horror of horrors, it wasn't him, and it wasn't her either." [32]

The truth is also a missed appointment. Back to the letter, and the tree. Meaning is a slippery thing. Lacan compared it to hunt-the-slipper, the game in which an object is passed from hand to hand and no one knows where it is. Lacan's definition of the truth was not merely mystical, as the *prosopopoeia* might lead one to believe. Truth is the relationship between a subject and the unconscious: impossible to grasp. Always a little off. In the classical philosophers one always finds in one place or another a fixed point, which gives the mind repose and makes truth into a stable relationship: with the known object, with the knowing subject, with Reason, or with History. But where the unconscious is involved, nothing is guaranteed. Lacan pulls the rug out from under the feet of the philosophers. No certainty remains, other than that of perilous speech, impossible reality, and an already-sealed fate. Actaeon came to the appointed place as a man; he turned into a deer and missed his appointment. It wasn't him, and it wasn't her either. Like Descartes, Lacan proceeds beneath the mask, but underneath the mask it's not even Lacan.

The Man with the Iron Skeleton

So now I'm looking for a phantom. That Lacan was the object of every conceivable projection is only too obvious. I've made no secret of my own. Here is one final projection, the epitome of all the rest.

In the depths of Siberia where the Yakuts live, shamans are found. They are sorcerers, endowed with powers that sorcerers commonly have. Their training is so special that it has become a model: all forms of initiation relate to it one way or another. You see me coming with huge feathers on my body. To become a shaman one must travel. Not like the young gentleman on tour in Englightenment Europe, who calmly set out in a stage coach and actually traveled about from place to place. The kind of trips I'm talking about can be taken without moving. They're dangerous in another way, as shown by the fact that the word has been taken up by drug users. Indeed, it is by means of drugs that future shamans set out toward their destination. Bear in mind that they do have a destination. In the land of the shades, in Hell, in the Other World, they turn into birds with iron skeletons. They return incorruptible, invulnerable, and hence, like the ramrod Andalusian bullfighter, immortal. From now on anything is possible. Two or three things we know about shamans deserve closer consideration, however. First of all, they have androgynous capabilities: the shaman can change sex without losing face. Better still, he can wear a woman's dress, transcending his sex. Shamans have a comic role to play: they amuse their public. They have the power to speak in unknown tongues, like nuns possessed by the devil in seventeenth-century France. They have astonishing powers to act on their own bodies: to do acrobatics, levitation, create stigmata—a bag of tricks worthy of a clown or a magician. They have a therapeutic function: in acting on their own bodies they heal the bodies of others. And they are repositories of their people's language and culture.

Lacan had none of the physical characteristics of the shaman. With him everything was transposed into the key of language. Acrobatics, levitation, poetic stigmata—all these were included in his panoply. A sort of linguistic transvestite, he found in the fantasies of women a passion for language that constantly obsessed him. He identified with their tortures, their anguish. Incorruptible, invulnerable, he gave the impression—he, the "subject-supposed-to-know"—of being untouchable and always ready to be reborn. A traveler in ancient and foreign linguistic realms, he was the repository of the language and culture of the psychoanalysts, notwithstanding their rejection of him—*meglio ancor.* A therapist, he treated his own language and hence the language of others as well. A comedian, he made people laugh, he was playful. He was strictly abnormal, as any man with the body of a bird and a skeleton of iron would have to be. Lame, awkward of build, he was both heroic and foolish, grandiose and ridiculous with his feathers and his bow-tie. Hopping about from place to place in the hope of avoiding his fate, he was old-fashioned, retrograde, obsolete—and timeless.

Old-fashioned is something he had been for all eternity. He is even more so now that the "human sciences," which in their halcyon days saw a hundred flowers bloom, have been relegated to the antique counter by the "philosophy of human rights," for want of anything better. Where structuralism, science, epistemology, and history used to be taught, now we hear only morality. Lacan's voice can no longer make itself heard, now that France is sinking into national torpor and its myth of liberty, briefly rekindled by the flames of a romanticism short on ideas, is subsiding into a cold ember. The real cause of Lacan's death is the deaf ear of his times.

But the shaman must "die" in his body if he is to be reborn as a bird. *"Si le grain ne meurt . . . ,"* as that other shaman [André Gide] once said. By steering psychoanalysis with a firm hand in the direction of language, Lacan forced it to undergo a fatal trial of initiation. For he was unsure that psychoanalysts were intellectually solid enough to receive the iron skeleton. And a shaman who fails the test is nothing but an impoverished intellectual. Of whom there are plenty around Lacan, some foolish, others wicked. More wicked than in other places, and also much more foolish. Failures.

As for Lacan the shaman, "death" attended each station of his passion. The time has come to tell his story in detail, like one of those legends first heard you can't remember when, on some night in the dim past. And we must begin at the beginning, at a time when nothing foretold the strange destiny of a sorcerer astray in an age that had forgotten its ancient customs and that took him for a clown. His story is not suited to today's France; the journalist from *Actuel* failed in his attempt to write the life of Lacan as Plutarch once wrote the lives of famous men. From rumor he learned what was grotesque about the aging shaman. But instead of Plutarch and the great men he described, we got Suetonius, and Agrippina rocking Nero in his cradle. Lacan said it himself, speaking of Claudel: the sublime is just a stone's throw from the grotesque.

He didn't know how truly he spoke.

CHAPTER 2

THE LADIES' WAY

The age of psychiatry; the fantasies of women and their attractions; the defenses of men; and the effect of the mirror

On Style, Once Again, and on the Madness of Women

Nineteen-eighty brought with it the revival of narrative. Narrative rushed in from all sides. It inundated writing and made inroads on theories that had grown old imperceptibly, while no one was looking. Theories that were impressive-looking machines: interpretations of Marx with all the old gears replaced by new ones and sparkling, nickel-plated new parts installed here and there by clever tinkerers; historical panoramas that had shrewdly divided time and space between beautiful madness and repressive reason; and scholarly reveries whose parts fitted together as cleverly as the parts of a Chinese puzzle and that presented a surface as smooth to the touch as Japanese ivories. All these intricate and elegant constructions had turned to rust or come apart before our very eyes. From this impasse—the situation I have just described is in some sense a pastiche of my own interests at this time and a fair account of what became of them— there was only one way out: disillusioned lyricism. The very existence of a journal of reportage like *Actuel* in its new format is proof enough of the saving vitality of the narrative. What is more, my daughter read *Actuel* and thought it "neat."

In a magazine article addressed to young intellectuals, Jean-

François Bizot wrote: "We were obliged to take note of the forced
retreat of hopes and utopias. Instead of the cynicism of *Realpoli-
tik,* we decided to resort to the narrative statement of fact as a
way of passing a life-jacket to our ideas, which had foundered."[1]
The constraint came from politics, and from revolutions, which
invariably baffled us: some because, just as we rolled up our
sleeves and got ready to go to work, they turned their backs on
us, and others because they showed signs of transforming themselves into dictatorships. Even now, writing these poor, empty
words, I am sure that I am still in some ways a dupe. But Bizot
for his part was not wrong: our ideas had foundered, our heads
were under water.

The narrative provided a kind of reef we could catch hold of,
just enough to indicate and describe what we had thought. As
Bizot put it, "The narrative remobilizes thought."

In narrative our thought lay curled up like an embryo, asleep,
caught in the toils of the deceptive passion to describe. The same
time saw the triumphant rebirth of the psychological novel in its
most formidably family-centered forms: love stories and stories
about mothers, fathers, and children raised to the level of relative
truths—better these than dashed hopes. The days of those for-
midable intellectual machines of yesteryear seemed far away indeed. And Lacan was still alive.

This same Lacan, at the dawn of his many long lives, was a
psychiatrist. He never turned his back on that part of his training. Even while he was holding his seminar, he continued to hear
students present their patients: an old French tradition. At the
Hôpital de Sainte-Anne, moreover, he listened to patients spill
out their fantasies, narrate their lives. He was a prodigious listener, who never took part in the cruel game—a pedagogical fiction which some doctors at the time took seriously for their own
amusement—of pushing patients to the end of their rope by pretending to go along with them, just for laughs.[2] In public, patients, when they speak, are storytellers. The purpose of the whole
exercise is to get them to reconstruct their lives: midway be-

tween a police investigation and a public anamnesis, the psychiatric inquiry is a search for clues, for traces of the past. Slowly a narrative takes shape: whether it is true or false is of little importance. The important thing is that it be uttered to someone. Having an audience gives a theatrical atmosphere to the event. Something of the spirit of Charcot is in the air: hysteria passes in review, offering bits and pieces of narrative as it struts upon the stage.

In order to succeed in an academic career the psychiatrist must produce case studies. Psychiatric papers are pieces of casuistry, so subtle that in some cases they are almost baffling. One disease shades off into another until everything becomes "schizoid." In fact, over the years the labels varied and shifted about so much that it became necessary to create a special category of cases impossible to subsume under any other label: the "borderlines," on the fringes of madness. But quite often the labels, like truth and falsehood, count for little: what matters is the underlying narrative. This is new and different in each case. And each case carries its own unique truth. Already narrative was mobilizing thought.

Jacques-Marie Lacan, chief resident of a psychiatric clinic, was no exception: he was a young psychiatrist with a bright future in store. He had been a student of Clerambault, a rather unusual psychiatrist who was mad about fabrics and woolens, which he collected, and who committed suicide—in front of a mirror—in 1934. Jacques-Marie Lacan wrote a thesis, which was published in 1932, a thesis with a long list of dedications that ended, so as to be sure not to leave anyone out, with the ritual formula, "Meis et amicis," to my family and friends. Its title was "On Paranoid Psychosis in Relation to the Personality." At the same time Lacan was publishing in the journal *Le Minotaure* articles of quite another stripe, from which all academicism was banished, this being an "arty" review.[3] There Lacan appeared in the company of Dogon masks and Ethiopian treasures, alongside those who made the trek from Dakar to Djibouti toward the end of colonialism's halcyon days. He shared the pages of the review with

Eluard, Reverdy, Picasso, and Masson, who became his brother-in-law, and with Dali, who borrowed from Lacan's thesis on paranoia the foundations of his own "critical paranoia," an aesthetic legitimation of insanity. The journal was a remarkable melting-pot, still ruled by the influential presence of André Breton. The revolution had turned cultural; the surrealists were becoming aesthetes. In this polyphonic concert Lacan's voice talked "cases." It told stories, all of which had this in common: they were stories of women, and they concerned the notion of style.

Yes, style—even at this early date. And not just any style, but the incoherent, disturbed style of inspired madwomen. In 1931 Lacan presented to the Société médico-psychologique his "observations" of one Marcelle, a thirty-four year old schoolteacher who had gone insane. Her malady was diagnosed as "schizophasia," a rather odd category. She produced "inspired" writings. "Inspired" like the writings of the prophets: but the madman is a prophet only in his own land, and a strange and solitary land it is. From what anthropologists like Marcel Mauss and Claude Lévi-Strauss tells us, we know that nothing distinguishes the madman from the prophet, the sorcerer, or the charismatic political leader—nothing, that is, except the greater distance that his delirium places between him and the group around him. Both the madman and the prophet invent a language of their own. Innovators, they do violence to grammar, to words, to the substance of language. But the prophet stands on the very edge of intelligibility, at the place where his linguistic innovations can still be understood by the group. The madman, in contrast, is too far out, isolated and out of touch: hence his inventions become "disturbances." When Lacan came, somewhat later on in 1933, to discuss the notorious crime of the Papin sisters, he took the view that their criminal madness was not so much a disturbance as a "social masterpiece" (*chef-d'oeuvre social*). Their inspiration inspired Lacan; hidden no longer, shamanism proclaimed itself, even to Lacan himself.

The fascination with the raving style of these writings, though it first appeared in a context already explored by the surrealists and later by Georges Bataille—who, rumor had it, was no stranger to Lacan's couch—did not remain innocent for long. Nor did it remain without effect. Lacan sucked milk from the neologism. He enjoyed the new words and the old, clichéd turns of phrase which, oddly enough, produced creative results only because they reverted to their ancient forms. Caught between the need to describe a pathology—and hence to describe the "not normal," almost equivalent, that is, to the "not good"—and the desire to understand "the great value" of inspired writing, Lacan wavered. To the Société médico-psychologique he said that this delirious writing was "brief and impoverished," that "nothing is, broadly speaking, less inspired than this writing, which is felt to be inspired." But his was not the only signature on this article. With his surrealist friends at *Le Minotaure* he took quite a different line. The writing in question, he said, carried "an eminent intentional meaning and [possessed] a very great ability to communicate tension." In itself it was a creation in no way inferior to the inspiration of the greatest artists; it recalled the mythical themes of folklore, which Freud had already uncovered in his psychoanalytic research. Whereas this frenzied paranoia was, according to the "official" textbook, akin to a kind of feeble-mindedness, impossible to confuse with any kind of mysticism, in the pages of *Le Minotaure* it became something else entirely.

Humanism's watchdogs, the guardians of its normative proscriptions, had scarcely any tolerance for madness. But Lacan, with the other hand, the "left" hand that was to guide him throughout his life, also wrote:

The life experience of the paranoiac and the world view it engenders may be thought of as a novel form of syntax, which enlists its own peculiar means of comprehension for the purpose of affirming the community of mankind. Understanding this syntax can, I think, provide an invaluable introduction to the symbolic values of art and, more particularly, to the problems of style—an introduction, in other words, to art's peculiar virtues of conviction and human communion as well as to the paradoxes attendant upon its creation. These problems will always remain beyond the grasp of any form of anthropology that has not yet freed itself from the naïve realism of the object.[4]

A novel syntax implying the need to understand a style, as against the impossible aim of communication: a fundamental contradiction—what the inspired madwomen write is often superb but it makes no sense, its meaning cannot be communicated. Only a person willing to hear what these women are saying, a person willing to become "crazy" in order to understand them, can gain access to this meaning and yet remain within the confines of the human community from which the patient has been cast out. The message is clear: Lacan proclaims it to himself. Style is the man . . . to whom one is speaking. In other words, how can one be teacher, theorist, and poet all at once? How can one be crazy and a public figure at the same time? In short, how can one become Lacan?

Marcelle: "I am the brother of the bad rat who makes you hoarse if you take mother's way, the marten and the fir close in, but, if you are sunshine and a poet with long deeds, I see You, yes I do, and I'll escape from that place. I put my lock in your woodcock."[5]

Lacan: "Before the upturned glove, suppose the hand knew what it was doing? Wouldn't it be to give it back, the glove, that is, to none other than one with whom La Fontaine and Racine would be willing to put up? The interpretation must be nimble to satisfy the 'interpreneur.' Pure loss endures: from him who endures it to him who does not take a chance is as from the father to the swine."[6]

Marcelle: "I am the handsome overfull of humor without pinafull and from the Vulture, the trial platoon that smashes the dirt to distinguish herself at all odds from others who want to surpass you because discretion is the better part of valor."[7]

Lacan: "The middy installed in his palace of ochre: 'Between middy-ochre and vile there is not a shade of difference' is a line I have a hard time attributing to the author of the poem that so effectively humorizes the word."[8]

Fluid are the boundaries that separate the play on words from the poetic invention, the premeditated device from the chance discovery, the frenzy of madness from the Lacanian norm. Once again, word play enters the discussion. But word play also has its roots in madness. What is the difference between Marcelle's pleasure in playing with words and Lacan's pleasure in doing the same thing? An ever so slight difference of communicability, an ever so slight concern with making one's meaning intelligible to everyone.

Lacan, then, felt the fascination of paranoiac writing in the very earliest stages of his work. So far did he feel this fascination that he incorporated in himself one of the most powerful effects of the paranoid style. Later, he would use the incommunicable strangeness of the delirious text with calculated effect.

I say again, with calculated effect. For invariably, along with the hermetic phrases, he slipped in a limpid sentence or two. Just when his meaning seemed most obscure there would glimmer a flash of logic that made it possible to put all the pieces together. Still, he took from his familiarity with paranoid inspiration his knowledge of a dangerous and subtle game; he walked the fine line between communication and non-communication, between light and darkness: the *midire*, or mid-speak, the art of the half-spoken thought. He learned a profound lesson from his paranoid female patients: in order to make oneself understood, it is sometimes necessary to play with a dangerously "open" language. Open, first of all, to invention, to words that do not yet exist. Open too to poetics—which comes to the same thing. Open, finally, where he was accused of being "closed," hermetically opaque. Such was the dialectic that Lacan chose for himself.

Closed—in other words, reticent to speak before crowds. He agreed to speak before the television cameras only on the condition that he could carry on with his "mid-speak," thus insuring that he would not be understood. Closed—in other words, deliberately selective. And open to the ears of the chosen few, his disciples and friends, all of them crazy. It should come as no surprise that this led to the formation of a school. To found a school was perhaps the only answer for Lacan. And when Lacan's words had circulated far too widely, when they became not his words but the words of his School, he dissolved the school. And started all over again. Yes, the first lesson of paranoia was the lesson of style. In one sense Lacan released the paranoid style from its confinement. He legalized it, bestowed upon it a patent of nobility, recognizing its "peculiar virtues of conviction and human communion . . ."[9]

This was not paranoia's only lesson. This "true madness," the easiest of all to diagnose, is often described, somewhat superficially, as composed of two interwoven themes: delusions of grandeur and delusions of persecution. At the simplest level this is true. Paranoia makes a man the bearer of a message revealed to him. So important and so urgent is this message that it provokes persecution of the messenger. The paranoid delusion is the story of this unknown prophet's tragedy, the story of a lost mystic to whom no one pays attention and upon whom the whole world heaps misery. The delusion speaks the truth. It aggravates what would elsewhere, in more banal social circumstances, be power relations. It is fabulously commonplace. If the delirium takes off, it links up with the most exalted forms of inspiration, possibly by way of crime, though the crime may in fact depart little from the status quo. Freud was aware of this when he analyzed the deluded writings of Judge Schreber, who was locked up for dreaming he was a woman who would receive a message from God through copulation, the fruits of which had been presaged by white geese. The delusion speaks the truth; it beckons to the prophet.

But Lacan did not concern himself with men. In the beginning Lacan was interested only in women.[10]

Jacques Lacan, Blessed Lady

Marcelle, Aimée, the Papin sisters—the whole cast of characters in his early work consists of women. Not a single man is present.

One of the most frequently encountered commonplaces about Lacan concerns his alleged aversion to women, his deep-seated misogyny. Everybody repeats this. In such unlikely places as the pages of a mass-circulation magazine, you find the same reproach: "He doesn't like women. He said they don't exist. He said that they are nothing." What didn't he say, he who never really "said" anything?

All of this is nonsense of monumental proportions. Here is a man whose thinking is founded entirely on the study of female paranoia. A man who never stopped talking about women. And finally, a man who dissolved his School and who, when this dissolution brought him into direct conflict with a woman—Françoise Dolto—took pains to clarify his thinking and to address himself to women analysts. That his behavior (whether apparent or real doesn't matter much to me) was that of an aging macho scholar and hardly a model of progressivism is beyond doubt. To deduce from this that his theory was misogynist is to disort that theory. The question is why such a distorted interpretation has been put forward. I personally know important leaders of the women's liberation movement who were helped to begin their political work by Lacan. If they later pushed their thinking further or turned in other directions, they have always paid their theoretical debts, as their own words attest.[11] But in this day and age the attitudes of militant feminists no longer prove anything, and I've even come to the point of wondering whether the charge of misogyny leveled against Lacan is not the paradoxical product of a period that for some time now has tended to dismiss women and their demands. The proof that "all that stuff" is just so much rubbish is that Lacan said that women do not exist. By "all that stuff" these critics presumably mean theory, thought, the human sciences—whatever makes life more complicated. How simple it is to declare oneself a woman against a man, especially when the man is named Lacan. How convenient—no further thought is necessary, all questions evaporate. This leaves the good gentlemen rubbing their hands with glee: they've stopped thinking, they're going to leave us in peace.

He did not say that women do not exist. He said, "Woman does not exist." To tell the truth, or to "half tell"*(midire)* even more of the truth, even this is not entirely accurate. One day, while lecturing, Lacan ventured to say this: "Woman *(la femme)* can only be written by slashing the definite article."[12] In print, then, we may represent his thought as follows: "L̸a femme n'existe pas," (t̸he) woman does not exist. Wave after wave of feminists have been saying the same thing for a century, and they were saying the same thing when Lacan made the point in his own way. When women rise up against the myth of women that men have foisted upon them in our cultures, they too (primordially they) are denying the existence of the eternal Woman, age-old and immutable, half of a Totality whose center is Man. A product of patriarchy, under whose domination we still live, this logical curiosity has enjoyed an extraordinary vitality. It has always functioned by placing man at the absolute Center of creation, the other half of creation at his side. The woman. And all too often, despite his denials, His woman. In endlessly varied, infinitely subtle and humanistic guises, Adam's rib continues to exert its mythical power: half of man, but emerged from his side, the woman does not in fact exist. This gender is not a gender. A few moments later Lacan made this point clearly: "There is no woman except as excluded by the nature of things which is the nature of words, and it must be said that if there is one thing about which women have complained enough for the time being, this is it."[13] Obviously Lacan's way of putting things has not been properly understood. It is perfectly clear that what he is saying is profoundly banal. Lacan, treating the definite article, was simply ratifying a point that women had been making for a long time, and he knew it. But he did not leave it at that.

Honesty compels me to cite his remarks in full. "If there is one thing about which women have complained enough for the time being, this is it—only they don't know what they are saying, that's all the difference there is between them and me." [14] A male chauvinist joke? Withering irony? The rest of the demonstration goes farther still. But it is advisable to take it slowly, like a piece by Schumann. And to dream a little while listening, to let the sounds blossom within, no matter whether the listener is a man or a woman. Woman, then, does not exist—not as an eternal myth, because, so says Lacan, "she is not the whole of her essence."

Mid-speak (*Mi-dire*). Not the whole truth. A treatise on the correct usage of reserve in literary style: Lacan's style is such a treatise—it is unceasingly reserved. His formulae, figures, and tropes are allied with negation, with the negation of negation, and with all resources of grammar that turn plain assertion around and stand it on its head. "I tell the truth—not the whole truth." When the truth is conceived "whole," it cannot be anything but the complement of the man. But the truth is not "the whole truth," it eludes the grasp of man, his culture, and his language. And since any privation dialectically entails a "surplus," since to assert without negation and to assert by means of double negation are not the same thing, if women is not "the whole truth" she will enjoy a privilege that men lack. To tell the truth, she will enjoy—simply that. For the "surplus," which Lacan says is a supplement rather than a complement, is female orgasm (*jouissance*).

A splendid dissertation topic and an absurdly difficult puzzle. Lacan is angry as well as joking: whenever women have been asked to describe their orgasms, they have shown themselves unwilling or unable to say anything about the subject. Haughtily, as was his custom, Lacan dismissed with a mental slap the bum-

bling of the physiologists with their talk of "the posterior pole
of the muzzle of the uterus and other nonsense"—the French col-
loquialism for nonsense, *conneries,* a derivative of the common
word for the female genitals, *con,* is here well chosen. On the
basis of his analytic experience he even went so far as to say that
women become concerned with their frigidity only when orgasm
is imposed upon them as a duty. He said this well before wom-
en's voices were raised to echo his point. He discusses "their"
orgasms as a man: with a mixture of lyricism, irritation, envy,
and admiration. And it was as a man that he went so far as to
say that he *knew* better than they what he was talking about:
"She has her own kind of pleasure (*jouissance*), 'she' who does
not exist and signifies nothing. She has her own kind of pleasure
about which she may know nothing, except that she feels it, and
that one thing she knows. She knows of course when it happens.
It doesn't happen to all of them." [15]

As a man, then, Lacan is reduced to *knowing* and to *speaking:*
not really to thinking. The female orgasm represents, within the
entire body of his work and thought, the absolute culmination:
there theory ends. His admitted tactical maneuver, carried out
with superb skill and straightforwardly explicated, is designed to
get around the unknown quantity of the female orgasm and at
the same time to appropriate some of that pleasure for himself;
this follows shortly after the remark on *La femme.* She is seeking
love. As for orgasm, nothing doing, but as for love, well, about
that he knows plenty! It has nothing to do with sexual intercourse. Lacan caused a scandal one day when he said out of the
blue that there is no such thing as sexual intercourse. Although
the seminar was normally enthusiastically docile, that assertion
raised quite an uproar. Suddenly a worry sprang up in everyone's
mind (and therefore in my own): so we weren't doing it, then?
We were wrong even about that? But the point of this little pronouncement was just as much a commonplace as the pronouncement on *La femme.* The thrust of the remark was the word "intercourse," not the word "sexual." In this respect Lacan remained

entirely faithful to Freud's thought and displaced sexuality from
its physical locus in the lower abdomen, in the "thing." Sexuality is constantly coursing over the surface of the body, but it
does not give rise to "intercourse" in the logical sense of the
word. Nor is there exchange, "relationship." If memory serves,
it was at precisely this point that Lacan began his discussion of
one of love's great myths, the myth of simultaneous orgasm,
about which he asked publicly why this, to judge by the evidence
of sex manuals, constituted the erotic ideal of Western civilization.

"Intercourse," "relationship," mutual exchange of pleasure,
Total Women, Eternal Mother, recovery of an original unity—
Lacan the Christian knew what he was about. The history of
ideas showed that he was right. Freud had defined himself against
Jung, the psychoanalyst who denied that sexuality was the source
of all desire, with his theory of "archetypes" situating that source
instead in the most archaic memories of the race. Freud wanted
a new science, not a return to religion. In Italy the strength of
Catholicism encouraged the proliferation of Jungian analysts. This
was no accident. In France, by contrast, the Jungians formed a
harmless fringe group. But then the left collapsed and the deck
was reshuffled after the debacle. In the changed ideological and
political climate, the Jungians came roaring back to life, bolstered
in part, but only in part, by the resurgent ideas of the right wing.
Freud's star was declining along with Marx's. The time had come
for the return of the Eternal Feminine, the return to the womb,
which neither women nor Lacan nor Freud had wanted. Regression was in full swing. As if by accident it was at this very moment that some people began to criticize Lacan for having said
that woman does not exist, etc.

To recapitulate: woman does not exist, nor does sexual intercourse, but love does exist. It depends upon God's *jouissance* and
is best expressed in mysticism. Here Lacan began to speak ten-
derly for a few minutes about Saint Theresa, as depicted in Bernini's sculpture, and of Hadewijch of Antwerp, a Beguine [the

Beguines were lay women who chose to live a semicloistered life in enclosed areas or *beguinages* constructed in various cities during the Middle Ages—trans.]. In speaking of these women, Lacan repeated what he had said earlier about all women: "And what is the substance of their ecstasy? Based on the testimony of the mystics, it is clear that they did feel pleasure, but that they knew nothing about it."

He went on: "These mystical ejaculations are neither idle chatter nor inane verbiage but, broadly speaking, the sort of thing that is best read at the bottom of the page, in a footnote. Include the 'Ecrits' of Jacques Lacan, because these are of the same order." [16] Here, then, Lacan classes himself among the mystics—as I was telling you.

"Excuse me," objects the Prudent Scholar. "You just defined Lacan as Freud's heir in the battle against Jung and religiosity, and now he turns out to be a mystic. Which is it?"

Sure, why not? There's nothing so astonishing in that. From Baudelaire to Klossowski, to say nothing of Hegel and Goethe, the names of those for whom mysticism and religion have nothing to do with each other are legion. And don't forget that one of Lacan's intimates was Georges Bataille. The same Georges Bataille who, in *Madame Edwarda,* described a madwoman who, while exhibiting the spread lips of her vagina, said that she was God.[17] Lacan is part of this intellectual tradition, which dwelt on the mystical experience, stripped away the surrounding husk of institutionalized religion, and rediscovered the true nature of mysticism by sublimating it. From the mystic to the madman is but a stone's throw; and as with the madman in the modern age, it was the social group—the sect, the monastic order, the Church, the physician's guild—that had the power to classify the mystic as falling on one side or the other of the dividing line between abnormality and charismatic function: the experience in both cases was the same. And Lacan situated himself inside it.

Thus it was logical that Lacan should have begun this thinking with insane women—and the logic of that choice became more and more evident with each new page that he wrote and each new word that he uttered. He never stopped thinking about women: Hadewijch of Antwerp followed Marcelle, Saint Theresa followed the Papin sisters—always the women were the same. Whether locked up in hospitals where Lacan discovered them or sanctified by a tradition that idealized them even as it misunderstood them, "inspired" women inspired Lacan throughout his long life. This was one of his principal lives: the most enigmatic, most difficult, and most recalcitrant of all, just like female ecstasy (*jouissance*), with which Lacan, in declaring himself to be a mystic, sought to identify himself.

The Eternal Couple: The Criminal and the Saint

In the age of asylums and cathedrals, women found their rapture in the convents, which had become harems set aside for the exclusive pleasure of the Lord. In the nineteenth and twentieth centuries they were sent to the hospital. No longer were they beatified or sanctified. Jean-Noël Vuarnet, examining the history of feminine mysticism from the time of the Beguines down to the children Bernadette and Thérèse of Lisieux, who saw the Virgin Mary, ends his grand survey with a portrait of a "real" madwoman: Madeleine of the Salpetrière, who was a patient of Pierre Janet.[18] The Physician has supplanted God, verifying the stigmata, recording the ecstatic pleasures of a body that is immutably passive and possessed. The mystics who aroused Lacan's interest were of a quite different sort. Their raptures were criminal; their pleasures took the form of actions. Aimée and the Papin sisters were insane and they were mystics, but they were also criminals.

Le Mans is a perfectly French town in the region known as the Sarthe. It is a town where not much has happened over the years, in which the bourgeoisie has managed to gain the upper hand over the aristocracy, which remains shut up in its drafty castles.

It is a wealthy region in which domestic servants were treated little better than animals: not so long ago it would have been possible, in this adorable little town, to hear a fine lady asking her butcher to cut a roast for her family and some lungs for the maid. Christine and Léa Papin were maids who did everything around the house. Sisters, they were inseparable from one another. They were also a little odd: they never went out. On their days off they both remained locked in their room. They said very little. But they were good servants. Living in the house were a woman and her daughter: not easy people to get along with but hard women, not unusual for this time and this social class, with its fierce habits.

One stormy night lightning caused a power failure. That night the two mistresses of the house had gone out. When they returned they reprimanded the two servants: no doubt it was the maids who were at fault if the lights were out. They had done nothing about it but remained together as usual, waiting for the power to come back on. Usually the two sisters did not respond to their employers' anger. But this time was different—very different.

Each of the sisters grabbed a victim; they tore their victims' eyes from their sockets. Then, with their victims on the ground, they quickly grabbed up all the tools from the area of the house given over to them as servants, kitchen tools and whatnot. Hammers, pitchers, and knives were all wielded in the sacrifice.

They crushed their victims' faces, stomped on their bodies, and then, to finish things off, slashed the thighs and buttocks of the two dead women and poured the blood of one over the sex of the other, marrying them in a ritual of mayhem. When it was all over, they carefully washed all the knives, hammers, and pitchers in the sink. Then they washed themselves and went to bed together as always. According to their own testimony, the only word they exchanged was, "That's a clean job of it!" Perfectly in character for kitchen maids. The rest of it was no concern of theirs.[19]

Another story: one spring night in Paris, a great actress—someone of the stature of Eve Lavallière, Cecile Sorel, Sarah Bernhardt, or, later, Huguette Duflos—arrives at the theater where she is supposed to perform. An unknown women approaches her at the stage door, as fans and autograph seekers will. Madame Z's suspicions are not aroused. The woman she is speaking to seems quite normal, quite decently dressed, wearing gloves, carrying a handbag, with a fur collar and fur bands around the wrists of her coatsleeves, as was later reported. She is no beggar. The unknown woman asks the actress if she is indeed Madame Z. After admitting that she is, Madame Z moves on. Or rather she tries to move on. The unknown woman takes a knife from her handbag and attempts to stab Madame Z. Madame Z grabs the knife by the blade, severing two tendons in her hand. The unknown assailant is arrested and hospitalized.[20] Lacan dubs her "Aimée." She will become "the Aimée case."

What do these two stories, one of which Lacan discussed in a long article in *Le Minotaure* (the Papin sisters) and the other of which became the subject of his thesis in medicine, have in common? In the first place, crime: the transgression of the social norm, the sudden, dramatic act committed by an unknown person whose action stupefies society at large. Aimée's petty crime would have remained a commonplace incident of psychotic aggression but for the celebrity of the victim—but this was precisely one of the motives of the act. As for the crime committed by the Papin sisters, all of France was profoundly troubled by the implications of the act publicized by Jérôme and Jean Tharaud in a series of articles appearing in *Paris-Soir* in 1933. The crime left such an indelible mark on the French imagination that Jean Genet used it many years later as the inspiration for his play *Les Bonnes* ("The Maids"). Even today the crime haunts the collective memory. In Le Mans it is never mentioned. Nobody will say where the house is located. On the subject of crime, the illegal action, the criminal deed, psychiatry has had something to say ever since the nineteenth century, when some psychiatrists were anointed as experts on criminal insanity in the midst of a crime wave best exemplified by the case of Pierre Rivière.[21] But psychoanalysis, with no claims to expertise in criminal matters [in France the exclusive province of psychiatrists—trans.], has nothing to do with labelling criminals or deciding upon their responsibility or lack of responsibility for their acts. Rather, it explores their childhood, looking for causes while the police are looking for motives. Almost the same thing, but not quite: the psychoanalyst traces the criminal's whole life since childhood, whereas the police confine their investigations to the adult life of the accused and to his or her most immediate desires—what we call "motives," the forces that set the criminal act in motion. Last but not least, psychoanalysis has a concept that corresponds to the uniqueness of the act, nowhere so apparent as in the case of the Papin sisters. Nothing foretold the murder they were to commit, much less the extraordinary way in which they were to go about it, and no act of violence followed the crime, at any rate none aimed at another member of civil society. Psychology, in the early days of its association with criminology, referred to such unique acts as "monomanias," a convenient term for describing a form of madness that manifests itself only once. This concept broke new ground. The psychoanalyst refers to the act as an instance of "acting out."

If the insane act is a question of acting out, this means that it is the result of an implacable logic that has been in preparation for a long time—not to say forever. For it is not only the childhood of the person concerned that shapes the sudden act of violence—or in less dangerous cases the action that is merely out of the ordinary—but also the childhood of his mother, or of his father; at one further remove, it is the institution of the family, as far back as memory can go. These are the root causes of a social malady that may ultimately take the form of true insanity. We now know that family memories rarely extend back more than three generations or so. This is the pattern revealed by the oldest known myths and cultures. Nevertheless, every act of

madness has in some sense been in preparation since the beginning of time: as the psychoanalyst sees it, the question is always
why it should be acted out in any particular instance. But then
the act vanishes behind the process of anamnesis and the interminable search for the past. It is abolished by all that precedes it.
As for its consequences, society decides what is to be done about
them. Christine and Léa Papin were at first sentenced to be guil-
lotined on the town square of Le Mans. Aimée was confined to
a mental hospital. And yet the difference between the two acts
was not one of kind but one of degree. To be sure, social aggression had assumed ancient proportions, and the open-mouthed
horror of civil society in the face of such acts accounts for the
primitive harshness of the sentence, proportionate to the dispro-
portionateness of the crime. Later the sentence was reduced, as if
society finally took note of the fact that the act committed was a
question not for the courts but for the hospitals. Had the sentence been maintained, it would have confirmed the existence of
crimes that had long since been wiped from the slate of the Law.
A dead past had worked its way to the surface, and this past was
not simply that of two sisters who had been reared in a climate
of extreme emotional deprivation. The prudent thing to do was
to entrust the whole matter to the psychiatrists and the analysts.
For the "acting out" had transgressed the boundary between the
imaginary and the real, the myth and the fact, the repressed history and the sudden actuality of the deed.

The first point of similarity linking Christine, Léa, and Aimée
is their status as women. Just as women alone can experience
ecstasy without knowing what its nature is, so these women were
able to act out their conflicts once and for all, releasing all their
tensions and deciding their fate. In prison the Papin sisters became what they had previously been only in principle: stark raving mad. Once hospitalized, Aimée was delirious at first but
within six months was cured. For acting out, however dangerous
it may be, is also therapeutic, monstrously so. A conflict that
becomes a deed, a fact, ceases to exist. Mental calm can then be

restored. Such acts are little different from those that have been part of female mythology from time immemorial: from Penthe-silea who devoured Achilles raw and then fell asleep quite rested to Pentheus' mother, Agave, a Bacchante subject to trances, who mistook her son for a wild beast and tore him limb from limb; from Corneille's Camille to Michelet's witches, from Judith to Charlotte Corday, the list of women who owe their renown to crime is endless. These women are heroines, and it is as heroines that they fascinated Lacan. Consider the conclusion of his article in *Le Minotaure:*

> They plucked out their victims' eyes as the Bacchantes castrated their victims. The sacrilegious curiosity that has anguished men since the beginning of time moved them in their desire for their victims, in their search in the dead women's gaping wounds for what Christine, in all innocence, later described to the court as "the mystery of life." [22]

Calmly, he foreshadows the final explanation, the revelation of the secret shared in common by these two female crimes. In order to discover what this secret is we must trace the histories of both crimes back through time, step by step. We must follow Jacques Lacan as he makes the discovery that became the source of all his subsequent thought. The enigma stands before us: we must now decipher it.

When Christine was imprisoned, she was, as is natural in a French prison, separated from Léa. Five months later the effects of this separation made themselves felt. Christine suffered hallu-cinations; she attempted to tear her eyes out. Confined in a strait-jacket, she refused to eat, she engaged in acts of self-punishment, she "expiated" her sins, and of course she began to rave madly. When Lacan learned of these facts—from the press and from the court psychiatrist, Doctor Logre—he immediately under-stood that the separation was the cause of the delirium, just as the close relationship between the two sisters was the cause of the crime. He understood this because the case of Aimée had already put him on the right track, and because feminine paranoia, even more than its masculine counterpart, had shed light on what is known in Freudian jargon as repressed homosexuality. But this was not the first explanation: it was to be the final one.

The first explanation involved language: this trail is already familiar to us. It begins with words and leads to action. In order for a paranoid crime to be committed, a metaphor must enter into reality. "I'll tear her eyes out"—this is hatred speaking, hatred at its most harmless. But when the metaphor is realized and the barrier between fantasy, imagination, and reality is eliminated, most people, Lacan tells us, react to the magnitude of the deed: their reaction is "ambivalent, double-edged, a product of the emotional contagion of the crime and the demand for punishment raised by public opinion." [23]

The extraordinary crime of the sisters Papin could occur only on one condition: each sister had to constitute the entire world of the other. "Genuine Siamese souls, they formed a permanently closed world. Reading their depositions after the crime, Doctor Logre remarked that 'you would think you were seeing double.' With no other resources than those they found on their solitary island, they had to resolve their enigma, the human enigma of sex." [24]

In other words, here we have a couple of sisters who, because they were brought up together, never had to face up to the existence of the Other, man. Two sisters who found their pleasure together; who, in murder, found a sacred form of ecstasy; and who, after killing their victims and laying bare their sexual parts, fastened themselves on their thighs. "I am certain," said Christine, "that in another life I was supposed to be my sister's husband." Actually she was her sister's husband in his life as well. When another female couple appeared in a hostile guise, the Papin couple let go. Their "twin insanity" had done its work. Its root cause was the "difficulty of being two," the impossibility of distinguishing themselves from one another, to the point that the other ceased to exist. From these circumstances came loss of identity and madness.

Lacan himself compared the two sisters to Aimé. Just as Christine and Léa were inseparable, so Aimée was also "inseparable." Over the course of her life, however, she was "inseparable" not from a single woman but from a succession of different figures, and it was probably this that allowed her to stop short of murder. For Aimée, the primary object of identification was her mother—the same as herself. "We were such friends," as Aimée tearfully put it. Next came a fallen aristocrat, Mademoiselle C. de la N., "a subtle schemer." Reading Lacan's thesis, it is easy to imagine the woman: a person who looked upon work as degrading, who ruled her colleagues with the authority of a duchess rebuking her lackeys, and who laid down the standards of good and bad taste with an iron hand. Her swagger fascinated Aimée, who first heard about the celebrated Madame Z in conversation with this woman. This fallen duchess frequently told Aimée that she, Aimée, was "masculine." Here we detect a muffled echo of Christine's belief that she was her sister's husband. But Mademoiselle C. de la N. did not prevent Aimée from marrying, more for convenience and "Don Juanism" than for love. It was then that the third woman, the third double, entered Aimée's life: her own sister, who came to live with the young newlyweds. Aimée's sister had had a hysterectomy and so had no hope of having a child. Aimée twice became pregnant. The first child was stillborn; the second lived. In both cases the sister made no secret of her unsatisfied desire to be a mother herself. Christine had been so close to Léa that she could only project her hatred along with Léa onto another female couple. Aimée, on the other hand, would take some time to work out the amorous hatred that she secretly bore toward her alter ego, and the forms taken by the fantasies derived from this hatred became increasingly remote from their original object. Finally she left home in the grip of a fantasy that took her ever closer to those creatures of luxury and bright lights who were plotting against her, the courtesans and actresses of Paris. Love or hate? The word is am-bivalence. "Each of these female persecutors was in fact merely a new image of the sister whom our patient had taken as her ideal. In other words, they were mere prisoners of Aimée's nar-cissism. Now we can understand what the glass obstacle was that prevented her from *knowing* that she loved her persecutors, al-though she cried that she did: they were merely images." [25]

Woman to woman, Aimée assaulted Madame Z: paranoia as self-punishment. Woman to woman, Christine and Léa, whose unconscious minds did not admit the existence of the Other, as-saulted two women. They attacked, just as those mystics in whom Lacan later took an interest allowed themselves to be wounded by a God who loved them and hated them to the point of inflict-ing on them every imaginable suffering, in His own image, since He himself had undergone them. The "psychic inversion" that Lacan discusses in the case of Aimée and Christine, which made each of them a male figure in a homosexual couple, has affinities with the "eternal couple of the criminal and the (female) saint," and with the exemplary story of Jean Genet.

By other means—philosophy, dialectics, phenomenology—Sartre, despite his aversion to psychoanalysis, also discovered this same "game of doubles," these same glass prisons of narcissism, in his study of Genet: *Saint Genêt, comédien et martyr*. If the saint requires her raptures and the mortification of her flesh in order to accede to sainthood, the criminal commits murder not in or-der to kill but in order to accede to "criminal being. . . . For crime is election, and it cannot be attained without the aid of grace." Not everyone who wants to can become a criminal: signs of election are required. Through rapture the lover, male or fe-male, whether Genet or the saint, touches the disturbing place where Good and Evil connect. Genet experiences amorous trances that Sartre compares to the swoons of Madame Guyon. And the experience of Evil is a "princely cogito that reveals to conscious-ness its singularity in regard to Being." The experience of the Good is the same. In both cases, what Sartre calls "singularity"

and what Lacan calls the "subject" evaporate in what Sartre calls
"consciousness" (*conscience*) and Lacan calls *jouissance*. A strange
tourniquet, says Sartre. Feminine paranoia, says Lacan. The experience is the same. But Sartre was not interested in a woman:
his subject was Genet. Whereas Lacan delved into the depths of
feminine paranoia and its sudden criminal manifestations.

In the early stages of studying the feminine enigma, Lacan came
to a crossroads where two paths diverged. These two paths were
to rejoin one another only much later on. The first led by way
of the family to that eternal and interminable discourse on love
which involves the Plato of the *Symposium,* courtly love, medieval tapestries, the Marquis de Sade, and Immanuel Kant.[26] The
second path is more fundamental: what Lacan discovered in the
crimes committed by the Papin sisters and Aimée was the so-
called "mirror stage." Beyond the twin disturbances of Christine
and Léa and the series of masks whereby Aimée identified herself
with her various doubles in order to destroy them, Lacan
glimpsed the crucial importance of an essential phase in the con-
stitution of the human personality: the moment when one becomes oneself because one is no longer the same as one's mother.
What Lacan finally discovered in his studies of women and never
repudiated thereafter was the danger of too much closeness, the
misfortune of one person's identification with another. At about
the same time, in 1937, Claude Lévi-Strauss was first becoming
acquainted with the Indians of the Amazon. There, in exploring
the strange cultures whose hitherto unsuspected degree of sophistication and intellectual complexity he was to reveal to us
twenty years later, he came upon the ethnological equivalent of
the mirror stage. In both cases the question involved is one of
"correct distance."

It sometimes happens that, because of the hazards involved in
nomadic wandering or as a result of natural catastrophes, various
bands of Indians will unintentionally come together. The Mandans of North America are an example. A tribe from a neighboring civilization joined the Mandans and learned from them

how to grow corn. Before long, however, the Mandans asked
them to leave, and their elders still repeat the words that were
uttered to them on that occasion so long ago:

> It would be better for you to cross the river and build your own
> village there, because our customs are far too different from yours.
> Since our young people and yours are not familiar with each oth-
> er's customs, there could be disputes and these might lead to war.
> Do not go too far, because peoples who live far apart are like
> strangers and war may erupt between them. Travel northward un-
> til you can no longer see the smoke from our houses, and there
> build your village. That way we will be close enough to be friends
> and yet not far enough apart to become enemies.[27]

The Mandans had an idea of the correct distance. Such an idea
is found in myths wherever chance encounters have led to catas-
trophe. It figures in the story of Oedipus, who is reunited too
closely with his mother. And it also figures in the story of the
woman Semele, who is destroyed by lightning when she comes
too close to the god Zeus, so obliging him to take the child
Dionysus she is carrying, and sew it into his thigh until it is
ready to come into the world. Correct distance also figures in
stories of incest and love affairs that are too passionate: in the
story of the overly intimate love of Madame de Mortsauf for
Felix de Vandenesse as well as the overly distant love of the Prin-
cesse de Clèves. In the one case the hero dies because he is too
close to his lover, in the other he dies because he is too far away.
Lacan's paranoiacs lash out because they are too close to a threat-
ening female figure and too far from other figures, so remote
that they are inaccessible. But the correct distance exists: education, custom, law, civil society, and all of culture are there to
establish and maintain it, to preserve between individuals a relationship without the menace implicit in the frightful closeness of
Christine and Léa. When this perfect love was forced to confront
the Other, it exploded and issued in death.

Lévi-Strauss discovered the correct distance in the stark model
of primitive society; Lacan discovered it in the child. The correct

distance is the opposite of the feminine. A bizarre minuet: Lacan searched for the correct distance, but for himself he preferred madness, the result of incorrect distance. Mysticism is incompatible with maintaining the correct distance. And if Lacan's disciples stuck to him like glue, they were perhaps merely returning affection born of a dangerous proximity that was not their fault but Lacan's. If this is correct, if indeed Lacan owed his success and his fascination to a pronounced taste for the abolition of distance, then we must confront the crucial question of psychoanalysis. For psychoanalytic practice also relies on achieving the correct distance: along the way analyst and analysand are inevitably and necessarily drawn together, but one day their relationship must terminate. The analysis cannot end until the correct distance has been achieved. When the patient is finally ready to head north and pitch his tent at a place where he can no longer see the analyst's smoke—in other words, when he is no longer suffering—the analysis is terminated. What is ritually referred to as "liquidation of transference" takes time, and this is when the correct distance is established, the correct distance that customarily separates men and women from one another and that is far from passionate love.

Quite a few analysts have a hard time accommodating themselves to this idea. The quivering of madness obsesses them, even though they are paid to cure it. Flashes of heroic action haunt their minds, as though they themselves have not entirely overcome the disturbances with which they grappled on the couch. How could anyone think that Lacan was not obsessed by the love of madness throughout his life? That he was able to sublimate this obsession in his style, sometimes with genius, changes nothing. Which would he choose: the normal child or the madwoman? What inner Bacchantes tore at him each time he returned to the subject of women?

A Brief Philosophical Digression

Ideas are exhilarating because they always carry you beyond their own limits. Exhilarating but also dangerous: the power of an idea is analogous to the power of the pleasure in neologisms for Aimée, Marcelle, and company. But ideas, like neologisms, interact with one another of their own accord and carry us along with them.

That's exactly what I'm doing with Lacan, Marcelline answered calmly. One more step and the idea would have me writing that Lacan is a paranoid woman. That would be one idea, but . . .

But Lacan was a man. A shaman, yes, but also a man like other men. Aimée was immediately hailed as a success by his poet friends: Fargue, Crevel, Joe Bousquet, Eluard. Like Marcelle, Aimée wrote in what Lacan called "the fertile moments of delirium." Before coming to the point of committing her act of aggression, she had, at a very profound level, come closer and closer to severing the ties that held her prisoner to the beloved but evil image of the sister she both loved and hated. Each time she became more isolated and more delirious, but also more of a writer. In her case Lacan struck gold not only as a psychoanalyst but also as a poet. For the eye of the psychoanalyst Aimée was able to write: "I am going to be received as a bridegroom. I shall go to see my fiancée. She will always be lost in thought. She will have children in her eyes. I will marry her. She would be too sad, no one would listen to her songs." [28] And the psychoanalyst would have the clue he was looking for: the masculine dimension always present in the paranoiac. For the eye of the poet, Aimée wrote: "In the twilight, when my shadow falls upon the hill, I am not frightened by the sound of wings beating at the edge of the forest, nor am I afraid of the crossroads or the beagle's bark, or the fleeing litter, or the boar feeding near the marker stone, or the flight of partridges; my animal pricks its ears at the moths and paws the ground. I deliver a soliloquy." [29] Lacan the poet was always fascinated by the sublimation of violence in language, where knife can be brandished without endangering the person of Madame Z: it is the tongue that trespasses. Lacan does not really make the connection between the poetic and the patholog-ical. He dances about, he behaves seductively. From infatuated observer to therapist, he is first too far away, then too close. He stands aloof or swoops down close, dives and climbs, stumbles but regains his footing. To his poet friends he holds out a candle which they lose no time taking up.

Just after the war, in 1946, in that psychiatric crucible orga-nized by his friend Henri Ey and known as "the Bonneval days," Lacan found a theme he could grasp. A philosophical theme and so presumably a solid foundation: from Hegel no less. Hegel as explicated by an odd personality, Alexandre Kojève, who left his philosophical imprint and the mark of his teaching on intellec-tuals as diverse as [the writer Raymond] Queneau, Jean Hyppol-ite, the translator into French of Hegel's *Phenomenology of Spirit,* Jean Daniel [editor of the weekly magazine *Le Nouvel Observa-teur*], Georges Bataille, and Lacan. (When we're older, we'll say the same thing about the seminars of Jacques Lacan: such is life.) With a sense of history for which he deserves recognition, Ko-jève died in June 1968. His sons are everywhere. And Lacan was one of them.

Installed within the solid walls of Hegelian philosophy, female madness sobered up for a while. Long enough to be caught in the web of Hegel's dialectic, in the perfectly regular one-two of the Hegelian goose-step: one, the law of the heart, and two, the insanity of presumption. The law of the heart or the revolt of the madman—as well as the hero, the *condottiere,* the inspired prophet—and the insanity of presumption, whereby the madman seeks to impose his own order on what looks to him like disor-der. "His being is therefore trapped inside a circle, unless he can break out of it by means of violence, whereby, lashing out at what looks to him like disorder, he strikes at himself by way of society's reaction to his act." [30] The philosophical mill thus ground

away, round and round, and Lacan turned with it, carefully citing his sources and turning his back on his own thought.

Although Lacan does briefly summarize the case of Aimée in
his article "Propos sur la causalité psychique," it is already an old
story over which he can pass quickly: a, b, c, d. He devotes
considerably more space to a rather odd case: the case of a gentleman in love, an incarnation of the law of the heart and therefore
also of the insanity of presumption. This fellow ends up in a state
of bitter jubilation, seeking in vain to trap his young and pretty
Célimène in a place "where a man is free to be honorable." "Où
d'être homme d'honneur on ait la liberté"—the allusion, peculiarly enough, is to Alceste in Molière's *Misanthrope*. Thus we
have a literary model for a clinical case. Who but a psychoanalyst
would see Alceste as a madman, who but a psychoanalyst atten-
tive to the echoes of madness even in the most classical of social
comedies? We are shown Alceste as Narcissus, bent on bringing
about Célimène's fall, dreaming of her as poor, ugly, completely
abandoned. Alceste, as Lacan describes him, is the masculine
counterpart of Aimée.

The central panel, in which ecstasy takes the form of veils,
bubbles, rainbows, and dragons, is flanked by portraits of the
donors. On the left, the woman, insane, turned on her back, her
eyes rolled upward, hysterical, holding a weapon in one hand, a
book in the other, and frightfully beautiful. On the right, the
man, hands folded, looking wise, Hegelian, and literary. Or again:
on the left, Aimée, Saint Theresa, Marcelle, Hadewijch; on the
right, Alceste, Kafka, Schreber. In the middle, Lacan. The central panel, with its entwined bodies and open flames, resembles a
painting by Memling. The left-hand panel looks like the work of
Hieronymus Bosch. And the right-hand one like a Georges de la
Tour: the masculine side of Lacan. Alceste's diagnosis is not
"feminine self-punishment" but "narcissistic suicidal aggression." The woman will assault other women—her employers,
Madame Z. But the man will assault himself, through other men.
His pleasure will come from his rage at hearing himself humili-

ated in Oronte's idle chatter and bad sonnets. There is something of the man in Lacan—but it is the least important part of him. There was something of the man in the last example he cited, without love, without trepidation: "The old revolutionary of 1917 on the bench of the accused in the Moscow Trials."[31] Man, said Lacan, is a "marionette." The marionette of his culture. Here we are a long way from the fascination with women: the gaze is cold, the shadows are clearcut, the phantoms stylized. The text is that of Molière, not of a madwoman.

In 1948 Lacan had a hand in the preparation of the *Encyclopédie française* under the direction of Henri Wallon. He wrote the article on "the Family." This is a prodigious piece, one that has hardly aged at all. Though largely forgotten, it circulates from hand to hand among Lacan's disciples, disciples in search of their legendary leader's origins. Everything is in order. At the end, by way of conclusion, we find in a place of honor "the prevalence of the male principle." Together with a firmness of tone that it would be a pleasure to encounter today: "The origins of our culture are too closely bound up with what we can only call the vagaries of the paternalistic family for that family not to impose the male principle in the various psychological guises fostered by the family; the partiality of this principle is reflected in the moral dimension accorded to the term virility." In these days of racism and contempt, who could write these words without arousing masculine suspicions? But Lacan wrote them in 1948, while the world was busy with postwar reconstruction. (I was not yet ten years old. The family was doing rather well, with its cortège of horrors and distribution of lots. Colonial wars were simmering on the back burner of French politics, while at the lycée other children were already calling me a "dirty Jew." The moral dimension accorded to the term virility . . .)

The article does not end there. Because the male principle is paramount, it has another side, which brings us back to Lacan's theology. The other side of the male principle is the Virgin. The "Holy" Virgin, defined as the "dissimulation of the feminine

principle beneath the masculine ideal." The male Virgin is a mystery turned upside down, male as well as female. She is a woman
because she is a mother and a man because she conceives by herself. Occasionally one comes across an anthropologist's musings
on the truth of Paradise Lost: think of Claude Lévi-Strauss and,
much later, Pierre Clastres.[32] From both of them we learn of the
power of the notion, common to many cultures, of an ideal world
without women, where men can live among themselves, an
asexual world of warriors. The Virgin is androgynous—what a
marvelous means of oppression, what an age-old excuse for
alienation. In a culture in which the male principle predominates,
androgyny is not shared by men and women alike. She is a man.
This perfect myth yields tangible results each time a mother—a
real mother—almost always sailing in the sublime, imposes the
virginal image on her son, thereby transforming him into a homosexual.

Lacan had a deep sense of history. The prevalence of the male
principle leads to "psychic inversion," that is, to the monstrous
figure of the Virgin and to the most commonplace homosexuality. But the historical roots of psychoanalysis lie in certain forms
of homosexuality: Dora, Schreber, the hysterics. Psychoanalysis
began with inversion. Why? Because it was searching for the unconscious, for the underside of all norms. What culture con-
sciously prohibits it creates in the form of abnormality. As the
abnormal often tell us with justifiable indignation, they are non-
conformists. It is not by accident, Lacan tells us, that he ends his
article on the family on this note. The family is beleaguered by
its own models, caught in the "imaginary impasse of sexual po-
larization involving cultural patterns, mores, the arts, rebellion,
and thought."

Everything has its place. The female part and the male part.
The crazy part and the cultivated part. Lacan was not joking when
he said that what differentiated him from women was that he
knew what he was saying: he was a man, that is to say, a cultivated individual. The bearer of the principle of virility as against

women who cannot help being emasculating, so little are they caught up in the sublime. This line of thinking can only lead to the Mother. My philosophical digression is not quite complete: the Mother is first of all the image of the All.

The "good" All, the perfect All, nostalgic, integrating: the circle rejoined, the Magdeburg sphere, the ball, the complete organism, the mandala . . . the atom, the glass bubble, the earth as in Hieronymus Bosch's triptych, The Garden of Earthly Delights. A greenish-gray sphere speckled with tiny clouds and above it the trunk of God. The triptych opens up; the sphere explodes. This is the separation. We are still philosophers.

It is also the weaning. We are becoming psychoanalysts. Down to earth. The idea suffocates and seems ready to quietly disappear. The root of separation, then, lies in weaning—nothing new in that. But at this point of union between man and woman Lacan discovered a handy little device. A concept like the concept of "mana," astonishingly useful. This was nothing more complicated than a certain stage in the child's development: the mirror stage.

The Hen Pigeon and the Foster Brother

The scene is the home. The infant does not yet walk or talk. He is still a "baby," embarrassed by his body and by this babyish word that makes him a small toy, his parents' teddy bear. Still a nurseling, fed at his mother's breast. He is six months, perhaps a year old. He is a girl or a boy, no difference. He's already been crawling up and down the halls for a while and trying to stand up. And he's been laughing even longer, in the way that babies laugh—absolutely. Suddenly the child finds himself in front of a mirror. The mirror has always been there. Nearby, loosely leading him by the hand or holding on to his arm, is another person: anyone you like. All at once, the child, who has never before faltered in passing before the mirror, stops.

He stops and his lips part in a smile. Not for nothing this time, though. He turns around toward whoever is with him and looks at his father, his mother, or his little cousin, and then looks again at himself. Because this is the first time he has seen himself in a mirror. A common enough scene, that Greuze might have painted and Rousseau might have waxed lyrical about. A far cry from Aimée's rages and Alceste's neurasthenic grumblings. A family event. And what is more, if a child does not smile at the mirror, if it (he or she) stands and looks with a grave face at the reflection which belongs to it but which it does not recognize as such, its behavior is taken as a troubling symptom, a menace to its future well-being. But our child has laughed at its reflection, turned to look at the other person with it, and then turned back to look once more at itself.

The laugh is important. With his genius for the bizarre, Lacan called this laugh "the jubilant assumption."[33] Assumption? Sure, it sounds like August 15, the holiday celebrating the transporting of the Virgin Mary to the side of her divine son by legions of gorgeous angels with lovely wings. But it's also a derivative of the verb "to assume," as in assuming responsibility. The assumption here is the assumption of responsibility for oneself. This is the first time our little man assumes responsibility for himself. It makes him laugh. Not a sarcastic laugh or a chortle and not a philosopher's ironic chuckle either. This is jubilant laughter. A new game is starting. And what a game!

The story is a complicated one. The human child is not the only animal offspring to recognize its image in the mirror. Or rather, the human is not the only animal to react to a specific image. The real problem is to understand precisely why the child recognizes himself and not someone else in his place.

Even before the war, there was a great deal of discussion of animal "imagos" and reactions to them. Let me digress briefly on the subject of animals. The scene shifts to the laboratory of a researcher named Harrisson. The time is 1939. Harrisson took two hen pigeons and shut them up in separate cages.

The birds couldn't see one another but each could hear and smell the other. They squawked and beat their wings. Upon checking Harrisson discovered that they had not ovulated. Well and good. He then placed them back in their separate cages, but now separated by panes of glass. The two pigeons could now see one another and they immediately fell in love. After two months they ovulated. Harrisson then redid the experiment, this time with one male and one female pigeon. Ovulation occurred after twelve days. (Always the same moral to the story.)

The noble creatures. Although most animal experiments resemble the primordial one in which the scientist cuts the legs off a flea and then deduces that it has gone deaf because it won't jump any more, the conclusion in this case seems undeniable: the pigeon-image is the cause of ovulation. What is more, it is enough to put a mirror in the cage to get the pigeon to ovulate. The imago, therefore, is not a peculiar property of human beings. It exists wherever a change in the relations between one individual of the species and another must occur. The question is one of species: the reaction is specific.

But the child does not ovulate. It laughs. Ovulation comes much later. This insipid joke goes to the heart of the matter. The question is profoundly biological. It is one of the most radical tenets of Lacan's thinking: all that was later to be formulated in terms of fantasy, imagination, the real and the symbolic, all the subsequent theoretical ferment, depends on this first step and its prerequisites. These can be summarized soberly, stupidly, ponderously as follows: the child, you see, is not an adult.

By this I mean that the child is not a finished product. It is born unfinished. Consequently it can neither walk nor talk. "Specific prematurity" is the term for this: the child is in many ways premature, unable to stand up, to control its expression, and so forth. It is immature—and yet, unlike animals, it is capable of recognizing itself in a mirror. Of recognizing its own image as distinct from the images of others. You can't treat a child the way you treat a hen pigeon. Prematurity in the biological sense goes hand in hand with a sophistication not usually found in animal species, a sophistication that Saint Augustine, frequently cited by Lacan, noted in his *Confessions*. The horrible pallor of a child watching its brother at the nipple is at once the most terrible and the most beautiful manifestation of jealousy that there is. This brings us back to weaning: for this necessary stage to occur, the child must have been separated from its mother's body—weaned—and must be able to turn around and see someone else. This is the action upon which all subjectivity is based, the moment in which the human individual is born. It is also a necessary condition for the existence of language: the *infans* is one who does not yet talk. The "mirror stage," moreover, comes before the child utters its first words, which but for this stage it never would pronounce.

This is also the moment in which culture is born. For man, and man only, there is from the moment of birth a fundamental discord between the individual and nature. The infant arouses our tender sympathies because it is discordant. Because it is not yet truly human but dependent, uncoordinated, and chaotic. Culture first comes to the infant by way of an image: its own image, born of a separation. And the child laughs. Laughter is the quality unique to man.

This is the beginning of the story, not the end. Lacan was a fine dialectician. Madness and experience in psychoanalysis had taught him that every norm has its dark underside, as we saw earlier in the male fantasy of the Virgin who bears children without male assistance. The mirror stage entails consequences that range from the most secure normality to the most psychotic disintegration of the personality. Lacan put it this way:

> The mirror stage is a drama whose inner dynamic moves rapidly from insufficiency to anticipation—and which, for the subject caught in the snares of spatial identification, fashions the series of fantasies that runs from an image of a fragmented body to what we may

call the orthopedic vision of its totality—and to the armor, donned
at last, of an alienating identity, whose rigid structure will shape
all the subject's future mental development.[34]

Quite a sentence. At the time he uttered it Lacan had not yet
discovered the virtues of "midspeak" (*midire*), of saying things
by halves; he used to try to say it "all." I daresay he was rather
successful in this case. But we have to take things one step at a
time. In school this is what is known, in France at any rate, as
"explication de texte." This is an exercise at which it's easy to
shine. All you have to do is read slowly and carefully. Nothing
could require less effort.

The mirror stage is a drama. A drama without pessimistic connotations—these will come later. Drama means action. Lacan
borrowed the term from Politzer. The action is in fact a gesture:
the child stops, looks, turns around, looks at himself. This is the
drama: at once minuscule and enormous.

But what kind of drama? A drama played out between an insufficiency—the human child's resources at birth are insufficient
for its needs—and an anticipation. Anticipation: here we hit upon
the first crucial word. What is it that the child anticipates in front
of the mirror? His own shape as an adult. What he will become
later on, when he has finally grown up. This anticipation obviously does not take the form of conscious rumination within
the imagination. Rather, it happens all at once in an unconscious
"snap"—in the sense of "snapshot"—of a subject just then coming into the world. In order to understand the full scope of this
anticipation, we must skip to end of the sentence and read the
word "armor" while we still have the image of the laughing assumption of self firmly in mind. This suggests the hidden and
ineluctable alienation that lies in store. In order to be a subject—
in order to be oneself—a structure is required. This structure is
rigid. It encloses. It alienates. The words conceal nothing less
than a stark paradox, since alienation also means the fact of "being
other" (être autre), being someone else. Thus the insane used to
be called "alienated." The madman has "lost his head," "gone

off his rocker," he is "no longer himself." Conversely, however, the normal subject is also alienated: he is the prisoner of his identity, whereby he is a member of a group, the son of his parents, the bearer of a family name as well as a first name that identifies him as an individual. Which of the two is freer, then, the insane subject or the normal subject? You or I? The armor we normally wear is protection against madness. To shed this armor—a subject to which Lacan was frequently to return—is to pass to the other side of a delicate curtain, to take the plunge and choose to communicate no more. In order to speak, in order to make oneself understood, one needs this knight in shining armor armed with an identity, this knight that the infant staring at its own image in the mirror has begun to become.

Look at the Indians of America in their festival garb. Notice the incisions and gashes in their bodies, the way they paint themselves, the labrets they wear in their nostrils and ears. These are the mutilations that turn a child into a man, into a warrior of the tribe. And then look at that subject so often treated in television drama: the child's first day of class. Armed with a briefcase, the child confronts the stares of his little classmates, the departure of his mother, and the first day's teaching. Or look at the birth of a child, at the plastic I.D. bracelet fastened around his wrist in the hospital, at the filling out of the birth certificate. Look at children who grow up in institutions, shut up for long, lonely nights between childhood and maturity. Or look at the way fashions change, from high waist to low waist, from long neck to short, from straight hair to Afro. And then, finally, look at that most innocuous scene of the child before the mirror, laughing at its own image. All of these are variants on a single scene, which anthropologists refer to as rites of initiation: each initiation is a separation which marks the crossing of a boundary into a new world. There is a world of the child, a world of the adolescent, a world of the parent, a world of the aged, and finally a world of the dead. And then there is this other passage, barely noticeable, that takes place at home, this little family ritual on which the future of the little boy in front of the mirror will turn—the little boy who now "speaks" in his own name.

Remember that we are in the midst of explicating Lacan's description of the mirror stage. At this point in the key sentence—between the biological inadequacy of the infant and the anticipation of adulthood, of the armor of self—Lucan introduces a digression. He begins to speak of fragmentation of the image in an aside that is heavy with meaning and allusion. Behind this fragmentation is the shade of Melanie Klein, whom Lacan describes elsewhere as a "genius when it comes to guts." And it is true that this woman, whose calm, handsome face we can study in the obligatory photographs, delved into the human guts. Exploring the world of the very young child—the child's games, questions, worries, deductions, bodily contacts—she came upon horrible, murderous fantasies.[35] Stories of cannibals and vampires, of bloody massacre, of objects that enter the body and grow inside it. Stories of teeth that grow in the stomach of the child or its mother. The child no longer even knows whether it is devouring or being devoured, whether it is the stomach that is struck or the weapon that does the striking. Its body does not exist. It is a mere pile of parts. A piece of the mother's breast, a bit of skin, a fragment of shoulder, a part of a lip. It has no body of its own. At this early stage the child is a fragmented body, a violent body.

Now, consider the fragment of Lacan's sentence that refers to the mirror stage as the moment when the subject moves from a fragmented body to an "orthopedic form of totality." Orthopedic—the term is a happy one. Etymologically it means "that which helps the child to stand up straight" (*ortho*, straight, + Gr. *pais, paidos,* a child). But Lacan, who never leaves any term to chance, save for the logical chance introduced by the play of the unconscious, plays on the fact that we often speak of "orthopedic shoes" or of orthopedic devices such as crutches—corrective instruments. The identity of the subject, then, is a kind of prosthesis. Something added, something that did not exist at birth that helps you to stand up straight within yourself. It is a carefully located form, the form of the totality of the body, which the child sees for the first time in the mirror. There is no doubt that it finds plenty to laugh about.

And there is plenty to laugh about in this farce, specific to the human species. For in obtaining its identity, the child in fact only manages to achieve identification. The two things are not entirely the same. In fact they are radically different. The subject will never be truly "himself." He will be the son of, the brother of, the sister of, the cousin of, the lover of, the friend of. He will become stuck in the affections of others, in which he will be not himself but another—an other man, an other woman. Aimée, in order really to be Aimée, is driven to attack a woman, insofar as this woman is her sister, with whom she identifies. The Papin sisters attacked their own image and identified with each other. The patient identifies with the pyschoanalyst, and the psychoanalyst identifies with his or her own analyst or with Freud or with Lacan, who can do nothing about it. It is not even correct to say that the subject takes on a "false" identity, for there is none that is true. There is only your legal identity or family identity, the one you are forced to own up to when you are drafted or sent to school or go to vote or be married or haled into court. There is nothing but this abstract identity, which insures that one child will never be confused with another, not even with its twin. And that is not all: the child sees itself in the mirror, but the image is reversed. No philosopher even a little concerned with questions of structure has ignored this spatial conundrum: see Kant, for example.[36] Identity is a mere outer skin that constantly distorts one's relations with others. Yet there is no other way to have relations with others, since without identity there is no language, no speech to address to anyone else, no social life, only an autistic existence, only a walled up, incarcerated life. Psychoanalysts, unlike psychiatrists, have long maintained that the insane person is not "cut off from reality." On the contrary, the insane person is inundated by reality, overstimulated, overreceptive, completely porous to the outside world. He is a crustacean without a shell, a bird without feathers, a warrior without armor. No laughing matter.

My daughter was right. Lacan is not amusing. There is, however, nothing that says that the theory of the unconscious must wander off into the tragic, settle for the nostalgic, and wallow in love of the worst. Still, at the bottom of any fragment of Lacan's writing despair is always lurking like a hare in the brush, easy to start. Lacan does not care for either rigidity or banality. He is never so vibrant as when he is analyzing those moments in which the factitious identity of the subject disappears. In ecstasy, particularly of women; in rapture; in raving; and in acting out. When the subject stands there like a simpleton talking, walking, eating and sleeping, and nothing happens to him but life, Lacan gets bored. In this he is truly a psychoanalyst, gifted with a selective attentiveness focused exclusively on unhappiness. When gaiety surfaces in his writing it is because a patient has done something amusing, because language has made a joke of its own accord. Look closely at the mirror stage and the child's laughter: this is the only episode in the whole story that is anything like serene. And yet . . .

And yet the whole thing comes apart at the seams. The fragmented body is not merely a figment of the infant's imagination. At the first crack in the edifice it comes back home to roost. Let anxiety penetrate even a little below the surface, let aggression penetrate the armor even slightly, and the whole thing explodes. The subject disintegrates. *Membra disjecta:* scattered limbs. On two occasions Lacan dreamt of the works of Hieronymus Bosch, which he described as an "atlas of all the aggressive images that torment mankind."[37] Armed organs, ears flanked by knives in the shape of wheeled canons, perforated wombs, testicles as bellowing bagpipes, intestines devoured by dogs, whose bites overwhelm the knight in his armor, sticky kisses, fetid lakes, urine-filled ponds—Hell. All these images, says Lacan, are found in our imaginary anatomy—not the anatomy taught in medical schools but the archaic anatomy that acts upon us without our knowledge. And so we suffocate, we go deaf, we feel pain in our stomachs and ulcers in our wombs even though there is no somatic counterpart to our sensations. We fall apart completely: Hell.

All right, Hell. There it is, infected by the Egyptian wars and wounds of the fifteenth century in which Bosch lived. But there is also a Paradise in which tranquil, three-headed monsters drink from a fountain of pink crystal. In which herds of elephants and white giraffes graze beneath the gaze of a toga-clad god, while man and woman wake up naked. Only a small lynx discreetly carrying a field mouse in its mouth foreshadows the coming disruption. There is also, horrible to say, a Garden of Earthly Delights. A garden in which fruits, birds, and coupled lovers represent every pleasure, every calm transgression, every conceivable perversion. Do you suppose there is even one figure of tranquillity?

Not a single one. What about the great veined bubbles in which lithe, naked creatures are making love? Aggressive images are found "even in the narcissistic structure of those glass spheres in which the exhausted partners of the garden of earthly delights are held captive."[38] Captive, exhausted—a far cry from pleasure. Though unstated, a question is raised by three remarks, a question that Lacan constantly asked of both the "stupid" analysts and the "rabble" in his audience. A question of ethics, of the possibility of a morality. In theory the psychoanalyst should not concern himself with such matters, lest he become like American psychoanalysts a kind of guide to correct behavior. Neither pleasure nor happiness can be taken as points of reference; indeed, there is hardly time to mention them in passing—the window is opened luckily, but it is too late, the bird has already escaped and soared out of sight. On the other hand, unhappiness is always with us. Lacan says as much in his labored language. My friend Myriam, a psychoanalyst in the provinces not much concerned with Lacanism, said the same thing in her own way after many long years of practice: "You can never do anything for people."

The first axiom of psychoanalysis is not to confuse analysis with altruism. It is an unnatural axiom: for even if analysts, by delving into their own histories, discover that altruism is only a cover for sadistic impulses, it nonetheless remains true that psychoanalysis, viewed strictly in terms of its social function, offers help to its patients. Psychoanalysts, with their endless glosses on "the desire to become an analyst," have not yet managed to resolve this dilemma, which Lacan was not the first to notice: before him Groddeck fulminated against those who are always wanting to "help." Among the issues at stake in the conflict between Lacan and Françoise Dolto was a moral issue: for her part Dolto offered an evangelical ideology and a reassuring, grandmotherly message, whereas Lacan held out only his cultivated ideologies, his unhappy Hegelianism, and his absolute refusal to enunciate a message of any kind. But if his intention was antiprophetic, how could he hope to escape the contradiction implicit in the fact that it was couched in a prophetic, indeed a clerical, rhetoric? He enunciated no message, with the result that his words were overinterpreted or misunderstood. As a result Lacanian analysts, with few exceptions, have long been floundering about hopelessly, and still are.

The terrifying imagery of fragmented bodies found in the work of Hieronymus Bosch can be used to create a tragic landscape, but so can other kinds of imagery. When the fragmented body gives way to the armor of the subject—and to its identity, already alienating by definition—the "ego" is formed. It is an armed camp, surrounded by swamp and debris. What one finds in the complex mechanisms of obsessional neurosis is the "quest for the haughty and remote interior fortress." A castle: Kafka takes the place of Hieronymus Bosch. The world, whether defensively armed or shattered in a thousand pieces, is the same. The fragile "ego" is merely a feeble defense, an opening into the passageway to the Unconscious that Lacan would describe later on, after he had delved into linguistics in search of what he needed to pursue Freud's theoretical line of approach. On all sides the newly acquired unity is beleaguered by aggressiveness, and the child's laughter, like the philosopher's, is remembered as but a momentary outburst.

The original article on the mirror stage ends with two propositions notable for their stringent moralism. One is a vehement critique of altruistic feelings. The emergence of the Other, which coincides with the mirror stage, gives rise to a complex set of interactions that threaten the fragile subject's existence in its very first moments. The child looks first at itself, then at the other— and laughs. The Other warrants the existence of the child, certifies the difference between self and other. But aggressiveness is constitutive of the subject. "We place no trust in altruistic feeling, we who lay bare the aggressivity that underlies the activity of the philanthropist, the idealist, the pedagogue, and even the reformer."[39] Psychoanalysis must therefore seek means other than education. Between the lines, political action is also being dismissed, by its own arguments. There is no such thing as sexual intercourse; there is no such thing as education; there is no such thing as political action. "It is not within our personal power as practitioners to bring [the patient] to the point where the real journey begins."[40] As my friend said, "Nothing can be done to help people." The point is taken: but this is only the first phase of a long conflict between psychoanalysis and society.

Lacan's second proposition is no less vehement. "Only psychoanalysis recognizes the knot of imaginary servitude that love must either repeatedly untie or sever."[41] Servitude: the word recalls a certain Stoic tradition, which Etienne de la Böétie, with his notion of "voluntary servitude," endeavored to bring to bear on new domains. For the analyst, however, servitude is parental and the imagery of servitude constantly refers to the family. Love is mentioned like the brush of a passing wing—"Your head turns back/A new love." Only love is capable, barely, of combatting the indomitable power of the potent, age-old images stirred up by the mirror complex. The knot is inevitably a Gordian knot, and it is never the analyst who is able to cut through it.

Between Man and Egg

Thus the separation of the mother from the child and of the child from its image is paradigmatic of all separation. In his final paper Freud referred to the fundamental cleavage that defines every human subject as the "Ichspaltung." It may be that the formation of the ego begins at the time of weaning, the time when the child laughs at itself in the mirror. But separation involves far more than the educational steps that train the child to separate from the haven of its mother's body. To discuss this question Lacan spun a fable, something he did not do very often. He created a myth and told a story—Just as Aristophanes, in Plato's *Symposium,* tells the story of the androgynous, four-legged creature who is split in two by an angry Zeus. Since that time the two parts of the creature have been struggling to rejoin one another and to reconstitute the original spherical whole. Each half holds fast to any object it thinks might be its lost counterpart. But what Lacan borrowed from the *Symposium* was not this myth but Plato's very style: the dinner conversation that can switch at the drop of a hat from lighthearted banter to the purest of poetry, the tall story that embodies the truth in disguised form. And this tall story is sublime.[42]

Imagine, says Lacan, what takes place at the moment of birth. An egg breaks—the amniotic sac ruptures to make way for the child. Suppose something comes out of the egg at the very moment it breaks open. Something other than the "afterbirth," as midwives poetically call the placenta. Something that takes flight when the membranes are discarded. A thin wafer, as flat and slippery as a crêpe but as lively as an amoeba. Now suppose that this wafer, now free of the egg, is destined to coat the body of the newborn. It is immortal—a product of separation but itself resistant to any further division. It is also asexual; no obstacle stands in its way. Suppose it comes and coats the child's body while the baby is sleeping. "It's something that wouldn't feel good as it flowed soundlessly over your face while you were sleeping, to seal it off." The fable veers off into science fiction. The tall story becomes a horror story. The slumbering innocent wakes up with this liquid vampire covering its skin, and the vampire begins, slowly and calmly, to eat away at the newborn babe. Guess what Lacan chose to call this amoeba-like, baby-devouring crêpe. The Hommelette (a pun, of course, on *l'homme*, French for man, and omelette). "You can't make an Hommelette without breaking eggs." A compromise between Man and egg.

The Hommelette—for all that it was the jest of a man humorously pretending to be drunk—was not invented merely for the sake of a play on words. Lacan had not yet reached the stage where he played just for the fun of playing, assuming that he ever did. The Hommelette was what Freud called the "libido." The meaning of this Latin word with its thick consonants had of course never been very clear, and the fable helps us to understand why the libido is irresistible. It also helps us to see why it is indestructible, why Freud classified it among the life instincts. He was quite right to do so, according to Lacan: in this fable the libido is a living organ and essentially an immortal one, since it is the only "organ" born of the separation process, the only organ that cannot itself be split. It cannot become either male or female. In a manner of speaking it is the essence of the egg. It is the mythical equivalent of the tiny soul which, in the Middle Ages, was thought to fly from the body at the moment of death. Or rather, not the equivalent but the opposite, since our imaginary amoebic soul flies to the body at the moment of birth. And once it has taken flight it is lost forever.

From this banal story—a story of birth involving the breaking of an egg, the separation of the fetus from its amniotic sac—Lacan, myth-making like the ancients, invented something alto-

gether different. The Hommelette stands for every object of desire. Throughout his life, Man (*l'Homme*), separated from the
Hommelette, feels this other creature pressing upon one part of
his body or another, investing that portion of the body with a
temporary local desire. This has nothing to do with the misty,
idealized notion of desire, in which the body of the beloved other
stimulates total desire on the part of the lover. Growing in the
Hommelette, desire takes root in a specific place: preferably in
some minute detail, such as a slight infirmity, a winking eye, an
out-of-place curl, a minor defect, a tiny feature, a leather whip,
or an artificial penis—a fetish, in short. To make it easier to talk
about this subject—with respect to which Freud was hesitant to
speak, and stammered or beat around the bush—Lacan introduced a rather odd locution: "the objet-petit-a" [which Lacan's
translators have been instructed, by Lacan himself apparently, to
leave untranslated, as though it were an algebraic formula. The
objet-petit-a is obviously meant to contrast with capital A, *l'Autre,*
French for the Other—trans].

"The object-little-a." For a long time this was one of the most
widely recognized bits of Lacanian jargon. Lacanians were de-
lighted to be able to dazzle outsiders with this hermetic terminology, this slogan, this code word that served almost as the
badge of a secret society: the objet-petit-a. There's not quite
enough there to make a meal on, though, unless we add the egg
from the preceding pages. Once the subject is duly constituted,
covered from head to toe with its shining new armor and ready
to attack or to love—the two are the same—whoever appears
before it, it needs to feel desire. Freud made the discovery that
the object of desire need not in any sense be complete. Quite
simply, there is such a thing as an "object" of desire. The old
cliché of Renaissance poets speaking of "the object of their flame"
should be taken literally—again. Desire does not seek out the
subject, for which it cares nothing. Rather, it seeks out the object. This object is necessarily incomplete, a tiny, minuscule
thing—"the little thing," Freud called it, as did Georges Bataille.[43]

To take the argument one step further, the tiny object is also a fallen object. Something that has dropped out of the body along with the infant and the afterbirth: we thus come back to our Hommelette, which symbolizes the object of desire.

That desire feeds on waste is a superb joke, a joke that Lacan knew how to tell so as to maximize its shock. All things considered, the fable of the Hommelette was still cautious in some respects. In *Télévision* all caution is thrown to the winds, the game now being to be as rhetorically provocative as possible. And what could be more provocative than Beatrice, Dante's Beloved, the absolute symbol of the purest possible love? "A glance, Beatrice's glance, a trifle, a flicker of the eyelids and the exquisite secretion that follows: and suddenly the Other arises . . ."[44]

A trifle or a thunderclap. A trifle or the flower that Carmen throws to Don José. A trifle or the passion for leather and rubber manifest in the classified ads of certain magazines. A matter of waste, of secretions: the placenta goes into the garbage, but the libido is a living can of garbage. In the Lacanian lexicon the "objet-petit-a" represents the little machine that unleashes desire. The list of such objects is long—but not interminable. All the objects on the list have some relation to separation. The breast—to take one commonplace object—is on the list because the infant will one day lose it, and because it suggests the "mammalian organization," which also includes the egg and the placenta. The penis is on the list, because it is imagined to be detachable or severable. The child is on the list, the infant, because it has dropped out of the mother's body. Myth tells us as much: the child is the tip of Osiris' phallus. Torn to pieces by crocodiles, Osiris' body is the object of Isis' quest, and she will never find the one piece that the god, destined to become the model for mummies, will thereafter always lack. Or think of the head of Orpheus, torn to pieces by the Bacchantes and left to float from river to river until it reaches the isle of Lesbos, where it is picked up by a shepherd. The "objet-petit-a" is found wherever there is a passageway on the body linking the interior to the exterior. The breath and the voice, for example—as well as song, the most sublime expression of both; feces and urine, which fall from the body, true waste—all of these things can be objects of desire.

Lacan was without illusions as to the nature of the book. What is the page for the writer but "the turd of his fantasy"? Publication Lacan referred to in an untranslatable pun as "poubellication" [*poubelle* is French for trash—trans.]. A contemporary of Samuel Beckett, Lacan understood the meaning of the trashcan. The cradle of waste, the gathering-place of garbage, the trashcan, sublimated, became something grandiose. But a book could also become a piece of shit, something many books are judged to be.

Finally, the glance is an "objet-petit-a," which proceeds from within the skull of the Other. Beatrice's glance, for example. Through a hole in the body the flat amoeba slithers out, the libido slips through. And the little object that will arouse desire takes shape. What does Dante look like in search of an item of waste?[45] The Other is a masquerade—the feminine masquerade or the masculine parade. The Other is merely a support for an item of waste. Truly there is no such thing as sexual intercourse. "In other respects sexual relations are subject to vicissitudes attendant upon the fact that they fall under the domination of the Other: in what is no empty fable, Daphnis must learn from an old woman how to make love."[46]

Love is "made" without "relations," without relation to love: something about which Lacan was really passionate. Tracking madness in women took him down a path that led to the enigma of female ecstasy (*jouissance*), by way of a clearing in which he saw his own image in the mirror of a pond. This clearing lay at the crossroads of all possible paths. The path of madness as well as the path of the normal family; the path of the child separated from its mother, who looks at him as he looks back at her; the path of narrative and the path of theory; the path of style and the path of thought.

Lacan may not have had any idea other than that of the mirror stage. This was a true discovery. Not so much for the observation, which others made at about the same time, but for the elaboration of that observation that he was able to give. In this discovery we find all his future work in embryonic form.

All his future work—but what exactly was this? Nearly all the essential points have already been made. By the time the war came, Lacan's thought was already formed. All that was left was to establish a school. This Lacan would accomplish during his rhetorical period. But he would make no further innovations, except for a lavish method of teaching that he constantly pushed to its limits, always beset by the fundamental contradiction of his work: how to teach without teaching, how to be a subject without division—how to be Lacan, how to be a man, and a woman.

CHAPTER 3

NO CAVIAR FOR THE BUTCHER

The exclusion of Lacan; the direction of therapy and the ethics of psychoanalysis: questions and powers

A Silly Drama

One day Jacques-Marie Lacan, former chief resident of a psychiatric clinic, became just plain Lacan. This transformation was preceded by a series of personal splits, a factional division, and an expulsion, finally culminating in the founding of the Ecole freudienne of Paris in 1964. It was this school that Lacan decided to dissolve in January of 1980. How did a man born into a good family and showing promise of a great future as a psychiatrist and citizen wind up an excommunicate? Perhaps it is this part of Lacan's story that the editors of *Actuel* had in mind when they depicted him, on the cover of their magazine, as a man with a predilection for smashing things: his tie askew, his hand raised, a ridiculous and angry look on his face. Sure, things did get broken. But there was a reason for every smashup. Thus, in order to understand the dissolution of the Ecole freudienne—virtually a reenactment of an earlier dissolution—we must first look at the fits and starts that marked the period 1953 to 1964. For what happened in those years there were always pretexts and reasons. Some of the story remains enigmatic, and at some points things went wrong, but always at the center of the various possible true accounts we find a concern with the ethics of psychoanalysis: that

worm in the fruit, that knife in the wound. Lacan's highly deviant practices raised a moral issue, which he dealt with in his
own way, beyond good and evil. Where other analysts were satisfied to "fortify" their patients with a few psychic vitamins, Lacan searched for ways to break down defenses and set the subject
free: desire, need, destruction of the Ego. His means were radical. The Establishment was hardly pleased, nor was anyone else.

It was a funny drama. The characters are stuck in their roles,
as in a melodrama or an old film.[1] Among them we find the
friend who betrays, the old man off his rocker and in love with
his mimosas, the anxious, inflexible authoritarian ("Bizarre, bizarre, . . ."), and the professional nuisance whose penchant for
authority creates a mess. Princess Marie Bonaparte—who in her
day had saved Freud by paying the Nazis to allow him to leave
Austria—was during the period in question a power to contend
with in the Société psychanalytique de Paris. She seems to have
had an unparalleled ability to forge alliances and then immediately turn around and attack her allies. Her presence behind the
scenes is apparent in the papers collected by Jacques-Alain Miller
in two volumes entitled *La Scission de 1953* (The 1953 Split) and
L'Excommunication. Once again the small community of psychoanalysts was in an uproar. But its uproars were no more fre-
quent than those of any other institutionalized group, whether a
union, a political party, or a professional organization. (This is
worth pointing out explicitly in order to refute the false notion
that psychoanalytic associations are more prone than other groups
to fundamental disputes. Contrary to widespread opinion, psychoanalysts are no different from other mortals, not even when
they join together in groups.) This time, however, the uproar
centered on Lacan, for the first time in his professional history.

Why was he expelled? Unusual though the expulsion was, the
steps leading up to it were not especially dramatic. The Société
psychanalytique de Paris had been founded in 1926 and was active until the war. After losing a number of its members in the
conflict, it resumed its activities in 1946. Jacques Lacan, a psy-

choanalyst whose career had until this point attracted nothing but praise, was naturally a participant in the group. In 1948 he became a member of the "committee on teaching," thus involving himself in what was to become his "mission" and his cross: the training of future analysts, the transmission of psychoanalytic knowledge. Nothing happened until 1953. In that year Sacha Nacht, then chairman of the committee on teaching, proposed founding an Institute of Psychoanalysis, of which he would of course be the director. Students of the Institute would be awarded a diploma officially recognizing them as psychoanalysts. Only physicians would be admitted. (Similar projects are still being canvassed even today. Sacha Nacht is no longer with us, but others harbor similar designs.) Psychoanalysts who were not physicians understandably raised a protest against this proposal, led by Princess Bonaparte, who was herself not a physician. After a period of strain punctuated by a number of open battles, Sacha Nacht resigned his position. Lacan was elected director of the Institute. The way was cleared for his election as president of the Sociéteé psychanalytique itself. Everything was going well for him when, suddenly, the princess switched sides and made herself his opponent. Lacan had apparently forgotten—the fool—to assure her that she would retain her honorific positions in the group. In the ensuing confusion ("You did it."—"No, I didn't, he did."—"Why are you betraying him?"—"Me? It's not me, it's you." And so on.) and shifting of alliances, Lacan was elected anyway but resigned a few months later. Together with a few friends he founded the new Société française de psychanalyse.

Up to this point the story is just the history of one more split in the psychoanalytic movement. Lacan did not yet stand alone: this came only in 1964. Meanwhile the new society asked to be affiliated with the "psychoanalytic international," the International Psychoanalytic Association (IPA). This was a normal thing to do and should not have caused any problems. But it quickly became apparent (according to documents published by Lacan's supporters, whose veracity cannot be checked since his adversaries have thus far refused to make any documentation public) that the condition laid down for affiliation was that Lacan be dropped from the Société psychanalytique. In other words, he should be expelled, this time without any hope of return, along with his closest supporters. Most of his former friends were willing to go along with this. But not all of them: together with those who refused to accede to the demand for his expulsion, Lacan founded his own school, the Ecole freudienne de Paris. In 1980, by which time he had become as isolated as he had once pretended to be, he dissolved this school as a prelude to starting all over again.

What I have just described in very general terms is the way in which Lacan was expelled. Why he was expelled remains difficult to decipher: behind the voluminous correspondence and official documents, the deadly courtesies and petty betrayals, it is hard to make out the real reasons for his expulsion. One eyewitness, Jean Laplanche, who chose the side of the IPA in 1964, has revealed a bit more than most others. In a published article he has discussed the "major obstacle" that stood in the way of affiliation:

> The major obstacle was the special position that Lacan occupied in our group, together with the whole range of his teaching methods, plus the fact that his personality seemed in some ways refractory to the requirements of collective rule. To be blunt about it, this did not come as a surprise to anyone. We all knew perfectly well that this would be the sticking point, that it could not be otherwise. A thousand private conversations among friends, where the truth is more likely to come out than in public meetings, attest to the fact.[2]

Lacan, the sticking point, the refractory personality, refractory to the requirements of collective rule: a more elegant way of saying that he was a nuisance could not be found. And of course he was a nuisance. How could a shaman be anything else? Doubtless the key to the whole transformation lies here. During these years a sort of shamanistic revelation was taking place. Lacan was obviously suffering, as the letters he sent to his friends and his public pronouncements make clear. He would not allow himself to be expelled without a fight. He did not submit to his fate like a martyr. And yet, when it was nearly all over, in a declaration made on January 15, 1964, he himself alluded to the excommunication of Spinoza. Speaking of the demands of the IPA, he told his seminar:

> It has been proposed that this affiliation will be granted only if guarantees are provided that this society will never sanction my instruction for the purpose of training analysts. What is involved, then, is comparable to what in other places is referred to as major excommunication. But in the places where this term is current, it is never applied without allowing for the possibility of eventual return to the fold. Excommunication of this definitive sort exists only in the kind of religious community designated by the revealingly symbolic term "synagogue," and it is this kind of excommunication of which Spinoza was the object. On July 27, 1656 . . . Spinoza was first made the object of the "kherem," a form of excommunication that corresponds fairly closely with major excommunication. Not until some additional time had passed was he made the object of the "chammata," which consists in the further stipulation that no return to the fold is possible.[3]

Persecuted and then persecuted again: Lacan found in Spinoza— from whom he had already taken the inscription to his thesis—a perfect model for the life of a saint. The "kherem" corresponds to the 1953 split; the "chammata" to the 1964 expulsion. Lacan must have aspired to a unique destiny if he dared to compare his own life to the life of a philosopher whose isolation, eminence, and asceticism are for all philosophers standards of perfection! He must have identified with others expelled from their groups in order to have uttered these words in founding his own school: "Today, as always isolated within the analytic cause, I hereby found the French School of Psychoanalysis . . . ." These words were uttered on June 21, 1964. In describing the occasion I must sound like one of Napoleon's grizzled old veterans: I was there, by God, I saw it with my own eyes. And because I was there I can remember quite well that the old man was not alone in the slightest. Still, he was not lying. Something in him had found solitude.

How does a person become a shaman? It may be impossible to tell one child from another in a group of children all of whom are raised together. But sometimes the difference stands out at once. The child's two eyes are of different colors, or he has a club foot, or he is an epileptic. In other cases the individual is not distinguished by any outward feature. This was the case among the Surel of Nepal in the village of Suri.[4] Alain Fournier interviewed the shaman or "poembo" of this village in 1969 and learned the story of his vocation. When he was a child of nine or ten, his grandfather sent him to watch the water buffalo by the river. At nightfall he began to shake and fell into a trance. The next day he was found unconscious, blind and deaf. His aunt, herself a shaman, was consulted. After turning to the spirits for advice, she announced that the river spirit had been offended. The child had allowed the buffalo to cross the river at a forbidden place. In exchange for setting the child free from its spell, the river spirit demanded that the child be made a shaman. And so it came to pass. This is typical of the way in which the shamanistic vocation is received: the child's "flaw" is either marked on its body at birth or else reveals itself later on, when somehow the child errs. The flaw, always necessary, is almost always inadvertent. By a mischance Oedipus kills Laius at the crossroads and by another mischance he marries Jocasta, etc. Inadvertence and destiny combine.

The anthropologist Mary Douglas comes to the same conclusion in her study of "pollution." "The 'polluters' are always wrong. In one way or another they are not in their proper place or they have crossed a line they were not supposed to cross thereby causing danger to someone. . . . Pollution is usually caused inadvertently. . . . It is a danger that besets the careless."[5] Lacan once entitled one of his seminars "l'Etourdit" [punning on the French for inadvertence, *par étourderie,* and the past

participle of the verb to say, *dit*—trans.]. And it was no doubt
by inadvertence that Lacan found himself declared a deviant, expelled from the group in 1964. Like the shaman he was forever
cast out of the group, which nevertheless continued to draw on
and to venerate his powers. The family of the child in Nepal was
upset by the river spirit's dictates, but there was nothing to be
done. Similarly, Lacan was presumably isolated at the center of
a group whose members both loved and hated him, who rejected
him and used him at the same time. He was alone like the hero
whose destiny he tried to explain, hero of both the law of the
heart and the insanity of presumption: the rebel brigand, the Ro-
bin Hood of psychoanalysis. "The universal ordinance and law,"
Hegel wrote in the *Phenomenology of Spirit,* "it therefore now
speaks of as an utter distortion of the law of the heart and of its
happiness, a perversion invented by fanatical priests, by riotous,
reveling despots and their minions, who seek to indemnify themselves for their own degradation by degrading and oppressing in
their turn—a distortion practiced to the nameless misery of a deluded mankind."[6] For "fanatical priests and riotous, reveling
despots," read the mandarins of the Establishment. For "their
minions," read the French psychoanalysts who would soon be-
tray Lacan. For "perversion," read psychoanalysis itself, a discipline capable of repeating within itself the all-in-all rather banal
story of any group that has deviants in its midst, deviants who,
if they are strong enough, become shamans first and then go on
to found groups of their own. From this point on Lacan was
indeed alone. And no doubt this was the secret goal of his previous strategy.

What line had he crossed to cause his "pollution" and make
himself dangerous in the eyes of his peers? Rumor already had it
that he had been experimenting with analytic sessions of variable
duration. The French psychoanalytic establishment had fixed the
length of each session (why?) at an invariable three-quarters of
an hour. Freud, whose sessions had been quite long but whose
analyses had overall been rather short in comparison with the

years required for a normal psychoanalysis in France today, had established no firm rules in this respect. Through lengthy investigation Lacan had come to the conclusion that the length of each session should be adjusted according to what the patient was saying: some long, some short, in any case no predetermined fixed length. This was no minor issue, and Lacan never pretended that it was. The question of time is crucial; implicit in its answer is a whole moral position. And Lacan did indeed conceive of the issue in moral terms: for his ear had been pierced by moral considerations, just as Aimée may have been in the course of her quest for purity, or the Papin sisters in avenging their status as servants, or Alceste in search of freedom. The "insane," also deviants, are invoked as an implicit point of reference: part of the truth is in them, and as such they can be instructive.

After his expulsion, Lacan began thinking about the question from another angle, taking his stance between the imagination and reality. Madwomen, as we saw earlier, invert the order of the world: their ravings reveal the truth because they are deeply subversive. Lacan now embarked upon a systematic inversion of the world. The first paradoxical result was this: the psychoanalyst became the spokesman of silence. The analytic contract was the reverse of the normal contract, in which two human beings agree to communicate, to talk to one another, to respond to one another. In the analytic setting one person speaks, the other does not respond. Furthermore, the action of the psychoanalyst is the reverse of normal action: it is a neutral action, a "nonaction." In these various ways Lacan began to establish, along with his theory of psychoanalysis, a kind of "negative model" or hollow mold of communication, from which psychoanalysts derive their ideas of truth and therapeutic efficacy. Having felt for himself the effects of "the hard labor of the negative" (Hegel's law of composition), Lacan drew the appropriate consequences and rigorously applied them in his own practice. At the same time he began to teach, in the vacuum created around him by his expulsion. In fact he had no choice. Spinoza had opted for discretion and chose to have his work published anonymously after his death: his was a philosophical choice. Lacan made the opposite choice and decided to become a prophet. The prophet who, in the words of Pierre Bourdieu, is not so much " 'the extraordinary individual' described by Max Weber as the individual who rises to an extraordinary situation, a situation in which the usual guardians of order have nothing to say, for good reason: the only terms in which they can conceive of such a situation are the terms of exorcism."[7]

Ending the Session

The year is 1953: the turmoil around Lacan is at its height. The split is already taking shape. Lacan delivered a paper initially intended to be the report of the official "Congress of Psychoanalysts Speaking Romance Languages." The troublemaker was asked not to deliver the official report, however. He agreed but delivered his address anyway, to his friends and supporters. The place was significant: Rome.

Lacan was well aware of the significance of the locale. The "Universal City"—it was not Lacan who made it so—lent itself to his purposes in numerous ways, some of which he mentioned, some of which he did not. One explicit statement was this: "Well before the glory of the world's most exalted throne was revealed there, Aulus Gellius, in his *Attic Nights*, suggested that the name of the place known as the Mons Vaticanus derives etymologically from *vagire*, which refers to the child's first stammered utterances."[8] The meaning is clear: the Vatican represents not only the pope, whose image Lacan swiped in passing, but also the foundation of language itself. What he did not say, though he certainly had not forgotten it, was that Rome was, in Freud's personal history, a place invested with magic, a place both seductive and evil, accursed and necessary. It was a founding city for a community in the process of being born, be it the city of

Rome, the universal religion, or a new form of psychoanalysis. This report which was not a report appears in *Ecrits* under the title "Fonction et champ de la parole et du language en psychanalyse," one of Lacan's classic papers. But it is always referred to by another name: the Rome Report. The name has something of the resonance of the *Appel du 18 juin* [de Gaulle's call to Frenchmen to reject the armistice and continue to fight with him against the Germans—trans.]. The tone is new, solemn at times to the point of bombast. It is the speech of a magus. The Report concludes with an incredible invocation taken from the Upanishads. Legend has it that a group of novices at the end of their novitiate asked their master Prajapāti to speak to them. And Prajapāti did speak to them—a little. To each one he said the same word: "Da." And each novice heard what he wanted to hear: some interpreted this word as meaning submission, others as charity, still others as grace. To all Prajapāti responded, "You have heard me." Lacan's "midspeak" was in the process of being born; Lacan had discovered his myth.

Further proof that a new school of psychoanalysis was here being established may be found in the remarks Lacan himself made about the report when *Ecrits* was published in 1966: "The slightest trace of enthusiasm left in a piece of writing is the surest way to insure that it will date, rather than mark a date." Lacan always detested his past. Accordingly, the Rome Report, which struck him as enthusiastic, seemed to have dated. He was horrified, he tells us in the invocation, by the letters and articles he published at the time in *Ornicar?*. Lacan denied his past as he proceeded, in contrast to those authors who carefully classify their minor writings for ultimate inclusion in that fantasy, The Complete Works. Lacan's narcissism was not of this sort. It was more deeply political and religious—I almost said "national." De Gaulle had had a certain idea of France, Lacan a certain idea of psychoanalysis. That and that alone was what he was interested in identifying himself with. He made his decision in Rome, in exile like de Gaulle. He was alone when he did so, having previously laid down the basic features of his system, subsequently amplified in a series of lessons that began on that day in Rome. The hour of the prophet had come; and the prophet spoke, naturally enough, about speech, the one tool of the psychoanalyst. "Psychoanalysis—no matter what its wishes may be, to heal, to educate, or to plumb the depths of the soul—psychoanalysis has but one medium: the patient's speech. The obviousness of the fact is no excuse for neglecting it."[9]

On the couch the patient talks. That is, he "blabbers away," as Lacan put it: he was not unwilling to make select use of slang terms—like a schizophasic, though he had not yet come to that. Nothing else happens; the patient just talks. Nothing? Not quite. The patient is talking to somebody, even if the listener must remain silent. If the patient were alone, he would not be talking. His words are spoken only in relation to his listener. They count as speech, whether or not they speak the truth, whether brief remarks or lengthy discourse. The issue of the session's duration looms in the background. The psychoanalyst attends not so much to the meaning of the patient's words as to their form, or rather, as Lacan puts it rather succinctly in his Rome address: "The subject's discourse derives its meaning from felicitous punctuation." He immediately went on to explain what he meant by this. The ritual ending of the session after a predetermined fixed length of time is "a merely chronometric stopping place." By contrast, to find for each session a stopping place suited to what the patient is saying "has just as much value as an intervention (by the analyst) for hastening the final moments." The length of the session must therefore not be fixed. Nothing in theory warrants the setting of a fixed length. Rather, the adjustment of the length of the session should become one of the techniques of psychoanalysis.

In this way psychoanalysis carves out a space for itself, a tiny laboratory in which gigantic passions reveal themselves. The psychoanalyst listens according to rules that are the reverse of those followed in ordinary life. If what the patient says is boring, he will not force himself to listen more closely or try to under-

stand. Instead he will conclude that his boredom is the real
symptom that the speaker is trying to bring to light. If the patient falls silent, the psychoanalyst will listen to the tales embed-
ded in his silence. He will take "the telling of a commonplace
story for an apology that beckons to the careful listener, a long
prosopopoeia for a direct interjection, or again, a simple lapsus for
a highly complex statement, to say nothing of an interval of silence, which he will take to represent the lyrical development
that it replaces." [10] And rather than calmly allow the time to pass
and the patient to come to the end of his allotted three-quarters
of an hour, the analyst searches for the right moment to "punc-
tuate" his discourse, to stop his speaking. Thus the patient never
knows beforehand how long the session will last. "We know
how the patient reckons the passage of time and adjusts his story
to the clock, how he contrives to be saved by the clock. We
know how he anticipates the end of the hour, weighing the time
as though he were hefting a sword, keeping an eye on the clock
as on a shelter looming in the distance." [11] In this cat-and-mouse
game the analysand resembles a hunted animal, thrown back on
its own defenses. And the analyst is like a predator who tries to
penetrate those defenses by using one of the few stratagems
available to him: depending on the case he can get up and say
either, "That will be all for today," or "Fine," or "We'll see
about that tomorrow," dismissing the patient in the middle of a
sentence or a dream or an interval of silence and thereby provok-
ing him to make the clear revelation that he had been hesitant to
disclose.

To draw from this the conclusion that the "punctuation" of
the session invariably shortens its duration is to impugn the analyst's motives: in fact the end may be either delayed or hastened.
If the rumors are correct and Lacan's rates run on a sliding scale
from 50 to 1000 francs per session [approximately $10 to $200 at
the time of writing—trans.], the length of the session ranges from
three seconds to an hour and three-quarters. [12] Thus the power of
the psychoanalyst is effectively doubled: he is the sole "judge of

the value of the patient's words," and he is in control of the time. But the client is not defenseless. He can decide not to come back: the contract between analyst and patient is only verbal, and the analyst has no recourse if the patient reneges. It should come as no surprise that Lacan was a master of analytic technique; he also knew the loneliness and distress of practice. The technique that he mastered he took not from worn-out rituals, however, but from the heart of analytic theory itself. The analyst, he said, "remains above all the master of truth." [13]

The Old Man of the Sea

The master of the truth: we must go back to the remote past and to Greece, to the very source of myth, to understand the burden of such mastery. [14] The master of the truth is the "Old Man of the Sea," the sea-deity Nereus, at once the bearer of "non-falsehood" and "divination." These are the two faces of truth in its archaic form, before the advent of the logical principle of non-contradiction that still governs our thinking today and much closer to the "midspeak" rediscovered by Lacan in the course of his life as a shaman. The master of the truth is one whose scepter is at once a symbol of authority and an oracle. The sanctuary of the truth is a mythic place that seems to have been dreamed up expressly to serve as an ancient model for the psychoanalyst's office: the sanctuary of Trophonius at Lebadea. This was a tomb in the form of a beehive, into which the "patient" was not allowed to descend until a fast of several days had been completed and a ram sacrificed. Before entering the chamber of the oracle, to which he was guided by two youths known as "the Hermes," the patient had to stop and drink at two wells. The first was Lethe, the water of oblivion, and the second, Mnemósyne, the water of memory. After drinking the waters of both, the patient slid into a shadowy opening feet first, whereupon a divine force violently sucked the rest of his body into the hole. After a certain length of time the Hermes returned, pulled the patient from the hole, and set him upon the throne of Memory. There, upon emerging from his groggy state, the patient would laugh, like the child in front of the mirror. Truth, Aletheia, was closely related to Memory, moreover. It had nothing to do with what history and culture have since made it. The truth of the old Masters was at once poetry, divination, and justice. And Lacan, as we know, was always sensitive to poetry. Madwomen showed him the way to divination. As for justice, the ending of the session can be viewed as the administration of justice.

Not distributive justice, of course, not calculated justice, the justice of the city. But rather the administration of a rule according to which each man receives his due: each analysand is accorded a length of time depending on what he says that day and that hour. It is an idea of morality that is being proposed: a morality in which the psychoanalyst cannot and should not do anything more than clear the way for the desires he hears beneath the words that the patient actually speaks. Since the analyst will never lay down standards of good and evil, his morality is embodied entirely in this one decision, to stop. The procedure was not new: Freud had used it before Lacan. In deciding that each session could be punctuated by the analyst according to what he heard, Lacan was apparently doing nothing more than developing the logic implicit in Freud's approach. But in so doing he stumbled upon powerful archaic forces that left his person reeking with the smell of sulphur and seawater and quickly turned him into an outcast. Like the Old Man of the Sea he was alone. And like the patient in the depths of the oracle's temple he stood midway between memory and forgetfulness, halfway to the Truth.

He was not only a master of the truth but also, in a more mundane sense, a scrivener, a scribe, a clerk, a witness, that is, to the talking patient's words. "Our role is one of recording, our function, crucial to any act of symbolic exchange, one of apprehending that which *do kamo,* man in his authenticity, calls enduring speech." [15] Thus the psychoanalyst collects: that is what he is paid to do. Rules are rules, and the patient must know (a) that time is money in this world; (b) that he is not the analyst's only patient; and (c) that his primary witness, his usually silent auditor, cannot spend his entire life listening to him alone. So the end of the session does indeed stand for justice, intertwined with the exercise of memory. Nevertheless, it is based upon something of quite a different sort: the word punctuation is no mere metaphor.

The year, again, is 1953: the love of language and the study of its forms are just beginning to transform the history of ideas in France. After Lacan, who came to rhetoric by way of psychoanalytic practice, we find Roland Barthes, who held a long seminar on the history of rhetoric, [16] Louis Althusser, who studied rhetoric in order to interpret Marx, and the first works on semiology. These are so many signs of an ideological shift that was to endure until 1968. The effects of this change are only now beginning to subside, more than twenty years after their first appearance. Lacan abandoned the terrain of psychiatry for that of *belles lettres* and for *Retorica,* which according to medieval tradition consists of Grammar, Dialectics, and Mathematics. The clinical chapter of his work had come to an end. Hereafter his only contact with insane women was through the writings of the mystics. From this time on he almost never cited "cases" of his own. Thus the word "punctuation" may be take to mean the end of a period of formation. Lacan's *Bildungsroman* was over and his period of prophetic certainty was just begun.

Punctuation, according to Emile Littré's celebrated dictionary of the French language, is the "art of distinguishing by means of conventional signs between phrases and indicating the various levels of subordination between one phrase and another." [17] According to Lacan, punctuation is "the moment at which meaning constitutes itself as a finished product." [18] The two definitions are almost the same. Punctuation is an art whereby order is established in discourse which, without conventional signs to indicate breathing places (comma) would be nothing but disorder (colon)

Lacan points out that (comma) in the Bible and in standard Chinese texts (comma) the absence of punctuation makes it impossible to read the text (period). He was always taken with sacred writings, so it was a rather neat trick that he was able to turn the meager words of his patients into an old-fashioned sacred text. It was a trick Lacan worked not only on the utterances of his patients but on the discourse of any subject whatsoever. He did away with the distinction between clinical discourse and literature, between the written word and inarticulate speech.

This became rather humorous when the patient's name was René Descartes. Because Descartes was imprudent enough to express himself (in both French and Latin) in the first person, he became grist for the mill of "punctuation." The result was a fabulous *explication de texte,* a model of analytic interpretation, which will help us to understand the real significance of terminating the analytic session. Descartes established the coincidence of thought and existence in a straightforward, if celebrated, sentence: "I think, therefore I exist." Or, "I think, I am." The possibility of a real world, and of a God willing to guarantee its existence, rests on this fragile point of coexistence. When Descartes, that fine French gentleman, formulated this idea, it was the ultimate in thought. And what did Lacan do with it? He terminated the session just at the point where Sir Descartes is saying, "I think . . ." I'm exaggerating, but not much. For consider Lacan's translation of "I think, therefore I exist." In Lacan's hands this became, "I am the person who is thinking: 'Therefore I exist.' "[19]

The utterance is broken into two parts. One consists of the subject who is thinking, the other of the thought being thought. The two levels of utterance are distinct. This, however, was not what concerned Lacan, who lost no time distinguishing between the part of linguistics that interested him and the part that he called *"linguisterie"* (by analogy with such French words as *"plomberie," "blanchisserie,"* or *"pâtisserie").* What interested Lacan was the fact that the comma has been superseded by something quite different. What results is something quite different

from what Sir Descartes wanted, namely, to establish the coincidence of thought and existence, which had cost him some considerable effort, poor fellow, involving an act of mental "forcing" that eliminated everything from his vicinity except himself.
The Cogito thus became a ruse: an utterance issued from thought
like any other and yet different from any other utterance in that
only man is capable of thinking that he is the person who is
thinking: "Therefore I exist." A conjuring trick has eliminated
the need for any other guarantee of existence and along with it
the need for God. Descartes will begin the next session by saying, "Therefore I exist." And the analyst, in his armchair, will
burst out laughing.

The Descartes fable is a useful one. The patient also returns for
the following session. The effect of punctuation is not merely to
introduce order into the proceedings: the analyst is not the bailiff
of the Unconscious. The interruption of the session is disquiet-
ing, as though the rug were suddenly pulled out from under the
patient's feet. "This is one way in which regression may occur,
regression being nothing other than the actualization in discourse
of fantasized relationships reinstated by the ego at each stage in
the decomposition of its structure."[20] Ugh—things are getting
complicated. Regression, together with the whole metapsycho-
logical apparatus, is surely one of the most obscure points in
Freud's teachings. Various psychological systems act as the bars
of a cage enclosing a wild animal, bars that are raised and lowered at various times in order to liberate energies held prisoner
ever since some moment in the distant past—the imagery is quite
complex. In a somewhat vulgarized version regression is also a
way of "returning to one's childhood": this metaphorical way of
putting the matter comes close to suggesting that one really does
return. Following in Freud's footsteps various psychoanalysts have
reformulated this insight in a systematic form: in order to "get
off to a good start," one must first go back to the beginning, and
in order to go back to the beginning, the subject must be dissat-
isfied in the present. This is the basis of the well-known triad

"frustration, aggression, regression," a familiar part of every apprentice analyst's basic tool kit. I frustrate you, you act aggressively toward me, you regress.

Lacan was deaf in that ear. There is of course nothing real about regression. And yet regression refers to something quite real: the reemergence of infantile modes of expression. A person asks his mother for something to eat—in adolescence, when he enters school, when he is in the cradle—at each stage in the decomposition of his (ego) structure: in other words, as his armor falls away, piece by piece. The psychoanalyst is therefore a "decompositor." Elsewhere Lacan made this enigmatic observation: "The thought of the analyst is an action that undoes itself." [21] The mystic is back at center stage: a decompositor in distress, in ruin, the Master of Truth is an invalid.

The Marketing of the Analyst: Commerce Turned Upside Down

This does not prevent him from having a sense of humor, which from time to time forces him to stretch words to their uttermost limits. Consider the word "demand," for example. This will prove to be most enlightening to study and will show up regression in its true colors—but we mustn't get ahead of ourselves. As luck would have it this time, "demand" in psychoanalysis means exactly what it means in other contexts. One demands what one is lacking. The oldest law of economics dictates that a demand stimulates a corresponding supply. A demand for corn results in a corresponding supply of corn, a demand for petroleum leads to a supply of petroleum. Nobody would think of supplying more corn in a time of glut. For the superfluous sacks of corn would only have to be hauled back from the marketplace: potential buyers would turn up their noses. No one in his right mind tries to sell something for which there is no demand: no one, that is, but the psychoanalyst. And some ad agencies.

The psychoanalyst, though, offers something to the patient: speak to me, he says. This is the way it all begins, and this is the only offer the analyst can ever make, the offer of conversation. "Speak to me and I will listen." Once the patient begins to speak a demand becomes evident, a demand that is indeterminate, radical, and hard to grasp. In a word, it is a demand that is "intransitive, without any object." It is a demand for love, for affection, for—response. A demand for a cure, for a revelation, for training. A demand so broad and so confused that it cannot be precisely pinned down. This is the way that things can really begin. Proudly, Lacan observes that "I have succeeded in doing something that people would like to be able to do as readily in the ordinary course of business: with supply I have created demand."[22]

And so it all begins. "Demand—the subject has never done anything but demand. It is the only way he has been able to live. And we take up where he leaves off." Once the subject finds himself face to face with his own words, without response from the analyst, his whole past begins to open up. It comes back to him step by step. Frustrated by the lack of a response, he begins little by little to remember, and his language remembers even before he himself does: turns of phrase not used since childhood come back to him, along with angry outbursts, tics, and dreams—signs come from afar that tell of demands "for which prescriptions exist." Finished, done, Mama is old and Papa is dead and I am yelling and crying as though I were three years old. The analyst takes it in, he withstands the demand. The more he withstands, the less he speaks, the more the patient regresses. And in the course of this necessary collapse something like a story is pieced together.

Thus far, Lacan has done nothing but reformulate certain Freudian concepts: a return to Freud with new words substituted for old. Regression, frustration, demand, story—none of this is new. But Lacan's language is admirable, arresting, concrete, and poetic. In it Lacan formulated psychoanalytic theory in French, something no French psychoanalyst had done before. Lacan's reformulation extended even to matters of grammar: the story Lacan pieces together from the patient's regression—a theme that Freud touches on in "Constructions in Analysis" and "Analysis Terminable and Interminable"[23]—adds nothing new to Freudian technique but merely changes the tense of the verbs: "What takes place in my story is not the past definite of what was, because it is no more, nor is it the present perfect of what has been in what I am, but rather the future anterior of what I will have been for what I am in the process of becoming."[24]

This round-robin of tenses is perfectly logical. The past definite: dead history can be forgotten or it can be remembered; it will not repeat itself. The present perfect would be more suitable if it did not imply death: what has been presupposes the end of the present time in which I am "what I am." This leaves the tense that is truly that of psychoanalytic time, the only valid tense: the future anterior. I will have been this or that—the mute child, the angry child, the child afflicted by the fantasy of the wolf, the prodigal son, the abandoned daughter—just long enough to say it. As soon as the thing is said, I am already in the process of becoming something else. I will have been this, but this is over. The memory cannot be expressed in the imperfect or the perfect or the past: it is now in its proper place, classified, and from now on harmless. Lacan's concern with grammar focused on the place where rhetoric and invention coalesce.

What is this but the "return to Freud" that Lacan for so long made his rallying cry? Everything, surely, is in Freud: the truth, which is not so much discovered as it is "pieced together" after the fact; the ordering of memory as the goal of therapy; and the healthy oblivion with which the analysis terminates, when everything is finished. I will have been this child, then—but what child? The memory is forgotten so quickly that it has already given rise to the dawning of a new day.

On the other hand, nothing is really in Freud. For it was in fact Lacan who by fooling around with tenses found in grammar that needed resource, the form whose function it is to span the gap between past and future and link the two firmly together: the so-called future anterior, the future that comes before like the poetic life imagined by Baudelaire. Only one tense is truly dialectical: a logical shuttle between past and future. No one pays attention to it. But it is true that the locution "I will have been," oddly twisted as it is, contains seeds of the future that one finds retroactively. It is a memory curious about its own future. A memory with a gift for science fiction, which refuses simply to repeat the old saw, "once upon a time," over and over again. Everything is different if we say, "It will have come to pass . . ." The fairy, whether good or bad, wins in advance: the story is already sketched out, but it changes as it is being told. As if nothing had happened, the future anterior alters history: it is the miraculous tense. The tense of healing. Plainly nothing, not even grammar, escapes from psychoanalysis.

This is the way it will henceforth be in Lacan's teaching texts, once he begins speaking in the name of Lacan. The dazzling, detailed discoveries of the clinic years are superseded by work on the material of psychoanalysis itself—a translation, a hashing and rehashing of its substance. Is the subject transformed as a result? Think of the way in which wolves feed their young: they go in search of food, swallow it, return to the lair, and regurgitate it. Then they all eat what remains. So does the pelican. There is something of the pelican in Lacan's procedure. He regurgitates predigested nourishment taken elsewhere, in the Freudian forests or the philosophical swamps or the vast deserts of mathematics. He continues regurgitating until the moment when, as with the pelican in the poem, there is no more fish in his stomach and nothing is left but himself: the "subject-supposed-to-know," the image of the Analyst that allows every other analyst to exist. Beyond any teaching is the mystical pelican that tears open its own liver and offers itself to its offspring.

Lacan's work is not a work of invention but a work of transmission. Midway through the Rome Report, Lacan sketches in broad strokes a program of instruction for an ideal Psychoanalytic Institute. This was of course partly because the recent schism forced him to take a position. But it was still more because he had embarked on a new path: the path of teaching and regurgitation—that is the word for it, ingenious though it was. Much later, in *Télévision,* Lacan drops a line that says a great deal about his need to teach: "I expect nothing more from so-called analysts except to be the object thanks to which what I teach is not a self-analysis." Supply and demand are back at center stage: if Professor Lacan is offering to speak rather than listen, still the seminar represents a demand on Lacan's part, a demand to escape from his own analysis. Was the boundary between his teaching and his self-analysis really so tenuous? Was the mirror so necessary? His teaching became a multiparty analytic session. He offered to speak, and his listeners demanded that he speak. Once again he succeeded in creating demand with supply.

But the authentic psychoanalyst does not respond to demand. Throughout his life Lacan will have responded—I use the future anterior advisedly—to the demand for instruction on the part of the psychoanalysts who came to hear him. In *Télévision* he repeatedly turns the question around: "There is no difference between the television audience and the audience I have been addressing for some time now, which is known as my seminar. In both cases a gaze: to which I address myself in neither, but in the name of which I speak." A fine definition of teaching: to speak in the hearer's name.

The Story of the Beautiful Butcher's Wife, and Desire for the Other

We have already encountered some of the premises on which Lacan based this moral principle, to which he was firmly attached. The relationship of patient to analyst, student to teacher, is a swindle: demand goes unsatisfied, the promise of supply turns out to be hollow. Things are off to a good start. And yet Lacan was an innovator in the moral domain. The psychoanalytic literature is so full of covert moralizing that it was probably necessary to do as Lacan did and develop his own moral system explicitly to the point where it could be spelled out. At least Lacan did not try to cover the dry toast of moral preaching with the butter of good will or the jelly of charity to make it more palatable. Whether or not psychoanalysts are capable of formulating a morality, at least this fellow Lacan will have tried. His more cautious colleagues remained ensconced in their armchairs and refused to come out into the open for any reason: the patient—their patient—did not need to know. They weren't about to take any chances in any case. But our rhetorician Lacan took plenty of them, in public, and staked his reputation on what he said.

We still lack the main thing we need if we are to discover what Lacan's morality is all about: namely, the concept of desire. The term is at once prurient and enigmatic. As Lacan used it, it was always related to demand. You have to do business first with the small shops before you can deal with the big wholesaler, the psychoanalyst. But what a story there is in desire.

Once upon a time there was a beautiful butcher's wife who was a friend of Freud's. An intelligent, witty woman, the beautiful butcher's wife found the theories of her friend the doctor rather irritating. "You are always saying that a dream is a wish fulfilled. Now I shall tell you a dream in which the content is quite the opposite, in which a wish of mine is not fulfilled. How do you reconcile that with your theory?" She then recounts her dream: the story of a dinner that is not given. The woman wants to give a dinner, but only a single slice of smoked salmon remains, not enough to feed her guests. The Butcher's wife wants to go shopping, but it is Sunday and all the stores are closed. The telephone is out of order as well, so there is no way to organize the meal. The lady therefore has to give up her desire to have a dinner. Clearly, she then tells Freud with an amused chuckle, this dream is not the fulfillment of a wish but rather the opposite.

Cautiously, Freud at first admits that what she says seems reasonable. But stealthily he begins his analysis. "What occurrence gave rise to this dream?" he asks. "You know the stimulus of a dream always lies among the experiences of the preceding day." And the naïve and trusting woman answers his questions.

Sure enough, her husband, a wholesale meat dealer, had told her the day before that he was getting too fat. Accordingly, he planned to do exercise and go on a diet, so that big dinners were out of the question. (Well, well, whispers Freud's ear—his inner ear, concealed between his nose and his right eye.) While she is on the subject of her husband, she tells Freud a somewhat smutty story he has told, just to show what a lively fellow he is. A painter wanted to paint his portrait. But the butcher told him no thanks, he had no interest in "sitting" for a painting, and anyway "a bit of a young girl's posterior" (the part on which she sits, of course) would make a far better picture than his face. This butcher is obviously a rather ribald character. Where does Lacan come into all this? Here is the way he translates this story: "Her butcher of a husband is a great one for dotting the i's when it comes to satisfactions everybody needs, and he doesn't mince words with a painter who makes a great fuss, for God knows what obscure reasons, about his interesting mug: 'Balls, man! What you really need is a nice piece of ass, and if you're waiting for me to give you one you've got another thing coming.' "[25] Another way of putting it.

The butcher's wife was very much in love with her husband, fat, red-faced, and vulgar though he was. Suddenly, without warning, she tells Freud that she has asked her husband not to give her any caviar, even though she is crazy about it. Where did this caviar come from? A minute ago it was smoked salmon. (The inner ear is fully pricked by this time.) In response to Freud's questions, the butcher's wife comes up with an embarrassed ex-

planation and ends by revealing another bit of information. Quite
a juicy one at that! On the night before her dream, she says, she
visited a friend of hers of whom she felt jealous because her husband had been paying a bit too much attention to this woman.
Fortunately, this woman is quite thin, and the butcher only likes
full-figured women. Now, this friend, who wanted to gain
weight, asked the butcher's wife, "When are you going to invite
us again? You always have such good food."

The inner ear is exultant, for the secret has at last been found.
The meaning of the dream is clear: the butcher's wife must avoid
giving a dinner at all cost, lest her friend gain weight and seduce
her husband and . . . It was far simpler to fulfill the wish not to
have this dinner, and so Freud was right, as always: no beautiful
butcher's wife is going to catch him out. And coincidentally
enough, smoked salmon is the friend's favorite food, which she
begrudges herself as much as the butcher's wife begrudges herself
caviar.

Freud was not a man to be satisfied with an easy victory, however. The story of the fulfilled wish, the desire realized all the
more effectively for having been disguised, was good enough for
his pretty friend. But he seems to have kept a second explanation
to himself, to savor in private. This second explanation involves
the one element of the dream not yet explained, the caviar.

The beautiful butcher's wife seems to have had an odd way of
expressing desire: she has two desires and refuses to satisfy either
of them. These desires transpire first in her dream and second in
her strange refusal to eat caviar even though she loves it. By
contrast, her friend, who loves salmon but refrains from eating
it, expresses a simple wish: to gain weight. The butcher's wife is
punishing her friend in her dream: no dinner, no way to gain
weight. She is actually identifying with her friend. And notice
how she does so. Since she is jealous of this friend, of whom her
husband speaks so well, she puts herself in the other woman's
place and refuses to eat. In this way she completes one of the

most routine of all psychic structures, the hysterical triangle, consisting of the husband, the wife, and the wife's friend (notice I do not say the wife's lover—quite another story).

This all in all rather homely little story occupies three pages of *The Interpretation of Dreams*.[26] As the reader will by now have gathered, Lacan has as usual reworked Freud's text so extensively that he sees in it something quite different from what Freud saw. Lacan is emphatic where Freud is discreetly reserved, on the question of the good sexual relationship between the butcher and his wife: "Now there's a man a woman should not have to complain about, a genital type, and therefore a fellow who can be trusted to see to it that his wife, when he screws her, won't have to masturbate when he's done." The wife is therefore presumably a "satisfied" woman: but no, she isn't—that is precisely the point. For the butcher's wife, Lacan tells us, does not want to be satisfied through her only true needs. "She wants other, gratuitous needs, and in order to be sure that they are gratuitous, she wants not to satisfy them. So to the question, 'What does the intelligent butcher's wife want?' one can answer, 'Caviar.' But this is a hopeless answer, because she is also the person who doesn't want caviar."[27]

Now we can see the circuitous path that wends its way from the beautiful butcher's wife to her mad sisters, Aimée, Christine and Léa, Thérèse of Avila, and Hadewijch of Antwerp. She appears in *The Interpretation of Dreams* in order to prove to Dr. Freud that every dream is the fulfillment of a wish, even the must disgusting and negative one: the defeat of the beautiful butcher's wife assures the victory of Freud. But for Lacan her significance is quite different. Since this woman desires caviar, which she does not want, she represents what in the Lacanian lexicon is known as "lack" (*manque*); she is the symbol of feminine identification. Only by invoking the example of a woman can Lacan establish the connection between desire and the lack it carries within itself: it is like a bean that splits open (the technical word for the split is "dehiscence") to release its seed. Only a woman can desire something she does not want, because she identifies with another woman who also does not want something that she desires. Step one is the mirror; step two is the lack that comes into being as soon as the image forms in the mirror. Lack intervenes between the subject and the reflection, between one subject and another, between Christine and Léa, between "my sister's husband" and the sister herself, between the butcher's wife and the caviar, and between the butcher's wife and her friend. Step one, the mirror; step two, the lack; step three, the desire: now it is only the Other who is lacking. We are already a long way from Freud.

Still, the twist is minor. Lacan's text strictly follows Freud's. For it is true that the butcher's wife "has for a long time wanted to eat a caviar sandwich every morning" (Freud) and also that "she grudged the expense" (Freud again). Hence it is not wrong to shift one's ground slightly from the desire and denial to the assertion "she did not want it." But this is not the end result of Lacan's linguistic approach. The next step is to introduce the concept of "inversion," Lacan's own. Here is the rest of Lacan's account: "How can another woman be loved (for the patient to think about this, is it not enough that her husband is considering it?) by a man who wouldn't find her satisfying (remember, this is the fellow who mentioned the 'piece of ass')? This is the question in its sharpened form. More generally, it is the question of identification, the question of hysterical identification." Freud merely observes that the butcher's wife asks herself why her husband, who is so fond of buxom women, takes such an interest in her friend with the flat behind. A half-century later, Lacan carries the argument somewhat further: "The question—this question—becomes the subject at this very point: the point, that is, at which the woman identifies with the man, and the slice of smoked salmon replaces desire for the Other." [28]

The point seems trivial, doesn't it? Desire, the Other—the words have become so familiar that we've developed an immunity against the vocabulary. But try to imagine reading these lines with the fresh, astonished eyes of our great-great-grandchildren, when they come upon the forgotten books of the good Dr. La-can in some library. Hysteria is the identification of one woman with another, as people have known since Freud. As for the iden-tification of a woman with a man, that is pure Lacan. Jealous, the beautiful butcher's wife does of course try to understand why her husband desires the other woman. It is also true that the question, "How can another woman be loved?" (an essential ques-tion for any woman), becomes the butcher's wife's question, and that she in turn "becomes" the question. In order to answer it, she places herself in the masculine position and desires the other woman as her husband does. The caviar and the slice of salmon draw the two women together: both of them desire these deli-cacies, and both deliberately do without them. In the dream the slice of smoked salmon stands in the place of the friend and hence it also stands for the desire for the friend, which goes unsatisfied.

And that is not all (not the whole truth . . .). In a dazzling play of language and sleight-of-hand, Lacan transforms the flat slice of salmon into a whole salmon, and the desire for salmon into desire for the phallus. The friend is the phallus; the desire for the lacking salmon—or caviar—is desire for the phallus, "meager though this particular phallus may be." [29] Lacan did not pass up the occasion to point out that a woman (signifier slashed or no) could be substituted for the phallus, that a woman could, as in certain ancient rites, wear a dummy phallus to be revealed in a sacred ritual of unveiling, just as a man dressed in woman's garb might have his phallus exposed in the ritual act of *anasyrma,* the lifting of the skirt.

> It happens sometimes that desire, all too visible, cannot be hidden so easily, occupying as it does here the center stage, the middle of the banquet table, in the form of a salmon—as luck would have it a pretty fish, which is sometimes served in restaurants under a thin gauze, so that all we have to do is lift that veil of gauze to recreate the effect with which certain ancient mysteries culminated. [30]

Lacan pulled off his trick. *Saumon à l'antique* became a fad. The restaurant was transformed into a temple, the fish into a taboo prosthesis, and the decorative mousseline into a Pompeian veil. Later, the cover of *Télévision* would show the "terrified woman" of the Villa of Mysteries spreading her dark wings and extending a hand with fingers spread to ward off the nameless, invisible horror, the sacred phallus. Dressed in white and set against a red background, this figure of a woman is probably the most beautiful image there is of the hysterical butcher's wife. The woman is always the same, caught up in an endless round. The first women inaugurated the mirror stage, this one comes up against the Other: "Desire is what is revealed in the space that demand creates within itself, inasmuch as the subject, in articulating the sequence of signifiers, brings to light its lack of being by calling upon the other to make good the lack, assuming that the Other, the locus of speech, is also the locus of this insufficiency." [31]

The butcher's wife's demand is for smoked salmon, or caviar. The butcher's wife's desire is for what both the smoked salmon and the caviar lack. The demand is for an object—possibly the analyst himself—whereas the desire is for a lack, a lack referred to literally as the Other. Now we can begin to understand the meaning of one of Lacan's most celebrated formulas: "The Unconscious is the discourse of the Other." This is no more complicated than the rest. It's just a little more magical.

Questions without Answers and Answers without Questions: Oedipus and Perceval

What, who is the Other? In the example of the beautiful butcher's wife, it is a person, a human being equipped like any other human being with powers of speech, thought, reflection, etc. But this is just one of the forms the Other may take. More broadly, the Other is that which lacks. Or, to put it another way, the Other is a location, a place from which the human subject can draw what it needs to express its desire, desire notorious for its lacunae and always after what it does not have—what above all it does not want to have. The expression of desire is to be read literally, letter by letter—again we encounter the letter, which takes us back to the elementary component of language, the signifier. The smoked salmon is the signifier of the butcher's wife's desire, drawn from a living source, the Other, the woman's thin friend. The butcher's wife does not dream of her caviar but rather of the other woman's smoked salmon. The butcher's wife's Unconscious is thus the discourse of the Other, no?

Not entirely. The Other is also the law, the Father, the repository of language and culture (we saw earlier how a young girl could be aware of this). And if for a woman the Other is her friend, the reason is that the friend represents the phallus, the ultimate symbol. The ultimate symbol of human Law in phallocratic societies. The Other is a logical idea, one that Plato was forced to make room for within the bosom of the Same because he had fallen into such a metaphysical impasse that he could not conceive of the world, of reality, without introducing an idea of lack.[32] The lesson was not lost on Lacan: none ever was. And it was also as a philosopher that he spoke of the Other. Perhaps that was why he spelled it with a capital.

Where does the other fit into psychoanalysis? The analyst is in an impossible position if the following peremptory formula is to be believed: "What I look for in speech is the response of the other. What constitutes me as subject is my question."[33]

The analysand consents in advance to speak. He naturally expects an answer. But the analyst is bound by the same prior agreement not to respond to the content of the patient's demand. The subject will therefore "stay with his question," as the phrase goes: he will remain a question, by definition a question without an answer. The "hot potato" of morality continues to pass silently from hand to hand.

To digress for a moment, let us join the Pueblo Indians, or the Algonquins, or the Greeks. Lévi-Strauss offers several enigmatic Indian stories for our consideration. Enigma is a common enough word for describing something like Lacan's question without an answer. Take the questions raised for Oedipus by the plague that

besets his city at the beginning of "Oedipus Rex." These are
questions without any true answer, since the only answer to the
plague is Oedipus himself. "What I look for in speech is the response of the other," said Lacan-Oedipus speaking to the people
of Thebes. And from the horrified silence of his subjects he
learned that "what constitutes me as subject is my question."
And what a question! The question of incest. Enough to take
away one's breath, or one's eye. Now, according to Lévi-Strauss,
who never makes an observation without good reasons, there are
many cultures in which we find an extremely close relationship
between incest and enigma (or riddles). Oedipus is faced with an
enigma before he commits incest. Among the Pueblo Indians riddles are put to the spectators by ritual clowns, who according to
myth are the children of incest. Among the Algonquins heroes
must on pain of death answer questions put to them by owls,
which through a highly complicated series of stories are related
to a powerful sorceress who discovers that her son and daughter
have committed incest. Wherever there is enigma, then, there is
incest. Enigmas are of two kinds: questions without answers and,
more rare, answers without questions.

The latter are found only in myths that are less familiar to us
even if, paradoxically, they come from cultures more closely related to our own than the Indian myths cited above. Perceval,
the village idiot of the Grail cycle, is so stupid that, when he
comes upon a magic boat, he does not care to ask the question
that he is supposed to ask: the answer is there—it is the boat—
but the question is not forthcoming. The story of Buddha's death
follows a similar pattern: a disciple forgets to ask the anticipated
question, and disaster follows. Disaster follows either because the
enigma cannot be resolved (the Oedipal version) or because the
questions are not asked when the answers are waiting (the Perceval version). Where does the danger lie?

The answer is remarkably simple: the danger always lies in
incorrect distance, whether too close or too far—remember the
Mandan Indians we discussed earlier. "First we have a hero who

abuses sexual relations by indulging in incest, and then we have a chaste hero who abstains from sexual relations altogether. First a subtle character who knows all the answers, then an innocent who can't even ask questions."[34] Perceval, in other words, is an inverted Oedipus. But the real point is this: if chastity is the inverse of incest, then the "question without an answer" is the inverse of the "answer without a question." "Like a solved riddle, incest brings together terms that are supposed to remain separate: son and mother or brother and sister, as does the answer when, against all expectation, it links up with its corresponding question."[35]

It is therefore preferable, from Oedipus' standpoint, that the enigma not be resolved. To answer the question is to commit incest, to establish a link between terms too closely related. But Oedipus has been warned: Tiresias has advised him not to seek knowledge of the truth. Tiresias has himself paid with his eyesight for his desire to find out the answer to the question of feminine *jouissance,* judged too intimate. It was by prying apart two copulating snakes that he crossed the tenuous and terrifying boundary that divides the dangerous from the ordinary.

When an answer exists, it is better to formulate a question to fit it rather than leave the answer to splendid isolation as does Perceval the Mad. Not to answer the question is to practice solitude, a dangerous thing to do. The prohibition of incest has an ecological moral. The consequences of incest, of solving the riddle, are decay and flood. By contrast, the consequence of estrangement, of chastity, of leaving the answer without a question, is sterility (animal and vegetable). As always in myths there are two opposing dangers: the danger of too much and the danger of not enough, the danger of excess and the danger of lack. "To the two prospects that may beguile his imagination—the prospect of an eternal summer or an eternal winter, the one profligate to the point of corruption, the other pure to the point of sterility—man must resolve himself to prefer the balance and periodicity of the alternation of seasons. In the natural order the alternation of seasons fulfills the same function that is fulfilled in the social realm by the exchange of women in marriage and the exchange of words in conversation, provided that both are carried out with the declared intention of communicating, that is, without subterfuge or perversity and above all without ulterior motives.''[36]

Plainly, then, mythical equilibrium consists in not saying too much: exchange cannot operate without reserve. Don't say too much: a man and a woman should keep the same distance between them as neighboring Indian tribes keep between their respective camps. Any closer and the result is a fatal fusion, any farther and it is suppressed hatred. Closer together and the result is Tristan and Isolde, farther apart and it is Penthesilea blindly killing Achilles in order to devour him later on. Or Tancredes killing Clorinda. Exchange thus harks back to "midspeak." From mythical trials Lacan learned how to speak with a reserve that partakes of enigma: questions without answers, that is, no incest—how wise the old shaman was! The point (which Lacan also learned from anthropology) is that, curiously enough, alliance and estrangement have the same function. By respecting the nature of enigma, and "half-speaking" his theory, Lacan showed himself to be both a good husband and a good prince amid the society in miniature that he himself had assembled. He was, in short, a good Oedipus. And around him we find both of the temptations mentioned by Lévi-Strauss: the profligacy of an unbridled and inexhaustible style, and the sterility of a listener who no longer knew how to respond to any question or any utterance. In both we recognize psychoanalysts: the loquacious analyst in the first temptation, the silent analyst in the second. Neither partakes of the seasonal alternation essential to psychoanalysis.

To return to the main topic at hand, Lacan says that the subject, in analysis, is a question in search of an answer by way of speech. Lacan's thought has consistently remained open to the infinite perspectives of mythology, whose secret powers have helped to shape his ideas. The question must not link up with its answer, just as the son must not link up with its mother, just as the client must not link up with the analyst. The essential thing is to find the right therapeutic distance between the two, neither too close nor too far. Analysis is an enigmatic question and to some degree it must remain so. The answer to the analytic question is only half clear and must remain partly in shadow. It is enough to explore the birds' nests and climbing vines hidden in the labyrinth, enough for the mind to live at peace in partial awareness that it is governed by the tribunal of the unconscious in keeping with laws derived from its irreducible history. We can explore these laws and map the boundaries of the territories to which they apply. We will discover that the Other, the unconscious, the law, the father are one place. "We teach, following Freud, that the Other is the site of the memory that he discovered and called the unconscious, a memory that he regards as the subject of a question that remains open insofar as it conditions the indestructibility of certain desires."[37]

Indestructible desires. Unsatisfied demands. Armor, fortresses, wasteland, boundaries. Only the question remains open: no luck, it is precisely the question that constitutes the subject, and the subject is eager to have the question answered. The beautiful butcher's wife and her slim friend go to a lot of trouble for nothing, and so does every other subject in the world. They go on passing up their caviar and smoked salmon while satisfying needless desires. What they don't want, what nobody wants, is to be satisfied.

The Swaddled Girl

"What is thus given to the Other to satisfy, and which is, properly speaking, what he does not have, since he too lacks being, is what is called love, but it is also hatred and ignorance. And it is also the passions of being that are aroused by any demand that goes beyond the corresponding need, of which the subject is inherently the more deprived the more the need contained in the demand is satisfied."[38]

This further elaboration is very important. It enables us to glimpse what is legitimate in the refusal of the beautiful butcher's wife: she is siding with the child who refuses the excessive attentions of an overly maternal mother. If the mother offers "too much" satisfaction, the child will never feel hunger and therefore will never know the pleasure of assuaging its hunger. Thanks to her randy husband the butcher's wife probably never had the time to feel the slightest sexual frustration. Similarly, when the mother anticipates the child's hunger and stuffs it with the "choking porridge" of love, the child will cease to eat: it has no other strategic option, it can pose no other "question" in the face of an "answer" that is all too present. What was Lacan up to in January of 1980, then? The same thing as the child or the butcher's wife: he was giving himself the luxury of putting forth an as yet unmet demand for disciples. He dissolved his school in the same way that the child refuses its mother's breast.

One might even say that he was deliberately regressing. For the id regresses not only when a demand is not satisfied but also when it is oversatisfied. The child becomes anorexic and shrinks to a shadow. Kingsley Hall's nurse Mary Barnes became schizophrenic at the age of forty-two. She refused to eat and had to be fed through a tube, while other tubes carried away her liquid and solid wastes. She wanted to "descend" to the brink of death. With great difficulty she was finally persuaded to take nourishment from a bottle.[39] Clearly, the gulf between one's needs and one's demands can be infinitely wide, so wide as to be fatal. If the demand is circumvented or ignored, regression commences. Lacan did not escape the mechanism he had described by dissolving his school. Just as Mary Barnes succeeded in gathering around her worried people who fed her like a baby, Lacan succeeded in perpetuating his hunger: for a school, for listeners, for love.

When Freud heard Charcot say, loud enough for anyone within

earshot to hear, "That doesn't mean it doesn't exist," referring to hysteria, he understood that the imagination could make the body ill. And when he saw hysterics released from their symptoms by means of hypnosis, when he saw paralyzed patients walk and other miracles occur, he had his first confused insight into the therapeutic potency of transference. Thus began a long story that ultimately found its Savonarola in Lacan. And like Savonarola Lacan was quickly condemned by the equivalent of well-off Florentine citizens concerned to protect their possessions: his fellow analysts. In any case, to return to Freud, he quickly abandoned hypnosis, which had too much "mysticism" in it; manipulation of and pressure on the skull, which smacked too much of witchcraft; and face-to-face confrontations with the patient, which were too upsetting. Instead he chose to "require the patient to lie upon a sofa, while I sat behind him, seeing him, but not seen myself."[40] No more laying on of hands, crystal balls, or penetrating gazes, just listening.

This settled the question, or so Freud thought at first. But the same dangers that Freud sensed in hypnotism, which drove hypnotized hysterics into the good doctor's arms when they woke up, cropped up again with patients on the couch. True, the accesses of passion were over (still . . .). And true, the transference now unfolded between two immobile individuals, the one sitting silent in his armchair, the other chatting away on the couch. The location of the problem had shifted, but the problem itself remained. When Lacan first became involved with the question, French analysts were talking about something they called "oblativity" as a way of responding to transference. To help cure his patient the therapist was supposed to offer himself as fodder for the patient's fantasies and respond to the patient's demands, though not all the way. At about the same time Hartmann, Kris, and Loewenstein came up with the idea of what they called the "autonomous ego," an entity capable of escaping the dictates of the unconscious and, at the conclusion of the therapy, arriving by some manner of miracle at a condition of autonomy. This theme was much developed by psychoanalysts in the United States. It was soon suggested that the patient, in order to strengthen his "autonomous ego," should identify with the "ego" of his psychoanalyst, a "strong" ego par excellence. Hence it was the analyst's job to develop a powerful ego. This Freudian Superman was then supposed to reproduce himself in his patients, producing one "strong ego" after another. Psychoanalysis was on the verge of becoming a totalitarian discipline. This was a far cry from Freud. Once again therapeutic practice threatened to turn psychoanalysis into a form of white magic.

To respond to the patient's demand and create a sturdy ego by means of identification—here we get a good whiff of Oedipus. A strong smell of cabbage stew, the family, and incest, these being precisely the images that need to be distanced. But what are the limits of transference?

Among the Celts engaged couples were allowed to sleep in the same bed before they were married. And a guest put up for the night was entitled to sleep beside his host's daughter, who was tightly swaddled in a sheet. The girl, a living mummy, did not budge all night, nor did the man beside her. The practice was called "bundling." Not surprisingly it was carried over to America—where else?—by certain religious sects. The analyst is like the young girl swaddled in the sheet. Wrapped in a moral shroud, he "lies"—platonically—beside his patient, allowing him to burn chastely with unslaked desire. The erotic closeness is at once irritating and exhausting. Bundling is a brief game that pretends to separate when in fact it provokes and titillates. And so it is with charitable psychoanalysts who bind themselves too closely to their patients' loves and defenses—like Tristan and Isolde, whose myth, so Lacan tells us, "is henceforth supposed to be godfather to the psychoanalyst in his quest for the soul, destined to achieve mysterious marriage by extinguishing its instinctual fantasies." [41] On this point Lacan waged the same battle as Freud, a profoundly secular battle. Make no mistake, however: atheism can defy religion and batter it with every available weapon only

to end in mysticism. That the two attitudes are far from being
contradictory is shown by the fact that it was Rousseau who
wrote the *Profession de foi du vicaire savoyard* and Spinoza who
wrote the *Ethics* and the *Tractatus Theologico-Politicus*. Or, to take
a contemporary example, cultivated Iranians will testify how
scandalous it is, from the standpoint of traditional *shi'ite* mysticism, that members of the clerical hierarchy have put themselves
forward as temporal leaders in Iran.[42] Psychoanalysis faces a constant threat "from the right": namely, that its theory will be
turned into a form of spiritual initiation. Freud wanted no part
of Jung's magic tracks. Lacan, for his part, wanted no part of the
charitable therapies practiced by the analytic "bundlers."

For Lacan the analyst has nothing in common with the young
girl swaddled in her bedsheet. The best way to deal with transference and to allow the love story between patient and analyst
to run its course unfettered is for the analyst never to respond to
any demand. This means that he must endure the patient's anxiety, love, and anger without ever becoming involved in these
emotions as a partner. It means that he must resist his patient's
attempts to seduce him, to involve him in drama, or to break off
the relationship, just as if he had lived a hundred different unhappy lives in a hundred different families. Now and then, of
course, one of the analyst's patients may turn out to be a beauty—
and the analyst is, after all, a man, or a woman, just like anyone
else, or nearly so. But by refusing to respond to any demand and
by leaving the way clear for the expression of the patient's every
desire, without ever fulfilling those desires, without ever
stanching the flow, the psychoanalyst, as Jacques Lacan imagined
him, becomes extremely vulnerable. The analyst who swaddles
himself binds himself at the same time, but at least he is protected. The Lacanian analyst is as unprotected as a worm. He
abides by one absolute principle, a principle at once practical and
ethical: a principle of "non-intervention." This at any rate is the
theory as presented in *Ecrits*. For the practice one must turn to

analysts themselves, to their stories of their own therapeutic experience, including their gaffes and errors.

Psychoanalysis: Prophylaxis for Dependency

Lurking in the shadows, ethics is constantly raising new demands. Lacan spoke for a year about the ethics of psychoanalysis. This was one of the best years of his seminar, and yet, even though the text of his lectures had been revised and was ready for the press, Lacan persistently refused to allow publication. Ethics was his constant project. Totally unlike the altruistic theories put forward during the first fifty years of the history of psychoanalysis, Lacan's ethics did not lay down prescriptions but suggested avenues of escape; he established taboos rather than positive laws. But the "principle of non-intervention" was not precisely a taboo. Rather, it was a principle of neutrality. *Ne uter:* neither one nor the other. This definition of the word "neutral," a word so often misunderstood, is well suited to the true analyst: psychoanalysis is not a matter of diplomatic mediation such as the Swiss offer through their good offices but rather a question of finding the correct middle ground between passivity and active intervention. An analyst abides by the principle of non-intervention if he has the capacity to act but refrains from doing so. He can then suggest what his action would have been by the mere fact of not acting. He is the opposite of the shaman, in that he allows the patient to act unfettered. This bestows on the analyst a kind of power.

"We now come to the malign principle of this power, always subject to blind guidance. It is the power to do good. Power never has any other end, and that is why there is no end to power." [43] What is this? The "power to do good" does not exist. It is incompatible with Lacan's angry dismissal of "analytic charity" as practiced by American psychoanalysts. No sooner does

Lacan drop the phrase, however, than he corrects himself. "But here something else is involved: the truth, the only truth, the truth about the effects of the truth. Once Oedipus starts down this path, he relinquishes his hold on power."[44] Power, then, is what is "malign," blind, and dangerous. The analyst's embrace of the principle of non-intervention comes close to being a definitive renunciation of all power. Freud had discovered a form of power, a frightening form, and sure enough, he was frightened by it, so frightened that he worked out a technique for neutralizing the dangers of hypnotic transference and, more generally, of love suggested by the shaman. The ability to control his power permitted him to cure his patients. Before Lacan, psychoanalysis had always been based on the regulated, controlled use of symbolic power, of the power of language over the body. To renounce this power was to take a significant step in the history of psychoanalysis. Lacan attempted to do this by substituting "truth" for "power."

The project made sense, notwithstanding the mistakes to which it gave rise in the theory of Lacan's later years, when he had taken on too many professorial airs, as well as in the erratic practice of certain of his most dogmatic disciples. Not only did the project make sense, but the idea of truth kept faith with Freud, who besides coping with the dangers inherent in his power over his patients, was smitten with the same passion for the truth. The connection is obvious: "The id speaks where it suffers." The truth is the expression of a pain. Freud, for his part, said that "the hysteric suffers from memories." Lacan generalized this proposition: all suffering is the sign of some reminiscence, from the minor suffering of the jealous butcher's wife to the greater suffering of Judge Schreber in his madness to the suffering of Oedipus as he seeks to learn the causes of the plague. If, while the analyst abides strictly by the principle of non-intervention, the patient's ego disintegrates and its armor falls away, exposing his lost infantile desires, the patient's question will remain forever unanswered, forever an enigma. But at least this question will have been formulated in the terms of "full speech," as Lacan calls it: a form of speech that exploits the available resources to the full. Toward the end of one of his finest articles, "La Direction de la cure et les principes de son pouvoir" ("The Direction of Therapy and the Principles of Its Power"), Lacan sets forth the rules of the "analytic contract" between the patient and the therapist:

> (1) All the power in therapy belongs to speech. (2) Rules are not much help in directing the subject toward full speech or coherent discourse. He should be left free to find his own way. (3) This freedom is what he finds most difficult to tolerate. (4) In analysis it is appropriate to put all demands "in parentheses," since the analyst is not allowed to satisfy any of them. (5) Since no obstacle is placed in the way of the avowal of desire, it is toward such avowal that the subject is directed and even led. (6) In the final analysis resistance to such avowal can here be due only to incompatibility between the desire and what the patient is saying.[45]

Thus everything is clear except for one final enigma: if the objective of therapy is the avowal of desire far more than the treatment of symptoms, then Lacan is deliberately setting an impossible goal. Desire can never be expressed in words; hollowed out "in the space" between the demand and the subject, desire is a form of interrogation that leads back, once again, to latent mysticism, a mysticism fostered, moreover, by the Hegalian inspiration of Lacan's ideas. Lacan's analytic contract is fine except that it directs the subject toward an impasse, in fact toward an impasse that is like the situation of a person in love, since "love is giving what one does not have." From this mystical position, inherited from women who took from an absent God what he did not have—a body with a phallus that satisfied them—Lacan drew a lesson for psychoanalysis: the analyst too is one who gives what he does not have and who refuses to give what he does have. The psychoanalyst is a creature of love and psychoanalysis, an amorous discipline, an erotic theory, a craft of pure *jouissance*.

Accordingly, the analyst will not speak for himself, even

though he has this ability. "The analyst is distinguished by the fact that he takes a faculty common to all men (speech) and uses it in a manner not within everyone's grasp, namely, when he speaks for, and endures the speech of, the other."[46] [I have here rendered by periphrasis what Lacan is able to express more succinctly in French by saying that the analyst "porte la parole." A porte-parole is a spokesman, one who speaks for others, whereas "porter la parole" literally means "to bear speech"—the analyst is shouldering the burden of his patient's words. In other words, he endures his patient's confessions—trans.] This is the obverse of love, the "fundamental rule" firmly laid down by Freud for the early stages of therapy. The patient must say "whatever comes into his mind." This violates the most basic conventions of any culture. Just think what any group of human beings would be like if everyone went around free-associating out loud. All civility would go by the boards. But the patient, absolved of the need to appear civil, is obliged only to obey this one rule. The analyst also deals strangely with conversation, though Freud never offered any explicit rule in this regard. The analyst, no more civil than the patient, holds his tongue and does not respond to what is said to him. Thus he is not so much the spokesman as he is the person who receives the "idle chatter" of the other. To endure speech is to be able to make exclusive use of it: non-response, like non-intervention, is not a choice of muteness over articulate response. To make this clear, moreover, the analyst chatters away himself from time to time.

Non-response, non-intervention—this refusal of power on principle calls to mind certain other hallmarks of Lacan's thought, such as the doctrine of "not the whole truth" and the dictum that "sexual intercourse does not exist." Like pseudo-Dionysus the Areopagite, who proposed a negative theology, Lacan proposed a negative psychoanalysis. In order to describe the "universal Cause" pseudo-Dionysus listed a series of negative attributes: it is neither figure nor form nor quality nor quantity nor mass, it is not susceptible to change, destruction, division, privation, or flux. This interminable list of negatives fills several chapters that do not so much qualify the attributes of the universal cause (God) as they disqualify other possible definitions.[47] In order to describe the "analytic cause" Lacan does the same thing. He does not say, for example, that psychoanalysis seeks to promote the independence of the subject. Rather, he says that it is "prophylaxis for dependency," hygiene to prevent subjugation. The cast of mind is the same as in the principle of non-intervention: the aim is to preserve the patient from dependency, not to make him independent. Whatever is positive is suspect: a positive assertion would pretend to tell the whole truth; it would no longer be "mid-speak" but would give the appearance of revealing something "more" and would for that reason become false. "Prophylaxis" is the ultimate that can be expected: psychoanalysis reveals where the psychic microbes are, what emotions they may infect, what kinds of amorous epidemics may break out. As always, the point is to explore existing conditions, to find out what the limits are. No pretense is made of transforming them. Love is a kind of pox: the statement could not be more clear.

✳ At the conclusion of therapy what will have disappeared is the armor of the Ego, the fortress, the glass cage of narcissistic illusions. The enemy is the ego. This contrasts with the view of American psychoanalysts for whom the ego is to be reinforced and protected. Lacan attacked the ego from every quarter: by silence, by terminating sessions, by violating ordinary conversational conventions in order to break down the individual's defenses. There is a celebrated remark of Freud's: "Wo es war, soll ich werden."[48] It has to be cited first in German, since the issue involves the translation. For the tradition [of French psychoanalysis before Lacan—trans.] and for Marie Bonaparte, the translation should be, "The ego must drive out the id." But Lacan observes that Freud did not write *"das Ich"* but merely *"ich."* Thus he is not talking about the ego. Nor did he write *"das Es,"* so he is not talking about the id. Lacan therefore translates the passage quite literally: "Where it was, there must I come to be." Another version: "Where it used to be, it is my duty that I come to be."[49] But in this latter version, commentary is already insinuating itself into the translation.

In any case, one point is clear. The word ego has been eliminated from Lacan's translations. And the fundamental ethical law of psychoanalysis, from Freud to Lacan, has always been to find the way to move between the most repressed material in the unconscious ("where it was") and a subject free of all defensive dependency ("I must come to be").

Does such a subject exist? It comes close to freedom, the old ideal of freedom that has ruled men's minds since the Enlightenment. But Lacan does not say this, as if by design. He is far too aware of the three impossible wagers that Freud posed as a challenge to psychoanalysis: to educate, to govern, and to psychoanalyze. It is already saying a great deal to admit that psychoanalysis dreams of educating and governing. Therapy thus comes up against the temptation to impose limits on the subject's freedom. Against this, the principle of non-intervention is the appropriate antidote.

But, to repeat the question, does such a subject exist? On occasion Lacan went somewhat further toward answering it, in brief, allusive, sepulchral phrases. He once discussed an "ethics of celibacy, in a word, recently embodied in Montherlant."[50] An ethics, in other words, of non-relation to the Other, in the literal sense. On another occasion, in discussing the danger of hope, well before it had become commonplace to attack the "master-thinkers of salvation" [the allusion, which may be lost on the non-French reader, is to André Glucksmann and other so-called *"nouveaux philosophes,"* who launched an attack on those they called, as in the title of Glucksmann's best-known book, *The Master Thinkers*—trans.], Lacan said this: "I want to say just one thing. I have had several opportunities to watch hope, the promise of what is called a better tomorrow, lead people that I respected . . . quite simply to suicide."[51] This from a man who had had the opportunity to see many suicides. A man who could also assert that "suicide is the only act that can succeed without misfire." A man who could utter the following pronouncement, to be taken at face value: "Hope for what you (will) like."[52] Take that any way you like.

Once he said this in passing: "An ethics is taking shape, converted to silence, not through fright but through desire."

It was in order to speak of this silence that he began to teach. And this in turn involved him in the contradition from which he was never able to escape.

CHAPTER 4

THE GAME OF HOPSCOTCH AND
THE FOUR CORNERS

*"Structuralism"; the passion for games and graphs; for the Phallus
and its equations; Lacan enraptured*

Political Interlude

The year is 1964. Lacan had left the Saint Anne Hospital, where
his seminar had traditionally been held, and set up winter head-
quarters at the Ecole normale supérieure. Thrown out of one institution, he gained admission to another. His solitude remained
unchanged. Society had merely made a place for him in another
of its structures, indeed in one of its most prestigious institutions:
the Ecole normale supérieure, traditionally the breeding ground
of great careers and one of the most selective of all French institutions of higher learning. Lacan's seminar met in the salle Dus-
sanne, usually reserved for theatrical performances and large lectures. The room had velvet curtains and offered direct access to
the street. There he received the sonorous title of "chargé de conférences de l'Ecole pratique des hautes etudes": the "refugee" had
been taken in charge by his friend Lévi-Strauss, who attended
the first meeting of the seminar at the Ecole normale. Lacan
opened the session with exquisitely polite expressions of grati-
tude to Fernand Braudel, chairman of the renowned Sixth Section of the Ecole pratique des Hautes Etudes, who had given the
go-ahead, and to Robert Flacelière, director of the Ecole normale, who had agreed to provide space. The same Robert Flace-

lière later revoked his offer, for mysterious reasons. Lacan then moved his seminar to an amphitheater in the nearby law school.[1] In 1969, at the time of the educational reforms instituted by Edgar Faure, he was put in charge of the Department of Psychoanalysis at the Centre expérimental at Vincennes. The world of psychoanalysis had eliminated him as a paramecium eliminates a foreign body. The academic world received him handsomely. But to him the university was never more than a sort of antechamber. The break with official psychoanalysis had changed his style and even his theoretical orientation.

At about the same time, Louis Althusser, known in the quaint vocabulary of the Ecole normale as the *"caïman,"* or lecturer in charge of teaching students preparing for the *agregation* in philsophy, began to attract attention for his "reinterpretation" of Marx, much as Lacan had attracted attention for his "reinterpretation" of Freud.[2] It was a time of "return" to the great precursors as well as a time of methodological reflection, of epistemological inquiry into the nature of truth. Lenin's dictum that "Marx's theory is all-powerful because it is true" obsessed the current generation of philosophy students at the Ecole normale, and these same students now began to form a sort of honor guard around Lacan. They founded a new journal in his honor, the *Cahiers pour l'analyse,* and thus attracted a new and wider audience, "in the name of which" Lacan now began to speak. While internal battles raged in the world of psychoanalysis after 1960, Lacan transformed himself. He created a new rhetoric of his own devising and perfected his teaching style. Lacan, the psychiatrist, began to speak of "the Hobson's choice of the clinic." He began making use of Lévi-Strauss's works and conceptual tools. And he wholeheartedly adopted the "structuralist" style. Structuralism was just then beginning to sweep France. The changes it introduced were few but important, and these had not escaped Lacan's notice. The really important contributions had all been made by just three men: according to no less an authority than

Lévi-Strauss himself, these were "(Georges) Dumézil, (Emile) Benveniste, and me (Lévi-Strauss)."

⋇ These three men are authentic structuralists, whose work seeks to uncover the complex forms hidden in various bodies of material. Dumézil's work is concerned with Indo-European mythology, Benveniste's with linguistics, and Lévi-Strauss's with kinship structures, spatial structures and social organization, and American Indian mythology, on which he had just begun work at this time.

Lacan, along with Foucault and Barthes, quickly came to be labeled a "structuralist," which, in his case at any rate, did not mean very much. At most the label can be read as a symptom of the respectful awe in which the structuralist "movement" was held in France for many years. Structuralism exerted considerable influence on French thought for a period of twenty years all told, until it was swept away in May 1968 in favor of a return to history, to events, to randomness. No doubt the structuralist label also connotes a constellation of themes common to Lacan, Foucault, and Lévi-Strauss, a constellation commonly subsumed under the rubric, "the death of humanism." At stake were many issues that had been the subject of endless debates between the true-blue Marxists and the structuralist heretics who rejected the Marxists' mechanistic analyses of history (ruling class, ruling ideology) in favor of an analysis of more enduring structures— structures that survived one social change after another and yet remained all but invisible to Marxist theorists, whose view of society had remained, as Sartre called it, "skeletal." Sartre himself was nearly forgotten. His *Critique of Dialectical Reason* was largely ignored, even though it put forth a theory complex enough to be proof against easy refutation by historians and sociologists, had they paid any attention to it at all. In the shadows Sartre began work on his masterpiece, *L'Idiot de la famille,* which, though ostensibly concerned with the biography of a man, Flaubert, and the history of a work, *Madame Bovary,* in fact resolved all the questions of the hour. By establishing, in painstaking detail, the complex relationships among the history of a period, the history of a family, the history of a neurosis, and the history of a social class, Sartre, without really intending to, cut his way through the morass of issues then agitating the intellectual world. But most people had forgotten about him. In May 1968 he resurfaced and remained in the limelight from then until his death. But his story shows what a wide gulf can exist between thinkers and their works on the one hand and the superficial judgments of public opinion on the other.

All the while there was plenty of talk about such topics as the "death of the subject," brilliantly inaugurated by Foucault, whose elegant writing made up for the deficiencies of his theory;[3] the "end of history," a fine dissertation topic first broached by Lévi-Strauss in his polemic with Sartre at the end of La Pensée sauvage; and the effects of intellectual fashions, which always exasperated the same people, the would-be mandarins waiting in the wings, the intellectual hacks, the people nobody was talking about, who could not forgive the stars for their success. In this respect nothing has changed. Today the targets of envy are different, but the envious are the same, full of hatred toward success so long as it is bestowed on one of their contemporaries. They are like the foam on the beach, the washed-up debris from the seas of the intellect, pitiful products of the vulnerable, lackluster university system.

Cartoons began to circulate in which the "structuralist" stars, Lacan, Foucault, Barthes, and Lévi-Strauss, were shown seated under palm trees and dressed in feathery loincloths chatting away happily, around a cauldron perhaps, suggesting that they were cannibals since of course all these prominent intellectuals were "against man."[4] This cartoon was a sign, a sign of the rumors, flattering as well as spiteful, that circulated around what was called "structuralism" and brought notoriety to theories that were otherwise little read and poorly understood. It was also a sign of the Vietnam War era, a period in which the ravages of American imperialism were plain to see. In this respect it is correct to call Lacan a "structuralist." There was nothing new about his warnings against the dangers of American humanism, which, on the pretext of helping mankind, whether by means of psychology, psychoanalysis, or military aid, was in fact helping to subjugate not only individuals but whole peoples. The attack on old-fashioned humanism, which, with its good intentions and noble words, had wreaked havoc by means of colonialism, had political significance. So did the later revival of philosophies that accorded, more or less clumsily, a central position to questions of human rights. And it was at the height of the structuralist vogue that Régis Debray, a brilliant philosophy student at the Ecole normale, left that institution to follow Ché Guevara, leaving us to our studies.

History is cunning. One of its shrewdest ruses was to assign to Lacan and Althusser disciples who later came to reject their masters. The young philosophy students at the Ecole normale, who listened with equal enthusiasm to the "new wave" Marxist and the fashionable psychoanalyst, became ardent Maoist activists in the final days of the 1968 movement. There was nothing illogical in this. But they must have apprehended the lectures of their two masters in a rather peculiar way. From Althusser, or from his various subconscious minds, these young philosophers learned of the need to create a new communist movement based on a model different from the Soviet model and hence also from the French Communist Party as it was then constituted, even though the secretary-general at the time, Waldeck-Rochet, was quite different in style and manner of thinking from the present leadership of the party. China was thought to provide a reasonably acceptable new model, especially since so little was then known about it that it was possible to project whatever theoretical fantasies one wished onto the exotic Chinese reality. From Lacan's lectures Althusser's children learned of the implacable determinism of the unconscious and of the illusions of freedom. The belief was that education could supplant imagination if coupled with a "cultural revolution" whose dogmatism excited the passions of these noble young souls precisely because it called for splitting skulls filled with nothing but noble thoughts. But in this respect too the unconscious had done its work well: for Lacan was indeed searching for a system of education and a consequent system of ethics. It is hardly surprising, then, that he turned out so many young Maoists bent on cutting their roots, whether social, emotional, or cultural. The Maoists "interpreted" Lacan and Althusser; they were true analysts.

A few of them, with various backgrounds and qualifications, became so-called *nouveaux philosophes*. After a period of conscientious exploration of the working-class terrain, they returned to the self-conscious world of noble bourgeois souls from which they had sprung. Some of them attacked the curtailment of freedom wherever they found it, but primarily in the Soviet Union. They also gave renewed currency to the well-used term "antifascism," which took on topical significance in France under the presidency of Valéry Giscard d'Estaing. It was as if they remembered the strange answer Lacan gave, in *Télévision,* to Jacques-Alain Miller when the latter asked, "What makes you so sure that racism is on the rise, and why in the world do you say it is?" "Because it's no joke," Lacan answered, "and in any case it's true." This was in 1973, and Lacan was right. Other disillusioned explorers became ardent exponents of religion, political angels first of all and conscientious exegetes of various forms of spiritualism later on. Meanwhile, with Giscard, the NATO alliance was showing new signs of life. Gaullism was crumbling and with it the Gaullist version of national independence. China, like the rest of the world, had contributed its share of disappointments. The time of disillusionment had come. For that intellectuals are always in demand.

Lacan was never involved in politics in the traditional sense of the word. In 1968 this was held against him. Nevertheless, he always did what was necessary, suspending his seminar when there was a strike and not shrinking from confrontation. Each time he took a theoretical stand, in some cases anticipating later events: in regard to racism, for example, or again, in opposition to Noam Chomsky as early as 1975 for reasons having to do with nothing less than the existence of the subconscious. A mimeographed report of a memorable encounter between a group of Vincennes students and Lacan, entitled *L'Impromptu de Vincenes* (published without Lacan's review or approval), tells us a great deal about the prevalent misunderstanding of the then-fashionable structuralism.[5] Lacan, already old, plunged into a world of which he knew nothing. Vincennes, he said, was "an experiment, I thought an exemplary one." An experiment whose aim was to develop new and critical forms of knowledge. But Vincennes had become something quite different from what it was intended to be. "Knowledge is useless" was the battle-cry of the real Vincennes. The students wanted "to look outside for the means to blow the University sky high," or again, "to find an outlet for our desire to change society and among other things to destroy the University." To these outbursts Lacan, the fall-guy, responded that "in sum, then, what is going on here is the building of a critical university." But he also became exasperated. Outside what? "When you leave here, you become aphasic." Aphasic—no doubt there were students in the audience who didn't know what the word meant. Their prodigious lack of culture dumbfounded Lacan, who had spent most of his life defending "literacy" among psychoanalysts and who now had to face the negation of all culture, the non-negotiable demand for the establishment of a non-culture. Whatever he said, he got himself thrown out of the auditorium.

If he failed to grasp the political content of this encounter almost entirely, still he was not mistaken about the crucial point of the protest. He made two points whose validity later became evident. The first was that, if he, Lacan, was "antiprogressive," the psychoanalysis he dreamed of was progressive and would enable the rebels to analyze "what it is you are rebelling against." He told the students that they were playing "the role of helots

for this regime. . . . The regime points to you and says, 'Look
what a good time they're having.' " And when the regime tired
of watching the students of Vincennes having a good time, it
dispatched a female phallus of the sergeant-major variety who
quickly had them moved to Saint-Denis. The second point has
to do with the essence of all protest and as such might also be
applied to those who protested against the Ecole freudienne.
"Protest," Lacan said, "reminds me of something my late good
friend Marcel Duchamp once said: 'The bachelor makes his own
chocolate.' Take care that the protester doesn't wind up making
his own chocolate." About this too he was right. How many of
the protesters of yesterday are today neatly dressed corporate
managers with attaché cases? How many read *Actuel* because it's
an "in" magazine with a whiff of nostalgia about it? Still, it's
true that Lacan, with his "good friend Marcel Duchamp" ("Who's
that?" muttered the aphasic on the platform), understood nothing of May 1968 or, more generally, of the social changes that
put an end to his own era. His old friends were more important
to him than political commitments: he dined with Salvador Dali
during a stay in New York, at a time when the handsomely mus-
tachioed painter was describing himself as Franco's last champion. Lacan's past youth remained his one point of reference,
along with the mythology of creation.

The Man of Truth

In 1965 Lacan, now in his second year at the Ecole normale,
devoted his seminar to the subject of "Science and Truth."[6] Because the psychoanalyst must eschew power and abide by the
principle of non-intervention, he must devote his efforts to the
truth. Oddly enough, Lacan organized his lectures that year so
as to begin with a "return to Freud" of a rather startling kind: a
justification of Freud's scientism. A whole body of psychoanalytic literature was conceived with the opposite intention, namely,

to show how Freud had parted company with the science of his day, and Lacan himself had previously shown little apparent interest in Freud's "scientific project" or in the various "mechanisms" he invented to explain the Unconscious. But now Lacan saw reason in Freud's scientism. He began by bringing Freud's original views back to life and went on to explain their significance. He described Freud's links to Brücke, the "patron" of Viennese science, to Helmholtz, and to Du Bois-Reymond, whose research in neurophysiology was based on thermodynamics and laid the groundwork for the discovery of the unconscious, originally conceived in terms of energy. Lacan further pointed out that it was in the name of the scientific ideal that Freud split so rancorously with Jung, whose explorations of subjective "depths" and immemorial universal archetypes brought psychoanalysis closer to religion than to science. Finally, he observed that, whereas Marxists criticized psychoanalysis for being a "bourgeois science" and a "reactionary ideology," [7] they were not (much) given to challenging Freud's thought "on the basis of its historical origins." Jacques Lacan then concluded with an ambiguous panegyric to Freud, which, but for the first detail, can also be seen as a self-portrait of the teacher who had already become "Lacan."

What were Freud's historical origins? Lacan tells us:

The society of the Dual Monarchy, with its Jewish ghettoes in which Freud remained hemmed in by his own spiritual aversions; the capitalist order, which conditioned his political agnosticism (which of you will write us an essay, worthy of Lamennais, on indifference in matters of politics?); and, I should add, the bourgeois ethic, for which the dignity of his life inspires in us a respect that serves to inhibit recognition of the fact that his work, misunderstanding and confusion aside, provided the place for the coming together of the only men of truth left to us, the revolutionary agitator, the writer who by his style leaves his mark on the language—I know who I'm thinking of—and the thinker of that life-renewing thought whose precursor we have here." [8]

Who was the writer and who was the thinker? The thinker was probably Heidegger. The writer may have been Aragon, Ponge, Char, Klossowski, or Leiris—there is no dearth of possibilities. Lacan had a way with puzzling allusions. There is no doubt that he put himself alongside these men, that he shared Freud's political agnosticism and bourgeois ethic. Nor is there any doubt that his ambition was to be remembered as a "man of truth."

And so he began to earn himself a reputation as one. Along the way he broke with Paul Ricoeur, who had earnestly attended Lacan's seminar and drawn from it enough material to put together an enormous book on interpretation that combined Freud, Hegel, and Christian hermeneutics. Lacan did not mince words, characterizing the whole approach as a "makeshift" last-ditch attempt by someone with whom he had "patiently cohabited for ten years to provide our narcissistic companions in shipwreck with their pittance, minus Jaspers' understanding and (Mounier's) personalism, painstakingly trying to spare all of us from being smeared black by the liberal communion of souls."[9] Casting these ties aside and relegating Jaspers and Mounier to the scrapheap, Lacan began his cleansing operation.

The first step was to dispel the illusions created by linguistics or any other branch of science that pretends to provide the means "to speak the truth about what is true." Lacan disposed of this claim in one of those negative pronouncements he knew so well how to make: "There is no metalanguage." There is no superlanguage for separating the true from the false in ordinary language (at the time semanticists were making efforts to establish systems for deciphering languages on a scientific basis, the results of which were to say the least disappointing). No metalanguage meant no "gimmick" for discovering the keys to the truth, "since the basis of the truth is what is spoken, and it cannot be any other way." Freud had also "allowed" the truth to speak. Lacan chose to have the truth speak through him: "I am the truth who is speaking." He preferred mythological bombast to illusory formulas.

The second step: to deal with magic, which, like psychoanalysis, has the capacity to heal by means of language. The use of transference and the power of words are the same. But in magic knowledge is concealed from the subject of the operation. "Magic is the truth as cause under the aspect of efficient cause." Only the effects are visible, not the truth of the cause. Lévi-Strauss comes to similar conclusions at the end of the second volume of his *Mythologiques:* "savage thought"—which functions in magic— works according to the same logic as science, but this logic is still caught up in a net of myth and image. In order for science to exist myth must reflect on itself. This is what happened when the Greeks began reflecting on their myths after maritime trade "opened" their minds, so to speak. In magic the shaman and his patient are both situated in the same natural whole, of which both the operator, the shaman, and the operee, or patient, offer a global interpretation.

Step three: religion. Here the subject ceases to play much of a role, since all causes emanate from God. "The religious person leaves God in charge of causality, thereby cutting himself off from access to the truth. This leads him to ascribe to God the cause of his desire, which is strictly speaking the object of sacrifice."[10] The "cause" is understood to be divine. And truth is held to be suspect: Giordano Bruno was burned at the stake. In conclusion Lacan said this: "Ecumenicism in our view has a chance only if it is based on an appeal to the poor in spirit."[11]

On that day Lacan was settling some old scores and no longer felt the need to spare anyone's feelings, except those of his new audience of young students, no longer sensitive to enlightened Christianity but enthusiastic about Marx. The encounter was spectacular. It changed the nature of Lacan's theory.

For if psychoanalysis is neither religious nor magical nor semantic, what has it become? The science of the material cause, that is, of the signifier. The theory of the objet-petit-a, the famous fallen object. But above all a science capable of communicating its knowledge, something that magic cannot do and religion refuses to do. Whence the need for "the logical form given to this knowledge." Gleefully, Lacan embarked once again upon this path, which he had already carefully explored. Ages ago, in any case at least a decade earlier, he had played with geometrical models of every kind, one after another in endless succession. The earliest were zig-zag models that looked like large Z's. Then there were odd-looking bottles with no inside or outside, what mathematicians call Klein bottles. There was a jar of mustard, half empty, half full, that lasted a whole year during which Lacan gave a seminar on anxiety. There was the famous Möbius strip, which was featured on the cover of Lacan's review, *Scilicet,* in which all articles were anonymous except those signed by Lacan ("We've got to sell them somehow," the publisher said). There was a bottle-opener. And finally, until the end of the Ecole freudienne, there was the period of the Borromean knots. These were sometimes represented by drawings on the blackboard— "graphs"—or constructed out of cut strips of paper or else piously pieced together out of bits of string by enraptured Lacanians. Two periods stand out in the "era of models." The first or Primary Era was one in which the Master was satisfied with two-dimensional representations: lines, arrows, points, symbols. The Secondary Era began when he realized that two dimensions were not enough to make his audience understand the theory of the unconscious as he conceived of it: specifically, he wanted to show that the unconscious is a structure with neither an outside nor an inside.

To tell the truth Freud had preceded Lacan down this path. Freud's "scientific project" and his predilection, throughout his life, for discussions involving systems of circulating energy, psychic barriers, and whatnot represented a similar kind of research. But Freud harbored no illusions as to the nature of these heuristic instruments, which he never claimed to be "science," any more than he claimed that the myths that he constructed in *Totem and Taboo* or *Moses and Monotheism* were science. Freud's little blueprints and beautiful stories functioned like the myths in Plato's Dialogues: they were another "manner of speaking," another manner of demonstrating, a kind of laboratory for thought. Lacan on the other hand was always ambiguous about the use of his "devices." Were they scientific? Or merely educational? It was tempting to believe that they were science, and many succumbed to the illusion. This turn marked the real end of Lacan's discoveries. His fascinated audience watched him gloss old ideas ad infinitum with the help of his mathematical objects. But he never again regained the inspiration that had led him to reinterpret Freud or discuss cases from the clinic—no more hysterical butcher's wives. The "Hobson's choice" of the clinic was gone, and with it a certain form of life, a certain relationship to the world. What remained was a man playing with his mathematical toys.

He modernized Freud's scientific project and discovered the joys of topology, of those mathematical spaces of which Euclidean space is only a special case. His manner of approach was quite simple. He began with Freud's last paper, in which the word *Spaltung* appears. Lacan translated this into French as *"scission"*— the splitting or division of the subject [the author raises an eyebrow at Lacan's translation, because *scission* in French also means "schism" or "secession" and strongly connotes a split in a group or sect—trans.]. The result is a "gap" (*béance*) or hole. But this gap is not located "inside the subject." Interpreting it this way would merely reintroduce the old idea of a separation of mind and body, which Freud tried to avoid by various means (inventing such structures as the id, the ego, and the superego, or again, the preconscious, conscious, and unconscious). Lacan's mathematical objects gave him the means to represent forms without insides or outsides, forms without boundaries or simple separations, forms of which a hole is a constitutive part. Take the Möbius strip, for example: if you start at any point and trace along the axis of the strip with a pencil, you will come back to the starting point and the pencil line will cover the entire surface, for the surface has only one "side." Alice in Wonderland would have been overjoyed—not surprisingly, since Alice was the creation of Lewis Carroll, a mathematician. A graphic artist like

Escher can make the phenomenon in question perfectly visible by drawing processions of ants marching along the closed strip in a labyrinthine world from which there is no escape into "another" world, no breaking of the mirror to cross the boundary into a distinct "other" place. Lacan invented none of this limpid mathematical logic. Its use merely complicated the exposition of his ideas.

It also complicated his own past. He had discovered the significance of the mirror in the life of each individual. Now, the mirror creates an illusory space. Lacan discovered when the child first recognized himself in the mirror and what the function of that recognition was. But he did not discover the structure of the illusion, nor did he discover what was hidden behind it.

> Consciousness distorts perception. What is the reason for this peculiar distortion? The mirror is defined only as this surface that divides, and thereby doubles, the three-dimensional space that we regard as real. The image would not have this value of *méconnaissance* if a false bilateral symmetry were not already in evidence: two eyes, two ears, etc. But inside the body everything is a little bit twisted. And how can we explain that the divided subject can be embedded in a world whose topology is spherical? [12]

This was the question that led Lacan down some crazy byways, full of topological games and a frenzy of words that began to talk on their own. Lacan became schizophasic, like his patients of the thirties: he was a passionate player.

The Player

Lacan had always had a passion for games. The first essay in (the French edition of) *Ecrits,* the only one not in its proper chronological place, is the account of his 1956 seminar on "The Purloined Letter," a sort of cops-and-robbers game in which a clever detective locates a missing letter by deduction. Just after the war he wrote a rather curious paper entitled "Le Temps logique et l'assertion de certitude anticipée" (Logical Time and the Premature Assertion of Certainty), in which he reflects on a riddle, a sort of party game.[13] The mirror stage itself looks a great deal like the child's very first game. Even psychoanalysis is a little like a game—the rather serious and stodgy game of bridge. The analyst plays the part of the "dummy," sitting out the hand, not intervening. But anyone who thinks that the "dummy" has nothing to say about the game has never played bridge.

Freud once discussed a game that his grandson played with a spool. The child kept throwing the object under the bed and making the sounds "ooh" and "ah," from which Freud deduced that he was trying to pronounce the words *fort* and *da,* over there and over here, and that the spool stood for the body of his absent mother, with which the child was playing by causing his mother to "come back" from under the bed. This story is a classic of psychoanalysis, something like the sacrifice of Abraham in the Old Testament. Since that time games have become one of the most useful techniques in the psychoanalysis of children. Pieces of wood, modeling clay, drawings, electric trains, and teddy bears are all indispensable to the practicing child analyst. With these items the analyst establishes an area in which the child is free to nip, break, twist, squeeze, separate, and bring together to his heart's content insignificant objects that stand for every person in the entire world. From another angle Lévi-Strauss has observed that the games that children all over the world play with strings express deep relationships between astronomy, kinship rules, cooking, and musical instruments. In short, nobody ever plays "for fun," "just for laughs." Lacan never played gratuitously.

In Lacan's game the stakes were not cash but a combination of prestige and knowledge. His ambition was a little bit like "encyclopedic" desire: he wanted to embrace everything in the culture of his time. And everyone: poets, novelists, logicians, historians, anthropologists, linguists (Roman Jakobson was one of his closest friends), filmmakers, painters . . . "Desire," he once said, "domesticated by educators, put to sleep by moralists, betrayed by the Academies, has taken refuge in the passion to know."[14] He made himself into his own personal Academy, in every sense of the word—a garden where classes are held, a school for a privileged social class, a part of a university, a kind of nakedness. He was a bit like the Académie française as it was originally defined: for Richelieu established the Académie "to observe and watch over the language and its correct usage." And there is, it seems, one further meaning of the word academy: a gambling hall.

A gentleman by the name of Winnicott with a background very different from Lacan's also discovered that the object of desire was a very interesting thing. Winnicott has proposed a very sensible theory of games. "In order to control what goes on outside, one must do things and not simply think or desire, and doing things takes time. To play is to do."[15] He also says this: "Play is natural, and psychoanalysis is a very sophisticated twentieth-century phenomenon. It is useful to remind the analyst constantly not only what he owes to Freud but also what all of us owe to that natural and universal thing, the game."[16] What if Lacan started playing with words, arrows, graphs, bottles, and knots simply in order to "do" something, having understood, correctly, that psychoanalytic thought is a self-obviating activity? What if, immersed in his own theory and determined to pass it on to others, unable to stop teaching without vindicating the inquisitors who had excommunicated him, he found repose in a "natural and universal" activity, a child's game? In my mind's eye I see him weaving strands of wool between his fingers and tying, without trying to understand, knots without theoretical significance. Repose—Lacan's paradise, with no mirror within reach, no ear to hear him, and no couch beneath his gaze.

The game creates a domain of omnipotence, the first domain over which the child exerts control. Winnicott again: "The precariousness of magic itself is in question, of magic born of an intimate relationship of whose reliability the child wishes to assure itself."[17] To denote those objects over which the child exercises omnipotence Winnicott coined the term "transitional object," which Lacan occasionally (very occasionally!) borrows. The transitional object in a baby's life is something that can be attacked, deformed, transformed, "enthusiastically loved and mutilated" and yet is always "affectionately fondled." Disfigured as it may become, it never changes. The child's favorite teddy bear remains his favorite teddy bear even if it loses its eyes, ears, paws, and insides. An adult would look at such an object as something that comes from "outside," like any other manufactured object. But the child sees it differently: it does not come from outside or from inside; it is a "transitional" object between the idea of an outside world and the idea of a barely hatched subject. The mirror phase is instantaneous and radical. By contrast, the transitional period and the reign of transitional objects lasts a long time, long enough for good relations to be established between the child and the world. The child never forgets the transitional object; he never loses it. It is an exceptional object in that it is one object for which the adult that the child becomes will never have to mourn, an object that is never lost.

Now, Lacan's mathematical accessories, by the duration of their usage and by the manifest pleasure Lacan took in showing them off and manipulating them, resemble transitional objects, and the theoretical space in which he used them resembles a transitional domain. Winnicott's observations, like those of Lacan in the thirties, touched on the problem of separation of mother and child. For Winnicott all cultural experience begins with the transitional object and the game in which it is used. If this first experience is a good one, the subject will have his own "sacred" space, a place for "creativity" (quite obviously Winnicott and Lacan do not speak the same language). But if the first experience is a bad one, "the exploitation of the 'transitional' area leads to a pathological condition in which the individual is literally overwhelmed by persecutional elements that he cannot get rid of."[18]

So, to continue my speculation: perhaps Lacan's indulgence of mathematical objects performed the vital function of preserving him from harm in a psychological climate that was in fact "persecutional." But Lacan had been interested in persecution from his earliest days in psychiatry. So? So these little games protected him, filled his days, occupied him, enabled him to "do" something. When the analyst is immersed in his patients' anxieties; when his thoughts disintegrate because they remain without effect; when he is obliged to hold his tongue and not intervene; and when he himself has been the object of hatred, expelled by his colleagues; play becomes a useful activity. Lacan set several generations of adults to playing. But the members of his audience thought they were learning something, when for Lacan himself the point was to establish himself as the ringmaster of a unique subculture. He had no need to mourn the loss of his graphs or knots, which he interpreted after his own fashion. Doubtless his mourning was reserved for other things.

The Four Corners

"Puss-in-the corner" was the first game.[19] Lacan drew the letter "Z" on the blackboard (Z as in Zorro or Zarathustra). Then, in each of the four corners of the Z, he put letters: a capital O, a small o, another small o with a prime, o′, and an S, and an $, with a slash through it. Now obviously $ is the subject, O is the Other (in French A for *Autre*), as always, the Unconscious. The small o is the object of desire. And o′ is the reflection of the whole picture in the subject's tiny imaginary world. Lacan put it all much better: "(The subject is linked by dashes to) the four corners of the model, i.e., S, his ineffable and stupid existence, o, his objects, o′, his ego, i.e., that which is reflected from his form into his objects, and O, the locus from which the question of his existence can be raised."[20] The terminology is not particularly complex. Lacan then reformulates the fundamental question, making the point even clearer. " 'What am I there?' refers to the subject's sex and to the contingency of his being: that is, first of all, he is a man or a woman, and second, he might not exist at all. Each question adds to the mystery of the other and the whole enigma is wrapped in symbols of procreation and death."[21] This helps, but we still haven't come to the real point.

For the thing to notice is that the game isn't over yet. Consider the same "Z" but now with different letters in the corners. The S remains where it was. But the O is replaced by an F, which stands for the Father. The little o is replaced by an M, which stands for the Mother. And o′ is replaced by I, which stands for Ego Ideal, Freudian terminology for the way in which the ego establishes a dream existence for itself. I also stands for *Infans,* one who cannot yet talk. And, lo and behold, there we have the good old family right before our eyes. The child, the mother, and the father: the triangle. But in Freud's work the family invariably consists of just these three terms, whereas in Lacan's model there is a fourth term, the subject. Furthermore, it is the subject that "conceives" the triangle from the time of the mirror stage onward. The subject is not a part of the game, any more than the analyst will be later on: "The fourth term is given by the subject in its reality, foreclosed, as it were, within the system and playing only a 'dummy's' role while the signifiers play out their hand, yet becoming the subject for real as the play proceeds and brings out its significance."[22] There we have our little fellow, then, standing on his own two feet, wearing his identity as a suit of armor, with a Z for backbone, equipped with an illusory but necessary imagination, and presiding over a card game in which the players are always the same: his father, his mother, and his self-image. An inevitable fantasy-circus—here the previous question comes into play: What sex am I? Man or woman, papa, mama, or myself? Where am I? (Shall I play in papa's place? etc.) There is only limited room for maneuver. But the game still has to be played, in other words, life still has to be lived: the signifier must be allowed to play its role.

We haven't yet finished substituting letters, though. Shuffle the

deck and deal out the cards a third time. The subject S, still with
a slash through it, does not change. In the place where O and F
were, however, I now put the letter S (but not the same S as the
subject, just to complicate matters a bit). In the place of o or M,
I now put R. And in the place of o' or I, I once again put the
letter I. S stands for Symbolic; R for Real; I for Imaginary. This
triad was dear to the Lacanians of a certain generation (around
1960 or so). You come across the letters RSI in all their haunts.
This doesn't mean that the triad in question is without interest.
Each of its elements harks back to Freud: the Symbolic to the
superego, the Real to the id, and the Imaginary to the ego; together, they figure in every individual's life game.

Let us begin with the Real, because it is always defined as "the
impossible." As Lacan conceives of it, it certainly is one of the
most refractory points of resistance. Obviously, if the Real has
something to do with Freud's notion of the id, the Real, like the
id, will probably be wild, crazy, and hard to control. But what
does Lacan mean by linking two notions as incompatible in their
traditional meanings as the real and the impossible? To begin
with, Lacan's notion of "the Real" has little to do with "realism"
or with any assumptions about the nature of the world. For Lacan the Real is a concept that cannot exist without the barrier of
the Symbolic, which predates the birth of the subject. This barrier forms the basis of the subject's perception of the world. This
perception is preserved; for the Real, when it really does rear its
head, is terrifying. This can happen, for example, when the subject, in the grip of madness, hallucinates the Real where it does
not exist and thinks that it is "seeing," or again, when the insane
subject turns the world upside and proceeds, say, to commit a
murderous act (or merely "acts out" in analysis for the benefit of
the psychoanalyst). These examples make clear in what ways the
real is impossible: it is impossible to see, to speak, or to hear,
since in any case it is "always-already-there." Adding additional
details, Lacan tells us that the real "causes by itself"; it "does not
wait, and in particular does not wait for the subject, since it ex-

pects nothing from speech."[23] It is "a punctuation without a text," pure act, raw behavior, sudden and unfettered. "It is there, identical with its existence, noise from which one can hear everything, and ready to demolish what the 'reality principle' constructs under the name external world."[24] This is the opposite of what one might expect to be called the real construed in the usual sense as an attribute of the world as perceived by man. When this reality appears, it is in the terror of psychosis and the disturbance of madness. The Lancanian concept of the Real, then, partakes of both the Id's disconcerting and unpredictable powers—always ahead of its time—and the terrifying archaic images associated with the Mother.

Next, the Imaginary: we have already witnessed its dawn in the mirror stage. There is nothing terrifying about the Imaginary. What would we do without its accoutrements, which the subject wears like a perpetual disguise? The Imaginary is a kind of garment, the first layer of which is armor, a protective covering that puts the subject beyond harm. When the Imaginary recedes, hallucination, or the passion of the subject, and "acting out," or the action of the subject, come to the fore. To reach this point some part of the structure in the mirror must be severely distorted, as for example when Christine is separated from Léa, and her one imaginary bearing, her security, her double, disappears. The Imaginary performs a function first adumbrated in Lacan's papers on the mirror stage: the function of *"méconnaissance"* [misrecognition, best left untranslated]. This is to be distinguished from "knowledge" (*connaissance*) presumably obtainable independent of the structure of the subject: *méconnaissance* is an intrinsic part of the structure of the subject.[25] This is what the Ego is. Reason—I use the word deliberately—is something one must forge for oneself.

Particularly because the whole process is governed by the Symbolic, the determining entity. The Symbolic precedes the game: in contrast to the Real, which is "always-already-there," the Symbolic endures forever. Even before he is born the child

has a place in a family and may even bear the first name of one
of his ancestors and possess a wardrobe of hand-me-downs: "The
book on the new child will have been opened some time before
his grandparents were born." Thus the symbolic function is associated not only with the father but also with the Name-of-the-
Father, an expression Lacan always carefully wrote with dashes
to signify that this was a concept of his own devising, a concept
on which he based his authority.

The Bankruptcy of the Fathers and
Its Consequences

Lacan worked out the theory of the Name-of-the-Father in re-
considering the case of Judge Schreber, over which more psychoanalytic ink has been spilled than over any other case, except
perhaps the Wolf Man. In so doing Lacan really went "back to
Freud," particularly since so many analysts writing since Freud's
day have highlighted the role of the mother in triggering psy-
choses rather than that of the father. Judge Schreber was a distinguished magistrate from a distinguished Prussian family. His father, Daniel Gottlob Moritz Schreber, had founded an institute
of "therapeutic gymnastics" at Leipzig and achieved some reputation as an educator, though not a particularly liberal one: he
believed in the virtues of physical training, organized frustration,
and the use of various kinds of corrective apparatus. Schreber's
psychosis therefore did not result from a real absence of the father. Rather, it had to do with the "bankruptcy" resulting from
a distortion in what Lacan calls the "paternal metaphor." To use
a metaphor is to substitute "one word for another." [26] The paternal metaphor establishes the correlation between the family
name—necessarily the father's name—and the subject coming into
the world. If the father, present or not, fails to occupy the symbolic position assigned to him by our culture, disaster ensues.

Judge Schreber met disaster in the form of insanity. The judgment that freed him from prison summarized his case as follows: "He believed that he had a mission to redeem the world and restore it to its lost state of bliss. This, however, he could only bring about if he were first transformed from a man into a woman."[27] This man, well brought up, the beneficiary, by his own (somewhat suspect) account, of an irreproachable moral education, and extremely reserved in all things, "particularly sexual matters," suddenly transformed himself into a woman, discovering erogenous zones and "nerves of desire," dressing before a mirror in women's clothing, and finding himself a bust convincing enough to fool any man. He was obsessed, moreover, by the fear of God, whom he expected to impregnate him as though he were an immaculate Virgin. A social disaster but a substantial insanity and a good defense. What had happened?

Unable to find himself in his father, the psychotic had turned instead to his mother. But the "place" of the father, the source of his own name, his family identity, and therefore his insertion into the world of human relations, remained empty. It did not disappear: it simply remained vacant. Lacan designated this mechanism "foreclosure." Foreclosure is a legal term implying the forefeiture (*déchéance*) of a right not exercised within the prescribed limits [and in French *déchéance* also refers to the "loss of paternal authority"—trans.]. The Father is there in flesh and blood. But paternal authority can nevertheless be lost in various ways, so that the Father forfeits his symbolic right, to the great detriment of the child. Lacan observes:

> The damaging effects of the paternal figure are especially common in cases where the father really has or exercises legislative powers, whether he is actually a lawmaker or simply one who sets himself up as a pillar of faith, a paragon of integrity or devotion, a virtuous individual or a virtuoso, by using a work of salvation, by means of any object or lack of object, nation or natality, safeguard or salubrity, legacy or legality, purity, impurity, or empire, all ideals providing all too many chances to be found wanting, inadequate, or fraudulent, opportunities for excluding, in a word, the Name-of-the-Father from its place in the signifier.[28]

The bankrupt father takes other people down with him. If one wants to be a reformer, a saint, a political leader, or the conscience of a nation, it is better to be a bachelor. Lacan never missed an opportunity to attack the foundations of bourgeois morality, of which in other respects he discreetly made himself the exemplar, keeping his "private" life private, free of the consequences of his public notoriety.

Bankruptcy of the paternal metaphor also lies behind a celebrated case of parricide: in 1835, Pierre Rivière, in the grip of a madness not unrelated to that of Judge Schreber, killed his mother, his sister, and his brother.[29] There would at first sight seem to be little in common between the case of Pierre Rivière, a poor, young Norman peasant, and the sophisticated madness and bourgeois incarceration of a renowned magistrate. The nature of the scandal was different, but in both cases there was a "scandal," a social shock. Pierre Rivière was at first sentenced to death. Bloody crimes had been committed at about the same time by the great regicides Lacenaire and Fieschi, and the monarchy, uneasy with the memory of Louis XVI's execution, thought it a good idea to let heads roll. Wanting to kill the king was of a piece with wanting to kill the mother. Pierre Rivière wanted to be executed; he was disappointed, because psychiatrists intervened and declared him insane. Rivière killed himself in prison.

Everything about his family history was of a nature to foster insanity. His parents' marriage was one of convenience. There was no love, only an arrangement made necessary by Napoleon's conscription, which in 1813 was emptying the countryside of men. Pierre's father married one Victoire Brion. There were complications: the couple became caught up in dark questions of dowry, land, and business. Ordinarily they did not sleep together, and when they did Victoire took the pillow and the blanket. She hated this husband who did not love her and compelled him to work for her as a sharecropper. They separated and fought over custody of the children. The usual horrors of divorce were magnified by peasant bitterness in a time of famine. Little Pierre

knew details of the family imbroglio, an indication that the Ri-
vières were the object of considerable comment. What is more,
he describes an episode that took place shortly after his birth,
probably told to him by his beloved grandmother. "Early in 1815
my mother gave birth to me, and she was very sick afterwards.
My father took care of her as required. . . . He said that when
he went to bed afterward, he could not sleep because he was so
used to watching over my mother in her sickness. Her breasts
went rotten, and my father sucked them to draw out the poison,
which he then vomited on the ground."[30] An incredible scene.
A mammary abcess became a Greek tragedy and the mother a
venomous serpent, or perhaps she herself had been bitten by the
little serpent to which she had just given birth. In any case the
scene became established in Pierre's mind once and for all: the
mother is poisonous, rotten, and the father is a saint. When he
sings in church, fifty people around him weep.

The mother gains the upper hand. The father is sent packing,
driven off the land, banished. Pierre begins to fantasize. Once,
women rebelled against tyrants: Judith, Charlotte Corday. Now
it is the opposite. A man—none other than himself—must rise
up against the tyranny of the woman. His model is La Rocheja-
quelein, the Chouan hero [the Chouans opposed the French Revolution—trans.], so young, blonde, and pink that he bore a feminine sobriquet. Incest horrifies Pierre. No woman shall touch
him. One day he puts on his Sunday clothes in order to bestow
the proper solemnity upon his act; then he reached for his weapon.
He killed his mother and sister and, so that his father can really
hate the murderer, his brother too.

Pierre thus decisively defeated Victoire for the first and last
time in her life. The process culminated with the " 'unleashing'
of the signifier in the real, thereby triggering the bankruptcy of
the Name-of-the-Father, i.e., of the signifier which, in the
Other, in its guise as locus of the signifier, is the signifier of the
Other in its guise as locus of the law."[31] The universe was turned
upside down: the mother was the signifier of the law, but Pierre

bore the name of his father. The contradiction was intolerable. With no paternal law and no effacement of desire for the mother, the signifiers could not link up and normal language was impossible. Language did exist, but it was "insane." The Symbolic referred all at once to the Superego, the Other, and the Father: all three were one.

Footnote one: it was in discussing the theme of the Father that Lacan began, in 1960, speaking of himself in the third person. A minor detail, but consider the context. The question was, "What is a father?" Every father, said Lacan, is "the dead Father, so said Freud, but no one listens to him, and therefore Lacan (remember, it is Lacan who is speaking) is renaming part of that concept the Name-of-the-Father, regrettable though it may be that a not very scientific situation leaves him deprived of his normal audience." [32] This calls for several obvious remarks: (a) it was the common and glorious destiny of both Freud and Lacan not to be heard; (b) Lacan, threatened with expulsion from the psychoanalytic movement, is nothing less than Freud's heir. Ill-tempered though it is, this declaration of filiation had to be made under the auspices of the paternal metaphor.

Footnote two: Lacan takes great pains to distinguish Schreber's insane relationship to God from "the Presence and the Joy that illuminate the mystical experience." [33] Schreber does not address God with the familiar "Du." A true mystic addresses the Other in person in the "Union of being to being." From the impasse he himself describes, Lacan holds out one hope of exit, doubtless the only one: mysticism, the only legitimate means of transgressing boundaries.

What is the upshot of this first Lacanian game? A triangle and a dummy, a fourth, silent player. A brilliant obligato to the theme of Oedipus, and along with this a formalized, reformulated interpretation of Freud. Lacan's teaching was sublime. He had the knack of renewing stale old texts, of bringing them back to life. In this area he never ceased to dazzle his listeners.

Figure 1

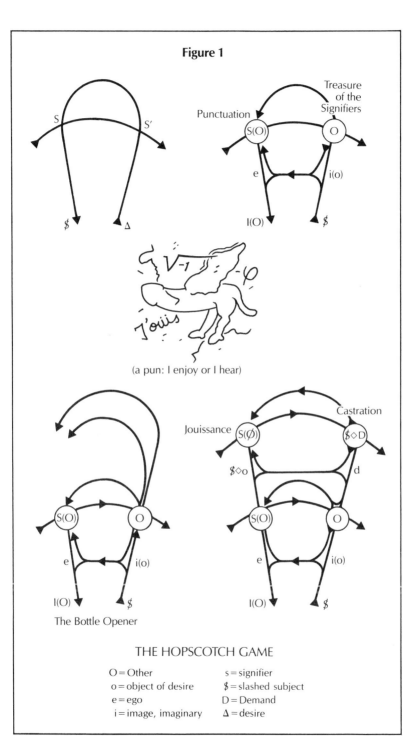

(a pun: I enjoy or I hear)

The Bottle Opener

THE HOPSCOTCH GAME

O = Other	s = signifier
o = object of desire	$ = slashed subject
e = ego	D = Demand
i = image, imaginary	Δ = desire

The Game of Hopscotch, or the Bottle-Opener

In the text of Lacan's "Subversion du sujet et dialectique du désir" ("Subversion of the Subject and Dialectic of Desire") we find many examples of yet another graph, to which Lacan refers in passing as "the bottle-opener." I see it also as a hopscotch board: when French children draw a hopscotch board on the sidewalk, the top box, which one must jump into on one leg, is always called "heaven" [rather than "home" as in the United States: one of those curious and perhaps revealing differences between cultures—trans.]. So let's hop: first one box and then another.

Beginning is simple enough. Take a piece of wire and bend it into a hook. Lay another piece of wire across it horizontally and you have stage one of the bottle-opener, the "elementary cell" of language and of the talking subject. In the accompanying figure the hook is oriented from right to left. It goes from desire (Δ) to the subject, duly slashed to certify that it has nothing to do with the game. The horizontal line is oriented from left to right: it runs from S, the signifier, to S', any other signifier: an unbroken chain. (Be sure not to confuse $, the subject, with S, the signifier.) Where the hook and the line cross, a circuit is formed in the upper portion of the diagram. The top of the hook and a segment of the horizontal line enclose a region of space. This is just what happens as a sentence progresses: it gropes blindly from word to word in an unbroken chain emitted by the talking or writing subject, and where it will stop, nobody knows. The punctuation—period or question mark—terminates the sentence. Its retroactive meaning becomes apparent only after it is punctuated, which only happens because the subject, like the psychoanalyst at the end of a session, decides to call a halt at this particular place. Stop here for the time being. A sentence is therefore a combination of subjectivity and language.

Now we are standing with one foot in the second box and the other in the air. Lacan marks the points of intersection with two letters—don't panic, we've seen them before. On the right is capital O, which stands for the Other. On the left, where the process of signification culminates "as a finished product," we find the expression S(O), which stands for the punctuation.

The first intersection, the one marked O, is a locus: the "locus of the Other," to which Lacan refers indifferently as the "hiding place" or the "treasury of signifiers."[34] These appellations are already more interesting than the previous formal designations. The point, first made by anthropologists like Marcel Mauss and Lévi-Strauss, is that there exists a—purely fictive—reservoir in which all the signifers of a language slumber in anticipation.[35] This is the common cauldron of the language, the repository of all its potential resources: the place to which the poet will go in search of new and hitherto unknown words, the place to which Lacan will go in search of neologisms. A place full of treasure, a real buried treasure: a hiding place in which worn-out treasures bury themselves in preparation for later reuse or for use in another place. Now we can see what Lacan was up to when he reused the old legal term "foreclosure" outside its legal context, or again, when he transposed the term "signifier" outside its linguistic setting. The procedure is that of all poets. If the Other has a locus, however, it is the place represented by the analyst in his armchair, not the "common place" of everyday communication, which does not readily accommodate the improvisational use of obsolete signifiers. Just try using a neologism without warning in conversation. At best people will laugh and treat it as a witty remark. At worst they will laugh at you, the first step of the exclusion from society that reduces the patient to insanity. The analyst at least offers a neutral place in which the most heteroclite signifiers can come to the surface—heteroclite, or, better still, heterodox signifers, at variance with the "doxa," or common opinion. It is this role that makes the analyst seem to be an otherworldly sage or nut and makes his approach seem so harsh: it is his job "not to be like other people."

The second point of intersection—second as the sentence unfolds in time—is the function S(O). This is not a place but a moment in time. If the Other is a "hiding place," S(O), the punctuation, is a "poking about for the exit": a way out must be found, this must stop now. The circuit is simple: I exist, I speak, fishing in language for my words, and I stop my words so that they will make sense. I therefore exist only after the fact, in the future anterior, after I shall have spoken. "An effect of retroversion whereby the subject at each stage becomes what he was as it were before and announces himself—he will have been—only in the future anterior."[36] The same process occurs in the mirror stage: there is no "ego" without a reflection in the glass. Hence we must add two more symbols to the hook and the line: i(o) for the image and e for the ego. Trifles. Time to get on with the game of hopscotch.

We now come to phase two of the bottle-opener: it is beginning to look more and mor like a hopscotch board. This is where Lacan's poetic inventiveness pretends to deck itself out in the plumage of a scientific peacock, not very convincingly. It's mere dust thrown in the eyes. Because he has already discussed the "question" of the Other, he now draws two arrow-tipped curves emanating from one point on the diagram, forming a sort of question mark. A pretty way of indicating the "question" of the Other. In this there is nothing very scientific, but since it involves a graph it looks serious. Still, Lacan is more inspired here, playing games with science, than he was to become later on, when he began using well-established objects from topology. By that time he could do no more than comment repetitiously on objects not of his own devising. Be that as it may, the two curves mentioned above are quickly closed up: their function was merely rhetorical.

Once closed, they duplicate the lower section of the drawing and thus complete the graph. But the symbols that are now placed, by similarity, beside the intersections forming the "heaven" of the hopscotch board call for further comment. Consider first the middle level of the upper section of the diagram, the line d—$◊o. The "d" is desire. It sets out in the direction of fantasy—for example, the smoked salmon that is needed for dinner and isn't there. For the peculiar symbol $◊o is Lacan's way of representing fantasy. All the terms of this expression are familiar to us: $, the slashed subject, o, the object of desire, tiny, lost, outcast, fallen from the body. This leaves the diamond, ◊, which Lacan calls the "chisel," like the chisel used in France to mark silver items and guarantee their authenticity. Fantasy requires a "chisel" because everyone has his own authentic fantasies, belonging to himself and no one else. There are as many fantasies as there are subjects. Kindly refrain from confusing your fantasies with the next person's: do not mix caviar with smoked salmon. To say nothing of the divine coupling of Schreber with the fantasy of Charlotte Corday, which belongs to Pierre Rivière.

The chisel, the individual's trademark, is not a symbol chosen at random. It is a combination of the mathematical symbols for "greater than" (>) and "less than" (<), an absurd combination, well chosen to signify the essence of fantasy, namely, its impossibility. Fantasy, then, is for each individual a private stage on which the subject's relationship to the object of its desire is played out, and this relationship is impossible in the real. Fantasy is a "paper brain" and it sometimes collapses: the image aptly conveys the fragile protection of the imagination, which gives way under pressure that is too great for it to bear. Fantasy then erupts into reality, and the result may be a murderous act, ravin, hallucination, madness. Though imaginary, fantasy is a structure absolutely necessary to the subject.

Finally, we come to the ultimate hopscotch board. On the right is the symbol of castration: $◊D. Again $, again the chisel, but this time a capital D which signifies Demand, now in its full amplitude, almost allegorical. This strange expression cannot be understand without first glancing at the lower level of the diagram: O, the locus of the Other, to which Lacan now attaches a new attribute, the instinct or drive (*pulsion*). Castration is therefore subsumed under the concept of place. It is situated, if I may put it this way, on the "desire" side of the graph, the right side, where we also find the locus of the Other, desire, and demand. Of course one can only address one's desires and demands to the Other. But the relationship is an impossible one: hence the chisel. There is no such thing as sexual intercourse. Castration signifies that the Demand is not granted. This we already knew, but now it has been put into a formula.

This leaves the "algorithm of ecstasy" on the left: $S(\emptyset)$, signifying a lack in the Other. (To love is to give what one does not have . . .) Ecstasy is on the signifier side. (For if the graph has a "right" side, all of whose symbols come under the head of drives, there is also a "left" side, where all the symbols are signifiers.) The signifier of ecstasy exists: it is nothing other than the phallus—not the penis but rather that which its erect form symbolizes, "the erectile organ (which) symbolizes the place of ecstasy, not in itself or in the form of an image but as a missing part of the desired image."[37] Since it is the signifier of a lack, the phallus is analogous in form to the square root of −1, the primordial imaginary number and generator of the whole field of complex numbers. It is in a sense the obverse of the *cogito*, a "phallic cogito" that is literally indescribable, since the subject, which can if need be prove that the Other exists, cannot prove its own existence and hence can know nothing of the phallus. Without this generic signifier of negativity, however, no other signifier would exist. It is from this that the phallus derives its generative power. It is not enough to call this power "phallocratic," since the "phallus," the triumphant opposite of the flaccid little penis, is the cultural foundation of language. And of the Virgin-Mother: the mother has no penis, she is endowed with a lack, and hence for the male populace she symbolizes the phallus. Women continue to cordon her off.

Enough of this cleverness and complexity. The digression was necessary to show just how far Lacan pushed his passion for teaching, his desire to formalize in order to transmit, to establish a doctrine so solid as to be beyond challenge. Like Freud, Lacan wished to make himself guardian of the tablets of the law. He wanted to be a prescriber of ideas and thus fulfill one of the most traditional, and perhaps one of the most contested, requirements of teaching. But the point is that all of this was merely teaching. In the days when Lacan was still making discoveries, he did not draw graphs. The vogue for structuralism—and the example of his friend Lévi-Strauss—may have convinced Lacan that without formalization there is no theory. It may be that all these mathematical devices and equations served merely to hide the shabby state of a theory that had come to the end of its rope.

Yet Lacan had no need of this formalistic game, amusing to play if one has a taste for such things but disappointing if one is looking for a systematic theory, not to be found here. In the next few pages we will learn far more from a still playful Lacan without the aid of a single graph. There is much more to sink our teeth into in the story of Socrates and Alcibiades than there is in the "bottle-opener," because Lacan is easier to take at "myth tempo" than at the fast pace of mathematics. Nobody can do everything.

Alcibiades loved Socrates, Plato tells us, but Socrates wanted nothing to do with this love. One night, they lay down side by side, and Alcibiades waited, certain that his seduction would work its effects on the shrewd old man beside him who, so Alcibiades believed, would be only too happy to be in the arms of the most handsome man in Athens. But nothing of the kind happened. Socrates remained quiet. Later, when the guests at a banquet tried their hand at defining love, Alcibiades took the opportunity to recall this episode and compared Socrates to *sileni,* figurines not beautiful to look at but enclosing golden figures within (*agalma* in Greek).

Contained in the objet-petit-a is the *agalma* or inestimable treasure that Alcibiades declares to be hidden beneath Socrates' rude exterior. But notice that this is assigned a minus sign. It is, if I may say so, because he has not seen Socrates' prick—for this we have the authority of Plato, who is not sparing of detail—that Alcibiades the seducer exalts his *agalma,* the marvel that he would have liked for Socrates to yield in an avowal of desire: the division of the subject that he bears within himself revealing itself quite splendidly on this occasion.[38]

This is not the end of the story. As the banquet wears on and dawn approaches, Alcibiades invents the fable of the *sileni.* But the object of his lust is no longer Socrates but Agathon.

Thus, by showing his object as castrated, Alcibiades paraded himself as desirous—Socrates saw this clearly—for the sake of another guest, Agathon, whom Socrates, forerunner of the psychoanalyst and sure of himself at this high-society affair, did not hesitate to name as the object of transference, thus giving an interpretation that highlights a fact of which many analysts are still ignorant: that analysis produces effects of love and/or hatred that manifest themselves outside the analytic situation.[39]

And we can also give another version of the same phenomenon, and in Lacan's favorite key, the key of love. If a woman wears a dildo, she is only more desirable. "Such is the woman behind her veil: it is the absence of a penis that makes her a phallus, an object of desire."[40] A woman is an object of desire if she wears a factitious penis, not her own; a man—Socrates—is an object of desire if one describes him as without a penis, though he has one of his own. Both perform the function of phallus.

"Nevertheless," Lacan concludes, "Alcibiades projected onto Socrates the ideal of the perfect Master, which he completely 'imaginarized' by the action of $(-\phi)$."[41] Here, $(-\phi)$ represents the absent phallus, which is transformed into a triumphant Phallus.

At the end of the banquet, when everyone else has fallen asleep, Socrates shakes the dust from his sandals and walks out alone into the light of day. And Lacan decided to dissolve his School.

From the Phallus to the Matheme

The bottle-opener, "universal key" and silly toy, was not part of a genuinely scientific approach to psychoanalysis. But Lacan insisted on pressing further and introducing what he called "mathemes," a course he was still, in his own word, "obstinately" pursuing when he decided to dissolve the Ecole freudienne. In the letter announcing this decision, he gave his real reasons for attempting to mathematize the subject.[42] The mathemes were the result of a strong critique of religion, and not only of the Christian religion (never mentioned by name) but of any institution producing "consolidated group effects" to the detriment of genuine discourse. "Everybody knows what price had to be paid when Freud allowed the psychoanalytic group to take precedence over psychoanalytic discourse and become a Church."

Psychoanalysis had thus become a corporate institution. At this point we might expect an allusion to the excommunication. Here it is: "The International, since that is its name, is reduced to a symptom of what Freud expected it to be. But its influence is small. It is the Church, the true Church, that sustains Marxism by giving it new blood . . . and renewed meaning. Why not psychoanalysis, if it turns toward meaning?" As I was saying, a critique of all religions: religion exists whenever a group of human beings fastens upon a meaning, be it divine or human, and takes for its ultimate aim a better world, be it Heaven or a society devoid of exploitation. The question of meaning remained crucial. As soon as Lacan became aware that his expulsion was imminent (i.e., that the group was determined to shun his influence), he launched an attack on the very idea of meaning: his was an anticlerical campaign. This was intimately related to the practice of "punctuation": "short" sessions of variable length gave "meaning" to the patient's discourse by stopping it at unpredictable moments. The struggle against the philosophical domination of the notion of "meaning" was thus for Lacan a way of defending both psychoanalysis and himself as a psychoanalyst. "It is not frivolous to say that the stability of religion is due to the fact that meaning is always religious," Lacan said when he dissolved his school.[43] Thus, in waging a campaign for his own rehabilitation, Lacan first took on the guise of an implacable foe of "eschatologies of meaning" and then became in turn a militant champion of the signifier, which abolishes meaning, a defender of Freud's scientism, and finally a champion of the "matheme."

As an idea the "matheme" makes sense. The word harks back to the Greek root of mathematics, the verb *manthanein,* to learn. Matheme first of all means study, knowledge. As Lacan conceives of it, it is also a logical anlysis of the fundamental division of the subject, the *Spaltung* discussed by Freud in his last paper. You might even say that the whole business of mathemes was intended to develop the following enigmatic statement of Lacan's: "Division of the subject? This point is a knot."[44]

Freud introduced the idea of a division of the subject in discussing the child's discovery that the mother lacks a penis. This lack reveals the "phallus"—"no penis" equals "phallus." From here it was but a short step to knot theory—the play on words was irresistible [to understand this, the English-speaking reader must know that le *noeud,* French for knot, is also slang for penis—trans.].[45] Lacan thus quickly plunged into topology, concerning himself particularly with objects such as Klein bottles and Möbius strips, which have neither an inside nor an outside.

He later went on to study so-called Borromean knots, "string rings" linked together in such a way that by cutting one, the rings all become free and fall apart. [The American reader may find the paradigmatic Borromean knot easiest to visualize as the familiar Ballantine beer symbol—the three linked rings that fall apart when the right one is cut.—trans.] The problem then is simply to figure out which ring has to be cut. Underneath this problem, so exciting to sailors, children, and faithful Lacanians, we hear an insistent melody, a melody that was not merely theoretical and was not concerned solely with the Phallus, woman, and truth, as Lacan would say, but also, as he put it, with "the function of the ONE."

"There is some One," he used to say. What was he looking for, at a time in his life when success was literally crushing him? A string ring which, when cut, sets all the others free, a liberating element. But the liberating element is there, Lacan adds, "only in order to represent solitude." [46]

This was not enough. He needed something else, something that would enable him to make clear the relations between the Other and the One, thus returning in a roundabout way to a very special subject, long left in abeyance. And thus returning in some sense to himself.

Himself, first, last, and always. What Lacan was pondering with the Borromean knots, first mentioned around 1972, became clear when he dissolved his school. "It is enough to take away one to set all the others free, a statement true of all Borromean knots, and as for that particular knot, my School, the one has to be me." [47]

Thus Lacan's theoretical research into the subject of the One, focused on the signifier and hence on the phallus, tended to transform Lacan himself into the person playing the role of liberator, terminating the institution and setting its members free. The dissolution of his school was strictly in keeping with the progress of his theory, which since 1964 had been intimately concerned with division and splitting. If one takes a broad view of Lacan's theoretical development, rather than the narrow view that results from pressing one's nose up too closely against all those graphs like a dog hunting for truffles, what one finds is a veritable theory of exclusion. His own exclusion—he began work on a theory of exclusion on the day that he himself was excluded. He managed to formalize his life, to transform it into a proof. "The subject," he once said, "is to its object in a relation of internal exclusion." [48] In part this is a general, abstract truth, as Freud's writings attest. But it is also a scarcely veiled reference to the story of Jacques Lacan, with its "passion to exist" and disappointed loves, Jacques Lacan who, in order to be the Other at last decided one day in January of 1980 to be the One, the ring that would set all the others free. He transformed himself into a living proof of his mathematical fantasies. He became the matheme, the signifier, the phallus, the lack: he excluded himself.

Since he was not in the least stupid, however, he knew this perfectly well, as he himself acknowledged a week later: "One can be content being the Other like everybody else, after a life spent wanting to be so in spite of the Law."[49]

In spite of the Law: he had come a long way. The phrase summed up the different stages of his destiny. When the *Memoirs* of Judge Schreber were translated into French for the first time in 1966, Lacan wrote the introduction and there began a retrospective assessment of his career.[50] He noted that the idea of "paranoid knowledge" put forth in his thesis was the forerunner of his theory of foreclosure. (He also noted that there had been a ten-year lag at each stage in his career: his thesis was not read until ten years after it was written, and his commitment to psychoanalytic teaching caused a public stir only ten years after it began.) To conclude the anamnesis he touched on the unavoidable question of mathematics, the only way, according to Lacan, of analyzing residues, divisions, and doubtless delayed acceptance as well. From thesis to dissolution Lacan had followed one unwavering path.

Lacan's thought can be taken one step further: in spite of the Law, Aimée, Christine, and Léa killed or attempted to kill. In spite of the Law, Lacan stood up against the attacks of the psychoanalytic community. In spite of the Law, he founded a School. In spite of the Law, he said time and time again that ecstasy exists, because it stands up to the Law. In spite of the Law—the very Law that he himself promulgated in establishing the Ecole freudienne—he dissolved it. In spite of the Law, he took it upon himself to commit an act in violation of the statutes of association. In spite of the Law, he was Other, not like everybody else.

To be Other like everybody else—now there was something to dream of. Which reminds me of the marvelous dream he told at the beginning of one seminar session in 1973: "I dreamed last night that I came here and found the room empty."[51]

O, Manes of the hysterical butcher's wife, protect your child against unsatisfied desires . . .

But this is where I stopped, in the years when Lacan began discussing Borromean knots. Perhaps they caused some kind of block in me. I thought about this a great deal but never really came to feel that it was the case. Every December I would give it one more try and return to the Seminar for a single meeting. Lacan, facing the blackboard, contemplated his knots. It was deadly. He spoke even less than before and in a muffled voice, as though unwilling to make himself understood. At the same time I began an analysis of my own. Love turned away and changed the subject. There was nothing to be done about it, and Lacan himself had explained why. I then had a strange experience: Lacan's writings, by themselves, without the support of the oral teaching, turned opaque and resisted all my efforts to penetrate them. I had no further investment in either the mathematical toys or the whole undertaking: my interest had depended, subjectively, solely on the rare, strong voice, so adept at making itself understood. As I found my own voice in analysis, droning on day after day, it gradually took the place occupied for so long by the voice of the schools. One day it was inevitable that I should cease to be a schoolgirl.

Odor di femmina, or Don Juan, Psychoanalyst

Beyond the increasingly sophisticated argument, I dimly perceived two contradictory passions in Lacan. The first was the passion for science that he praised in Freud, thus giving notice that he was committing himself wholeheartedly to the scientific project. In fact he used science as myth, and in this he was not alone among his contemporaries. Althusser too, in seeking to distinguish science from ideology in Marx, also toyed with the fantasy of a science untainted by the mentality of its times. The idea of structure, used in a rigorous fashion by Lévi-Strauss, was for Lacan a beautiful and pregnant image, a scientific allegory. In this period the journal *Scilicet* began publishing dizzyingly bombastic articles. The imposture reached such a height that it could not continue. Anonymous "autocritiques" (anonymity of authors was *Scilicet*'s rule at the time) were published by writers who accused themselves of having used topology without materialist dialectics: the two "methods" were said to be "identical." This claim was put forward not by Lacan but by one of his disciples, who, while elegantly allowing that "this theorem remains to be proven in detail," used it to attack contemptible revisionists who had not yet made the connection.[52] Page after page was covered with topological discussions and short courses in mathematics. Scientism flourished as never before, suffused with a deep-seated irrationalism that discouraged thought. An odd contradiction, since Lacan's passion for science was that of a teacher.

Lacan's other passion was truly his own and the one that I really loved: namely, his passion for love, which he never stopped trying to elucidate. This *idée fixe* recurred in the speech he made announcing the dissolution of his school. In that speech the verities to which Lacan truly adhered resurfaced like masts after a shipwreck. Woman, the phallus, *la jouissance*. The phallus—neither fantasy nor incomplete object but signifier of every signified. The whole business still obsessed him. It was also a justifiable concern of those who saw in Lacan the "ancient and enormous root" of a linguistic constellation that Jacques Derrida dubbed with the unwieldy title of "phallogocentrism": central to language and the world, sharing jointly in the same power, are the phallus, the Logos, and the Voice.[53] Women and writing, the repressed material of history, come second. No chance of such a statement being false: but wasn't Lacan saying the same thing? In his January 1980 testament he was at pains to clarify matters:

women have access, he said, to phallic *jouissance* (great!) but only on condition that they "do not lose themselves in an antiphallic nature of which there is no trace in the unconscious."[54] In other words: to get beyond the phallus you've got to change the world, and since Lacan always detested progress and reformers, it should come as no surprise that, here as elsewhere, he stubbornly insisted on taking the world as he found it and not as it ought to be according to the dreams and wishes of various reformists and revolutionaries. The "revolutionary of thought, the man of truth," may be a philosophical agitator but he has nothing to do with a utopian philosophe. The gates are closed—the gates to those other worlds that some women began around 1970 to model in their imaginations after their wishes.

Jacques Derrida based his extremely vehement critique of Lacan's "phallogocentrism" on a mercilessly minute analysis of Lacan's commentary on Poe's "Purloined Letter." Lacan thought so highly of this commentary in 1956 that he placed it first in the collection of articles published under the title *Ecrits,* the rest of which appear in chronological order. As with certain commentaries in philosophy, Lacan's article became more famous than the story on which it comments. "The Purloined Letter" is far from the best of Poe's *Extraordinary Tales.* But Lacan turns it into a striking myth: truth, woman, and castration are all clearly revealed to be lurking in the text.

The case is "simple" and "bizarre," we are told by the police inspector who assigns it to the rather philosophical detective Dupin. A letter has been stolen from the royal apartments, in fact from the queen's chamber. It is a letter "of the utmost importance." The thief is known to be the minister D. While reading the letter, the queen had been interrupted by her husband the king and forced to leave it on the table. At this point D. came along, saw the letter, noticed the queen's distress, and managed to abscond with the object by producing from his pocket a second envelope almost identical to the one containing the queen's letter and substituting the former for the latter.

The queen therefore knows that the minister has stolen the letter, and the minister knows that the queen knows that he is the thief. But where is the purloined letter hidden? The inspector has searched the minister's house from top to bottom: he has examined the floors, the rugs, the wallpaper, the cellars, all with a fine-tooth comb. Dupin finds the letter by a process of deduction: the minister is familiar with the methods of the police and would not have "hidden" the letter in any ordinary hiding place. Instead, he has put it in a shabby card-case hanging by a dirty ribbon from a copper knob. The letter is torn and neglected, whereas the minister has a deserved reputation for orderliness. This is the best of hiding-places: visible to all, the very obviousness of the location disguises the purloined letter and actually makes it invisible. Except to Dupin, who recovers the letter but not before taking one of its pages and substituting another in his turn.

Poe emphasizes certain details that could not fail to arouse Lacan's interest: the minister is a poet, a madman, and a mathematician, the author of a book on differential and integral calculus. This fantastic combination of attributes drew Lacan's attention to questions of inspiration, madness, and the matheme. He therefore analyzes "The Purloined Letter" from the minister's point of view, fascinated by the man behind the minister-thief and by his relationship to the woman. She is not just any woman: she is the queen. This changes the nature of the story: she becomes a possession. By absconding with the queen's letter, the minister takes possession of the sign of the woman and is himself possessed by it: it is "in his possession." We see him hide the letter by adopting a stratagem similar to a trick an animal might use to escape from a predator. Lacan calls this device the "policy of the Otherich."[55] [The neologism calls for explanation. In French the word is *autruiche:* a combination of *autruche,* ostrich, an animal that hides its head in the sand, believing that it will not be seen because it can't see anything, and *autrui,* "others," since the ostrich depends on the others who are looking at it.—trans.] The

minister's dependency is absolute: he is in possession of the letter, but he does nothing with it beyond hiding it by placing it an
obvious location.

The minister, moreover, becomes a woman. He gives off the
most obvious "odor di femmina." He turns the envelope inside
out as one turns the skin of a rabbit and writes—or has someone
else write—his own address in place of the queen's. So we have
a minister who writes a woman's letter to himself—whatever the
real contents of the stolen letter may be. "The purloined letter,
like an immense female body, is displayed in the minister's office
when Dupin enters. But Dupin already expects to find the letter
in this condition, and through eyes shaded by green glasses he
now has only to undress this immense body."[56] The minister
has been castrated by Dupin, who occupies a place analogous to
that of the psychoanalyst. From a neutral position he observes
the stratagems of one who thinks that he is not being observed
but who is in fact, like the ostrich, standing with his behind in
the air. The minister thus receives a message of his own, the theft
of the letter, but in an inverted form: the theft of the letter by
Dupin, who lets the minister know that he has stolen the letter
back by writing two verses from Crébillon on the page that he
substitutes for the letter in the envelope. A model of all communication: the transmitter receives his own message back in inverted form from the receiver.

"Simple" and "bizarre" too was Lacan's choice to begin *Ecrits*
with this analysis, a choice he explains in the following terms:
"Some people may say that this 'theft of the letter' is a parody
of our discourse." A parody in two senses: first, in the sense of
"par-odos," an accompaniment, and second, in the usual sense,
the ridicule being intended to ward off the "shadow of the master-
thinker." The concern is laudable. But if the purloined letter represents Lacan's career, does he occupy the position of the queen,
the minister, or Dupin? No doubt he is all three: obsessed by the
queen, as the minister was, and too completely identified with
this mad poet and mathematician not to feel that he too is a

woman; but also a psychoanalyst, and thus a Sherlock Holmes capable of unlocking every puzzle and returning his own message in neatly deciphered form. And the message never changed. Here is Jacques Derrida's formulation of it: "This proper place, known to Dupin as to the psychoanalyst . . . is the place of castration: woman insofar as she is revealed to be the place where a penis is lacking, insofar as she is the truth of the phallus, i.e., of castration."[57] The lady's way never deceived him.

Lacan republished the piece on woman-scent, behaving like a true Don Juan who knows that Leporello's catalogue is endless because "woman" is "not everything," she is the eternal "minus-One."[58] This time the blow was aimed at Michel Foucault, in particular at Foucault's admirable commentary on Velazquez' painting *Las Meninas,* published in 1966 as an introduction to *Les Mots et Les Choses* (translated into English as *The Order of Things*). The tiny infanta stands at the center of the painting in the midst of her entourage and in front of a canvas that we see "from behind." Velazquez himself stands in the background, facing us, paintbrush in hand. A man is exiting through a doorway, and at the far end of the room we see the reflection of the royal couple in the mirror. They are the subject of the painting, and Velazquez, the court painter, is preparing to paint their portrait. According to Foucault, the royal couple is doubly represented: once in the portrait of which we see only the frame, and again, indistinctly, in the mirror, where we can see them: Foucault sees this painting as a model of "classical" representation, in which the subject represented has disappeared. "Free of this fettering relationship, representation can at last put itself forward as pure representation."

Lacan at first greeted this truly admirable chapter with enthusiasm. But he quickly changed the subject and eventually produced his own commentary on *Las Meninas,* guided, as always, by the "odor di femmina." The object that occupies the geometric center of the canvas is not the king or the queen but rather, hidden beneath an enormous hoop skirt, the infanta's genitalia.

Velazquez, the one man in this gynaecaeum in which, apart from dogs and monsters, only women figure—Velazquez the de-miurge—has organized the whole painting around the child's hidden and prepubescent genitals. Peculiar enough to have inspired Picasso to imitation, *Las Meninas* arouses in the onlooker a desire to see what is on the other side of the canvas. "Show me," he says. "Show me the painting. Show me the underside of things. Show me what is underneath the hoop skirt." In Lacan's words: "The gaze flows from the painter's brush and out over the canvas, forcing you to lower your own gaze before the painter's work." [59]

The canvas is a stunning eye-trap. "Show me," says the spectator to the painter. The painter's answer, though, is this: "So you want to see? Well, then, look at this!" And "this" is another gaze, staring back. Lacan, the enemy of meaning, here makes himself the enemy of content. For him the best example is the anamorphosis that looms up at the feet of Holbein's two ambassadors, who seem to be laughing at it in a dignified way. This distorted form is of course the anamorphosis of a death's head, as can be seen by looking at the picture sideways from a certain angle. A death's head: what symbol of "subject nothingness" could possibly be better? The infanta hides a child's genitals beneath her dress; the ambassadors disdainfully point to "the apparation of the phallic phantom" at their feet. [60]

The Ravishing

Mathematics and topology never lured Lacan away from the lady's way. Beyond the phallus, the square root of -1, the diamonds, loops, volutes, and rings, beyond the equations and imaginary numbers, we find the familiar phantoms of mad-women, lovers, hysterics, and lunatics. Marguerite Duras wrote a novel entitled *The Ravishing of Lol. V. Stein.* Lacan took up his pen to pay her homage, something he did not do often. But this case fascinated him in many ways. For one thing, the author was a Marguerite, like the Marguerite d'Angoulême to whom he compared her. For another, the character Lol. seemed to have been written expressly for Lacan. The plot turns on a gaze and ends in madness. This novel restored Lacan's interest in insane women, an interest that he had never really abandoned.

Lol. V. Stein was born Lola Valerie Stein in an ordinary small town somewhere in the vast United States. She was engaged to be married. On the night her engagement was celebrated the man she loved walked out before her very eyes with a woman dressed in black with whom he had danced in an intimate manner. A primitive scene: Lola, her gaze fixed on the couple who were stealing her life away, was struck dumb and remained so for some time. She changed her name then to Lol. V., as though it had become necessary to amputate her true name. Then all her trouble seemed to vanish. She married and lived a quiet life. But the embers of madness smoldered beneath the ashes of the domestic hearth. One day she runs into a childhood friend, Tatiana, who has black hair. She conceives a strange passion, to watch while a man, Jack Hold, makes love to Tatiana. Lol. cannot rest until one night, stretched out in a field of rye, she watches while Tatiana and Jack make love at the edge of the field, where she can see them thanks to the light falling from a window. They know. Lol. then falls asleep, her blonde hair mingling with the rye in the field. When Jack Hold tries to bring things to a head by seeking Lol. out for real, she becomes mad, on the very spot where her reason was stolen from her by her fiancé and the woman in black some years earlier.

Lol. was "ravished," taken out of herself, made the cynosure of all eyes, a veritable eye-trap like the painting. She first became the center of attention when she was publicly abandoned by her fiancé. Later she arranged for the other couple to make love and watched herself. Lacan was enchanted by Lol.'s action, in which he saw the essence of "scopophilia," the location of the object of desire in the act of looking itself. Objet-petit-a, the gaze emanates from the body and is tossed away, like Beatrice's glance. Like Actaeon's desire to see the goddess: Actaeon is the symbol of the psychoanalyst, "excessively" eager to see what is forbidden. "The focal point of the gaze shares in the ambiguity of the jewel." [61] In other words, the thing looked at is a dark spot that dazzles in the sun.

One day Lacan went fishing in a boat somewhere in Brittany. With him was a fisherman by the name of Petit-Jean. This fellow was fond of telling a certain joke, which he thought hilariously funny. Some distance from the boat a sardine can floated on the surface of the water, glittering in the sunlight. Seeing this, Petit-Jean made the following observation to Jacques-Marie Lacan, then age twenty: "You see that can over there? You see it? Well, it doesn't see you!" [62]

Lacan naturally didn't think this was funny. In later years, having become an analyst with a strong interpretive bent, he thought about Petit-Jean's joke. The glittering can "looks at me," as all light does. It made a spot; it was a screen; it was looking at Lacan. Thus bringing home to Lacan, the intellectual on vacation, that he too, sitting in his little boat, constituted a spot. Petit-Jean had put his finger on the dark spot. Every gaze is like this: it designates, and it designates the person who is looking. Lol., by forcing Jack and Tatiana to be looked at, also forced them to look at her: they could no longer be oblivious of her presence. She was the sardine can: she did not "see" them, but their love depended on her gaze. Back to the purloined letter: like the sardine can, an object innocently exposed in an obvious place. Back to the purloined letter and to the woman hidden behind it, like a woman hidden in a field of rye. For Lacan, Lol. has been "stolen away," stolen away from herself at her engagement party. She can only find herself in the other couple, Jack and Tatiana. But when Lol.-as-question finally links up with her answer, she sinks into madness: the correct distance is the distance between the rye field and the brothel, the distance of an absent gaze. Lol. could be touched by love only at a distance.

"Hasn't enough taken place to enable us to recognize what has happened to Lol., which also reveals the nature of love? To wit, that love is the self-image in which you are wrapped by the other, which clothes you, and which leaves you when it is stolen away, to be what underneath?" [63] Nothing at all. Lol. could not be naked: only Tatiana could be, "naked, naked underneath her black hair," said Lol. to Jack Hold. Now and forevermore, love as Marguerite Duras described it in keeping with the dictates of Jacques Lacan's heart, "the taciturn marriage of the empty life with the indescribable object." Courtly love is the only kind; no love exists that is not "noble" love, a far cry from sexual intercourse. Does the message need repeating? For Lacan there is no love but in the most unabashed distance.

On one side, the stubborn road of science, playfulness, truth, and mathemes; on the other, passion for love, inspired madness, the gaze that looks without seeing and captures itself in capturing the other. On one side the learned founder of a discipline; on the other side, the poet. On one side the madman; on the other the mathematician. Lacan bore a striking resemblance to the minister in "The Purloined Letter." But no Dupin could ever take his letter away. He had taken it from himself.

THE FIREBIRD

It is nighttime. On my writing table lies neglected the issue of the magazine whose cover depicts an angry Lacan with his mouth wide open. Outside the air is filled with the noise of people returning home. Slashed subjects, $\$$, people internally divided from their objects, they return home now that night is fallen to confront the master signifier, $\sqrt{-1}$, with the impossible objet-petit-a of whose existence they know nothing. People with their I and their I(A), divided between their good and bad images, blindly kept under surveillance by their O, which stares at them wide-eyed and knits its brow whenever they wander from the straight and narrow. These people are hungry; they don't know that D cannot link up with $\$$ and that they're poking themselves in the eye, sticking $\sqrt{-1}$ in a, if they even so much as imagine . . . Behind that lighted window a child may be standing on its hind legs and laughing at itself. Fog is shrouding the dance of the signs, and a Fellinian piper is playing sourly. My daughter has just come home. It is time for the game shows on TV. She picks up the newspaper with Lacan's picture and without thinking throws it into the wastebasket.

It is nighttime. France is an old country, whose slumber conceals rebellions that have not yet found their voice. Lacan too has grown old, as biology dictates. Nothing can now cause him to deviate from his path, the path of the mathemes—nothing, not even the decline of a Republic that is allowing itself to be transformed insidiously into a covert monarchy, nor the abuses committed by the corrupt authorities, nor the upheavals of Islam, nor the turmoil in Southeast Asia, so many wounds on our minds. It is as though he has seen so much else that nothing more can move him, probably not even the dissolution of his School, one of his last outbursts. Absent from the scene, he watched his little world become agitated and his loyal followers divide into factions. He sent a formal, aloof message of support. Absently he watched the parade of faces in the hall in the Chemistry Building, watched but did not respond as people deferred to his authority. In his absence there was nothing of contempt, none of the hauteur of de Gaulle. He was simply not there, like Lol. V. Stein. What sudden arrival might have made him start, what approach might have moved him? Distance had become his world. He now spoke only in riddles, having imprisoned himself in silence. Around him the furor was extreme and the disputes violent and bloody. But no one really challenged him. Everyone felt that challenge had become pointless. He had become his own gravestone. He was making his way toward eternity with the halting gait of an old man. In this sight there was nothing ridiculous and nothing touching. Yet he always retained a certain grandeur.

He had said enough about death to suggest that he may have stopped thinking about it. Death recurred from time to time in the form of Hegel's Absolute Master, a frequent reference, and also in the references to the statue that came to dinner [in *Don Giovanni*—trans.], a symbol of the desire that never finds its object. Death "with its eyes of pitch."[1] Death is an integral part of the analyst's work. "It is here, then, that the analysis of the Ego finds its ideal term, in which the subject, having rediscovered the beginnings of its Ego in an imaginary regression, through a process of progressive remembering draws near its end in analysis: in other words, the subjectivization of his death."[2] Regression completes the loop. Imaginary though it may be, it comes back to its starting place, not birth, which is quite real, but the ultimate end, the final punctuation of the individual text. "And this may be what is finally due from the analyst's Ego, of which we may say that it should submit to the prestige of but a single master, death, so that life, which it is supposed to guide through so many destinies, may be its friend." In any case, the "subject-supposed-to-know," that figure of the psychoanalyst whose illusions Lacan had so vehemently criticized for the benefit of his disciples, so that they would not erect him as the absolute authority in matters psychoanalytic, did understood one bit of the truth. For Jacques Lacan, psychoanalyst, must indeed bow to the prestige of death, if he is to carry out his profession to the end.

Here we touch upon Lacan's real limitations, limitations he shares with all men. When he discussed female *jouissance* and the ignorance characteristic of it, when he attempted to establish an equation between desire, the phallus, and the truth, he was seeking, like Christine Papin before her judges, "the mystery of life." Doubtless he did succeed in finding the correct distance in his relation to death. He avoided the illusions of progress and all that goes with them: the false sense of mastery, the misguided reforms, the utopian illusions, happiness, salvation, charity, the imperialism of altruism in all its forms. He was a true stoic and sometimes a true cynic as well. He stubbornly persisted in his efforts to create a systematic inversion of the world, a mirror image.

Mirror images: Léa, the reflection of her sister; Madame Z. confronted with the aggression of Aimée, the cultivated peasant; madwomen; the Virgin, hidden behind the predominant male principle, the sublimated image of male desires; Lol.'s gaze; the butcher's wife's dream; Judge Schreber's copulation with God; the subject and the world—the subject, which is no longer, as Descartes' mad dream would have it, the "master and possessor of nature," but rather the slave of the signifier that represents it to another subject; the message as returned by its recipient, reversed by the unconscious. A ship of fools of which Lacan, standing on his head, chose to be the mizzenmast. But if "up" and "down" no longer have meaning, who is to say that Lacan was crazy because he chose to see the world upside down?

By doing so he realized his destiny as a shaman. For he was a shaman as well as a prophet—the two are not identical. The shaman is a solitary healer, a "medicine man," excluded from his tribe. His words are therapeutic but have no other power, and he can become a chief only thanks to his magic. By contrast, the prophet delivers a message for all to hear. Lacan became a prophet in 1953.

> The prophet and the sorcerer, both distinguished from priests in that they are independent entrepreneurs who carry out their functions outside the institutional structures of society and hence without institutional protection or sanction, occupy different social positions because of their different backgrounds and preparation. The prophet lays claim to the legitimate exercise of religious power . . . whereas the sorcerer responds case by case to specific and immediate demands, using language as one technique among others for, say, healing the body, and not as an instrument of symbolic power, i.e., an instrument of preaching for "healing the soul." [3]

Here, Pierre Bourdieu has put his finger on an important distinction. By deciding to teach a science, Lacan, who kept his shamanistic powers and continued in his professional role as a psychoanalyst, was seeking legitimacy. He got it with his School. The decision to dissolve the School in January 1980 was not so much the act of a prophet as a decision to return to the loneliness of the shaman. "If I should ever go away, tell yourselves that it is in order to be Other at last . . ." In order to be even more absent, even more resolutely "upside down"—more of a sorcerer and less of a prophet. Nevertheless, as an "independent entrepreneur," he conformed to the social rule. He was indeed independent, in spite of himself. The institution that excluded him by pronouncing the final "chammata" left him no other choice.

By contrast, the publication of *Ecrits* was the act of a prophet. Publication made the dogma available to everyone and opened it up to endless glosses and interpretations, as well as to misinterpretation and error. Publication also put Lacan face to face with a possible contradiction between shamanism and prophecy and placed him in a position of authority as the Teacher (in the sense of a master instructing his disciples in the true word), even though he had always opposed such authority. Lacan distinguished between the Teacher and the Academician (and the Academy met with even less favor in his eyes after he became part of it). He also distinguished between the Teacher and the Hysteric (whose discourse is like the painter's "Show me": "Show me if you're a man") and between the Teacher and the Psychoanalyst, who explores the impossible object of desire.[4] Was there a way out of this Teacher's role, which he said he did not want? He was so trapped that he wanted to get out at all costs, and so he dissolved the "glue" (l'Ecole, la colle). He did so in order to shed the authority that is inherent in all teaching. But he took this step only after filling all four roles at one time or another. For he was above all a psychoanalyst, and all his pronouncements were uttered in this capacity. He had spoken as a hysteric, determined to challenge each member of his audience to "Show me if you're an analyst." That he became an academic, a cog in the university machine, even Lacan could not deny. And finally, he was a Teacher.

He harbored a fear to which he gave vent in the essay on "The Purloined Letter" in *Ecrits*. "May it please heaven that the written word (*les écrits*) shall endure as the spoken word surely does; for the latter's unpayable debt at least impregnates our acts through its transferences."[5] This shows that he was afraid of not enduring. The *Ecrits* were not nearly as important to him as an audience accustomed to hearing him teach. A psychoanalyst to the very depths of his being, he placed his trust in the spoken word, not as a way of saying the truth, for the truth is impossible to say, but rather to shift the "unpayable debt" onto his audience via transference. The psychoanalyst "invests" in transference, as it were. But he also looks to "liquidate" that investment at some point in the future. If the debt were really unpayable, its transfer would amount to indentured servitude. The temptation to "endure" by such nefarious means was implicit in the authority of the teacher, and it was a temptation that Lacan never entirely resisted. Not even the dissolution of his School was sacrifice enough: no sooner had he announced the formation of his new group, "la Cause freudienne," than applications flooded in, and Lacan did not turn them down. The applicants were the same, apart from a few of the least indentured, who broke away. The prophet in Lacan had suffocated the shaman, the victim of the contradictions in the Lacanian doctrine.

But Lacan remained passionate about love, transference, truth, and the Logos—the Logos that was branded on the minds of his listeners with the red-hot iron of his passion. He did not care about publishing and in fact wrote very little. He appealed to another kind of memory, and he was a man of another era, not of this world, which nevertheless loved him before it hated him. He was determined to become immortal, the desire for immortality being an intimate part of the shamanistic myth. For it is the shaman and not the prophet who transcends human divisions and manages to be both included and excluded, inside the group and outside it, honored and reviled, but recognized for what he is. Only the shaman becomes the poet "who produces himself by being eaten by verse" [in French a pun on *vers,* verses, and *vers,* worms—trans.].[6] Eaten by words that pass through him, "obviously without worrying whether the poet knows anything about them or not."[7] In such terms Lacan explained why the poet is ostracized in Plato's Republic, led politely to the city's gates, honored of course but cast out nonetheless. Words ate away at Lacan. Ostracism made him a poet, and he developed a poetic style to the point of excess. But his passion for madwomen foretold his future ostracism long before it occurred.

Finally, it is the shaman who achieves androgyny. The same initiatory journey that gives him his iron skeleton also gives him the power to transvest. Neither man nor woman, he becomes something else, something superhuman, something beyond the culturally-induced distinctions between good and evil, master and slave, mother and father, boy and girl. Speaking an enigmatic, abandoned language, the shaman serves as the repository of his group's culture because he transcends and sublimates that culture. And so it was with Lacan, prodigiously well-read but determined to repeat what he had read in his own way, allowing language to make its own discoveries within his fertile imagination. Also shaman-like was his obsession with immortality, that shamanistic immortality best revealed in the myth of the phoenix. The phoenix, the firebird, rises from its ashes. But after a long journey up the Nile, the firebird sets fire to its own father, which it has carried on its back. Then, grazing its father's wings, it too catches fire and burns on a pyre of its own droppings, from which it takes a pleasant scent such as death gives to the body of the Christian saint: the droppings of the phoenix are cinnamon. Child of itself or of its own father, the phoenix is not subject to the law of generation. The offspring of neither man nor woman, it has something of the nature of both. In this respect it is immortal, indifferent to sexual boundaries.[8]

There is something of the phoenix in Lacan, in his identification with the ecstastic transports of mystics and in his enthusiastic and intimate encounter with existence. And there is something of the phoenix in Lacan's desire to endure at all costs, and in his consumption by language, which eats away at him like a worm, reducing him to dust from which he then rises. He has died two deaths: once when he was expelled from the psychoanalytic community and again when he was suffocated by adulation. And yet he has risen, as is attested by the joy of his followers, who, having buried him in their hearts, like Mary Magdalene at the gate of Christ's sepulchre discovered that the tomb was empty and the spirit risen.[9] The part of him that is like the phoenix is the source of his inspiration. It is the part that gives him the powers of exaggeration appropriate to myth: exaggeration is the art of metaphor. The phoenix in him is the source of his joy in language freed of all pedagogical constraint and ultimately liberated in pure play. The child joins hands with the bird, the old man with the child who laughs at recognizing himself in the mirror. Now the end is approaching, the Absolute Master, the final punctuation mark, death, the end of the game.

Lacan was a man with two destinies. A public destiny as a clinician and man of letters, a teacher, a prophet, and the leader of a school. And a private destiny of passion, poetry, madness, love, and shamanism. The psychoanalyst stood at the crossroads between public and private, between the prophet and the shaman—caught between two contradictory passions for language. The public life was ludicrous, the private life extreme owing to the force of its relentless passion. The firebird survived every attack, but it lost some of its feathers in each battle. It ended, as stands to reason, by setting itself ablaze on a pyre of its own excrement.

NOTES

All references to Lacan's *Ecrits* are to the original French edition published by Les Editions du Seuil. The page numbers given in parentheses are to Alan Sheridan's English translation of selections from *Les Ecrits* (New York: Norton, 1977). These are cited for the reader who wishes to compare my translations, given in the text, with the existing translations. For reasons outlined in the Translator's Introduction there are some differences between my translations and Mr. Sheridan's.

1. LOVE'S PLEASURES

1. François George, the author of *L'Effet 'Yau de poêle de Lacan et des lacaniens'* (Paris: Hachette, 1979). George's earlier works include *Prof à T, Deux études sur Sartre, La Loi et le phénomène,* and *Pour un ultime hommage au camarade Staline.* He was brought up by his family on the most thoroughgoing variety of dogmatic Stalinism, which inspired in him a passion for freedom, loyalty to Sartre, and intense admiration for the character of Arsène Lupin, to whom *La Loi et le phénomène* is dedicated. George's thought is a strange mixture of metaphysics and pataphysics [see Alfred Jarry's *Ubu Roi*—trans.]. His taste for the bizarre and for playing with words could hardly fail to arouse his interest in Lacan, if only to make fun of him.

2. On January 5, 1980, in a letter sent to the members of the Ecole freudienne.

3. "Lettre de dissolution," *Ornicar?* (1980), 2(20–21):9–10. (*Ornicar?,* the Lacanian journal, is published by Editions Lyse and distributed by Les Editions du Seuil.)

4. *Ibid.,* seminar of March 18, 1980, p. 19.

5. *Ibid.,* January 15, 1980, p. 12.

6. Louis Althusser at this point had the courage to take up his pen and write an article whose fame has endured, "Lacan et Freud," published in *Nouvelle Critique.* For the most part Althusser was unusually discreet as to his thoughts on psychoanalysis. He violated this discretion only once, in 1980, when he made a vehement and passionate public attack on Lacan, an attack that ex-

pressed irritations shared by a great many other people. Althusser's previous positions on psychoanalysis were as strong and courageous as the positions he took in the many other battles he waged over the course of a long career as a militant philosopher.

7. For example, in *Télévision,* this phrase, placed in the epigraph: "He who questions me also knows how to read me," signed J. L. It was Miller who questioned Lacan in the program produced by Benoît Jacquot. Or again, in a letter to the newspaper *Le Monde* prefacing the text of a January 1980 seminar, Lacan denounced those who "raise a hue and cry against Jacques-Alain Miller, odious for having shown that he for one has read him" (i.e., Lacan, here referring to himself in the third person).

8. As is shown by the Jacques Lacan issue of *Magazine littéraire,* "L'Impromptu de Vincennes." See discussion in chapter 4 of this book.

9. For example in the series published by Les Editions du Seuil under the rubric *L'Evangile au risque de la psychanalyse.* The interpretation is certainly Christian but remarkable for its simple directness and for its fresh insights into the Gospel texts.

10. In discussing the repression of Logos by writing in Western culture, Jacques Derrida gradually developed a critique of Lacan, whose views on Logos were the same as everybody else's, according it priority over writing. The critique became overt, and more sophisticated, in "Le Facteur de la vérité," where Derrida analyzed Lacan's repression in his interpretation of Poe's story, "The Purloined Letter" (presented by Lacan in his 1956 seminar). See chapter 4, and chapter 4, note 53. As for Felix Guattari, he was already in open rebellion with the Ecole freudienne. What is more, he had written, along with Gilles Deleuze, *L'Anti-Oédipe* (Paris: Editions de Minuit, 1972). This earned mixed reactions from Lacanians: it criticized Freud, but it also criticized Lacan. [Lacan's seminar on Poe is available in partial translation in *Yale French Studies,* 1972, no. 48, and Derrida's "The Purveyor of Truth" may also be found in *Yale French Studies,* 1975, no. 52. Deleuze and Guattari's *Anti-Oedipus* was translated by Robert Hurley, Mark Seem, and Helen R. Lane (New York: Viking, 1977).]

11. Patrick Rambaud—like all the reporters for this fine magazine—is a shrewd young man with a keen eye for "what's happening." He spent a decent amount of time interviewing one person or another and nosing about, not without results but also not without finding some lips sealed and certain doors closed. Ultimately tired out by his efforts, he had to settle for publishing a compendium of all the rumors he had heard, some of which were exaggerated in the process.

12. A film produced by the Research Department of the French television network, broadcast under the title "Psychoanalysis," and subsequently published under the title *Télévision* by Les Editions du Seuil (1974).

13. Montherlant, *Le Génie et les fumisteries du Divin* (Paris: La Nouvelle Société d'édition, n.d.), pp. 32–33.

14. Althusser was able to gain access to a working session not open to the

general public thanks to one of his former students, a member of the Ecole freudienne. On this occasion he read remarks that attracted considerable attention, remarks polished the night before to be sure they would not go unnoticed. The text of these remarks—read to me over the telephone by Althusser himself the following morning—has never been published in its entirety, though I did publish some excerpts in (the newspaper) *Le Matin*. Althusser's analysis was highly critical, highly relevant, and quite hostile not only to the Lacanians but also to Lacan himself.

15. Surprising light has been shed on Edouard Pichon's position by the remarkable work of Elisabeth Roudinesco (*Confrontation,* no. 3, published by Aubier-Montaigne, pp. 179–225). Pichon said the following to Lacan: "Continue then, Lacan, blazing your own trail through the wilderness, but leave enough nice white pebbles behind you so that others can follow where you lead. Too many people, having lost all contact with you, imagine that you've lost your way." Pichon gave two reasons for thinking that Lacan had gone off the track. For one there was the "armor consisting partly of sectarian jargon and partly of personal preciosity," and for another Lacan's "Frenchness" was tinged with what Pichon regarded as an excess of "Germanic varnish." When this was written Lacan had recently published an article in the *Encyclopedie francaise,* under the general editorship of the psychologist Henri Wallon, who was a Communist.

16. In Martin Buber, for example; or to a lesser extent in Levinas and Jabes; and even in some respects in the most recent work of Jacques Derrida.

17. Jacques Lacan, "La Direction de la cure et les principes de son pouvoir," *Ecrits* (Paris: Seuil, 1966), p. 642(276).

18. *Ornicar?,* 1980, 2(20–21):10.

19. [I have substituted a Shakespearean example for a Lacanian flight of fancy involving an extended pun on the French words *rideau* and *ris d'eau*—trans.]

20. In an issue of *Delenda.*

21. I have taken this "defile of signifiers" from Sandra Thomas's story "La Barbaresque," which appeared in *Mercure de France* in 1980. Or perhaps I took them from her true private story, which she told me in terms somewhat different from the public story a few months prior to its publication.

22. "La Psychanalyse et son enseignement," *Ecrits,* p. 458.

23. With the two volumes of *Avant-Mémoires* published by Gallimard and based on the records of his own family up to the sixteenth century. And finally, in spite of everything, he came to write about the seventeenth century, where we encounter some of the characters from Alexandre Dumas's *Les Trois Mousquetaires*. Jean Delay has confined himself strictly to history, but history that one feels is rather novelistic. A "family novel" is bound up with the pages of the history written by this psychiatrist and psychoanalyst of peculiarly wide-ranging interests.

24. "L'Instance de la lettre dans l'inconscient," *Ecrits,* p. 501(153).

25. *Ibid.,* p. 500(152).

26. *Ibid.*, p. 501(153).
27. *Ibid.*, p. 504(155).
28. Supplement to *Ornicar?*, subtitled "La Communauté psychanalytique en France," part 2 (1977), no. 8, published by Lyse.
29. "La Chose freudienne," *Ecrits*, pp. 408–9(121).
30. *Ibid.*, p. 411(123).
31. *Ibid.*, p. 436(145).
32. *Ornicar?*, special issue entitled "Après la dissolution," 1980, 2(20–21):12.

2. THE LADIES' WAY

1. *Le Débat*, published by Gallimard under the general editorship of Pierre Nora.
2. Henry Ey, for example, with whom Lacan worked for a long period of time and together with whom he staged major colloquia at the Bonneval Hospital. Ey was a great psychiatrist.
3. This review has just been reissued in part (1933) by Skira-Flammarion. The articles by Lacan appear in the reissue, which offers remarkable evidence of the intellectual fecundity of this small group, which is immortalized by a Brassaï photograph (Sartre and Simone de Beauvoir also appear).
4. The two articles by Lacan published in *Le Minotaure* have been collected, together with his thesis in medicine, under the title *Premiers Écrits sur le paranoïa* (Paris: Seuil, 1975). The passage cited is found in the first of these, which dates from June 1933 and is entitled "Le problème du style et la conception psychiatrique des formes paranoïaques de l'expérience," pp. 387–88. On page 384 Lacan notes ironically that "of all intellectuals the physician most frequently bears the mark of a slight dialectical backwardness." This was the opening shot in Lacan's critique of psychoanalysts, which he resumed later in almost the same terms.
5. "Ecrits 'inspirés': Schizographie," *Premiers Ecrits . . .* p. 372. In another place Marcelle speaks of a "merle à fouine" rather than a "mère la fouine."
6. *Télévision*, p. 72.
7. "Ecrits 'inspirés' . . ." *Premiers Ecrits . . .* , p. 371.
8. *Télévision*, p. 72.
9. "Le problème du style . . . ," *Premiers Ecrits . . .* p. 388.
10. To the list of Lacan's major works we should add "Parkinsonnienne post-encephalitique" (1930) and "La traumatisée de guerre" (1928).
11. I have in mind the series of publications with the collective title *Des femmes*, not "De la femme," which for part of their history took a Lacanian approach. This is not altered by the fact that they later criticized this approach.
12. "Encore," *Seminaire* (Paris: Seuil, 1981), book 20, p. 68.
13. *Ibid.*

14. *Ibid.*

15. *Ibid.,* p. 69.

16. *Ibid.,* pp. 70–71.

17. Georges Bataille, *Œuvres complètes,* vol. 3: *Œuvres littéraires* (Paris: Gallimard, 1971), pp. 20–21. "Seated, she raised her leg and spread it wide. To be sure the slit was wide open, she pulled the skin apart with both hands. Edwarda's 'lips' stared out at me, hairy and pink, as full of life as some repulsive snake. I gently stammered, 'Why are you doing that?' 'You see,' she said, 'I am GOD . . .' "

18. Jean-Noël Vuarnet, *Extases mystiques* (Paris: Arthaud, 1980).

19. *Premiers Écrits sur la paranoïa,* pp. 389–99.

20. "De la psychose paranoïaque dans ses rapports avec la personnalité," *Ibid.,* p. 153.

21. *Moi, Pierre Rivière,* a collective work under the general editorship of Michel Foucault (Paris: Gallimard, 1973), pp. 199–201. It was in 1835 that young Pierre Rivière hacked to death his mother, his sister, and his brother. The years before and after this celebrated parricide saw equally surprising crimes. [Available in an English translation by Frank Jellinek as *I, Pierre Rivière* (New York: Pantheon, 1975).]

22. "De la psychose paranoïaque," *Premiers Ecrits . . . ,* p. 398.

23. *Ibid.,* p. 393.

24. *Ibid.,* p. 397.

25. See also "Propos sur la causalité psychique" in *Ecrits:* "The series of female persecutors who figure in her story all personify, virtually without variation, an ideal of evildoing, against which her need for aggression increased constantly." This implacable mechanism, in which aggression turns outwards to strike at another self in the other, Lacan calls the "paranoia of self-punishment."

26. "Kant avec Sade" is the title of one of the more austere and difficult of the articles republished in *Ecrits,* in which Lacan relates the Marquis de Sade's *Philosophie dans le boudoir* to Kant's *Critique of Practical Reason,* within a few years its contemporary. In this piece Lacan shows, in a rather elliptical fashion, that Sade is the absolute opposite of Kant. Though Sade describes a variety of transgressions the work has an air of "reason" about it. For both Kant and Sade what is at issue is the relationship between Desire and Law. In Kant Law dominates Desire. But the same is also true in Sade (*Ecrits,* pp. 765–90). This article is also one of the very rare ones written by Lacan. It was intended to be used as a preface for *La Philosophie dans le boudoir* and was actually published as an afterword to that work in the 1966 edition published by the Cercle de livre précieux.

27. Cited (in English) by Claude Lévi-Strauss in "Rapports de symétrie entre rites et mythes de peuples voisins," *Anthroplogie structurale* (Paris: Plon, 1958), vol. 2, p. 299.

28. "De la psychose paranoïaque . . . ," *Premiers Ecrits . . . ,* p. 185.

29. *Ibid.*, p. 193.

30. This passage, astonishingly Hegelian in style (apart from the last two words of the sentence), is taken from "Propos sur la causalité psychique," *Ecrits,* p. 172.

31. *Ibid.*, p. 175.

32. At the end of *Structures élémentaires de la parenté* Claude Lévi-Strauss used the expression "keep to oneself." These are the final words of the book. Pierre Clastres, in the posthumously published collection of his essays, *Recherches d'anthropologie politique* (Paris: Seuil, 1980), suggests that this is an entirely homosexual notion.

33. Or *affairement jubilatoire* [instead of *l'assomption jubilatoire*] as it is put in the primary text on "The Mirror Stage," in *Ecrits,* p. 90(2). The other texts on the mirror stage are "L'agressivité en psychanalyse" et "Propos sur la causalité psychique," also published in *Ecrits,* pp. 101–24 and 151–93. Harrisson's work was done in 1939.

34. *Ecrits,* p. 97(4).

35. In the *Essais de psychanalyse,* published by Payot. [See Roger Money-Kyrle, ed., *The Writings of Melanie Klein,* vols. 1–4 (London: Hogarth Press, 1975).]

36. *Critique of Pure Reason.*

37. "L'Agressivité en psychanalyse," *Ecrits,* p. 105(11).

38. *Ibid.*, p. 105(12).

39. "Le stade du miroir," *Ecrits,* p. 100(7).

40. *Ibid.*

41. *Ibid.*

42. "Position de l'inconscient," *Ecrits,* pp. 842 ff. See also "Les Quatre Concepts fondamentaux de la psychanalyse," *Séminaire,* book 11, pp. 179–81. [Available in a translation by Alan Sheridan as *The Four Fundamental Concepts of Psychoanalysis* (New York: Norton, 1978).]

43. "One day, a naked girl lying in my arms, I carressed the slit in her behind with my fingers. I spoke to her softly of the 'little thing.' She understood. I didn't know that they sometimes refer to it that way in bordellos. If I describe a dirty childhood, mired in filth and condemned to dissimulate itself, it is the gentlest voice in me that shouts, 'I myself am the "little thing," which has no place but hidden.' " Georges Bataille, *Œuvres complètes,* 3:38, in the text entitled "Le Petit."

44. *Télévision,* p. 40.

45. One of the most enigmatic objects in the list of "objets-petit-a" is the pound of flesh desired by Shylock in *The Merchant of Venice.* If the judgment were awarded and the Jew were to get his pound of flesh, the young Christian in his debt would die. In Shakespeare's play this does not occur. Lacan sees this as one of the possible figures of the objet-petit-a: an object that is part of something else from which it cannot be separated, an inaccessible part of a larger whole.

46. "Encore," *Séminaire,* book 20.

3. NO CAVIAR FOR THE BUTCHER

1. Reminiscent of Jacques Prévert's and Marcel Carné's immortal *Drôle de drame,* with, in order of appearance, Michel Simon, Louis Jouvet, and Françoise Rosay.

2. In the special issue of *Ornicar?* entitled "L'Excommunication" (1977), p. 96. These remarks, assented to by Pontalis, Lang, Smirnoff, and Widlöcher, were offered in response to the opening address by Serge Leclaire on November 10, 1963. Leclaire discussed the open conflict that surrounded the figure of Lacan. Jean Laplanche simply stated the problems raised by the very existence of Lacan, in particular "the revelation of the meaning, in terms of desire, of the enthusiastic assumption of the master's role, which is beyond the scope of what is possible in a group such as this one." The problem was a real one, whatever the role played by the incredible pressure brought to bear by the International Psychoanalytic Association. This was summed up quite well at the time by Jenny Aubry: "The present state of the debate comes down to this—'Do you want Lacan or do you want the International?' " By paraphrasing the Gospel (Do you want Jesus or Barrabas?) she put her finger on the deeper mythical significance of the conflict.

3. The text is reprinted on the cover of the "L'Excommunication" issue of *Ornicar?* (1977).

4. Alain-Fournier, "Note preliminaire sur le 'Poembo' de Suri," Special issue on "Shamanistic Journeys," *L'Ethnographic* 74–75(1977):239.

5. Mary Douglas, "De la souillure," in *Essais sur les notions de pollutions et de tabous* (Paris: Maspero, 1971), pp. 128–29.

6. G. W. F. Hegel, *Phenomenology of the Spirit,* cited hereafter in J. B. Baillie's English translation (New York: Harper and Row, 1967), p. 397.

7. Pierre Bourdieu, "Genèse et structure du champ religieux," *Revue française de sociologie* (1971), pp. 295–334.

8. "Fonction et champ . . . ," *Ecrits,* p. 238(31).

9. *Ibid.,* p. 247(40).

10. *Ibid.,* p. 252(44).

11. *Ibid.,* p. 313(98).

12. According to the testimony of François Weyergans, who wrote *Le Pitre* (the clown or stooge) and gave a judicious account of his analysis with Lacan. *Le Pitre,* a novel published by Gallimard, describes a clownish Lacan caught up in his patient's mythology. It is a splendid treatment of the Lacan image and a superb novel.

13. "Fonction et champ . . . ," *Ecrits,* p. 313(98).

14. See Marcel Detienne, *Les Maîtres de vérité dans la Grèce archaïque* (Paris: Maspero, 1967), p. 45.

15. "Fonction et champ . . . ," *Ecrits,* p. 313(98). *Do Kamo* is the title of a celebrated work of ethnography by Maurice Leenhardt (Paris: Gallimard, 1947), according to whom the Melanesian "do kamo" refers both to the man and to what he says.

16. Published in *Communication*.

17. The Grand Larousse gives the following definition: "Punctuation marks: various signs used to indicate the boundaries of, and relations between, the various parts of a sentence or discourse." This is followed by a lengthy article on punctuation. "All punctuation marks denote a pause, which may be either optional or compulsory, indicating a linguistic or psychic demarcation. In the spoken language, this pause is always accompanied by inflections of the melodic curve of the utterance more than the flow of speech, signifying much the same thing as the corresponding written marks."

18. "Subversion du sujet et dialectique du desir," *Ecrits*, p. 806.

19. See especially "Les Quatre Concepts fondamentaux de la psychanalyse," *Séminaire*, book 11, p. 36.

20. "Fonction et champ . . . ," *Ecrits*, p. 252(44).

21. "La Direction de la cure . . . ," *Ecrits*, p. 616(253).

22. *Ibid.*, p. 617(254).

23. Freud, *Gesammelte Werke*, (London: Imago, 1940–1968) vol. 16. [*The Standard Edition of the Complete Psychological Works of Sigmund Freud*, James Strachey, ed. and trans. (London: Hogarth Press, 1964), vol. 23.]

24. "Fonction et champ . . . ," *Ecrits*, p. 300(86).

25. Freud, *The Basic Writings of Sigmund Freud*, trans. A. A. Brill (New York: Random House, 1938), pp. 225–29.

26. "La Direction de la cure . . . ," *Ecrits*, p. 625(261).

27. *Ibid.*

28. *Ibid.*, p. 626(262).

29. *Ibid.*, p. 627(263).

30. *Ibid.*, p. 626(262).

31. *Ibid.*, p. 627(263).

32. In the dialogues "Parmenides," "Theaetetus," and "The Sophist," which gradually make clear the need to point up what is lacking before the nature of reality can be grasped.

33. "Fonction et champ . . . ," *Ecrits*, p. 299(86).

34. Lévi-Strauss, *Anthropologie structurale* (Paris: Plon, 1958), 2:33.

35. *Ibid.*, p. 34.

36. *Ibid.*, p. 35.

37. "Du traitement possible de la psychose," *Ecrits*, p. 575(215).

38. "La Direction de la cure . . . ," *Ecrits*, p. 627(263).

39. Mary Barnes and Joseph Berke, Un Voyage à travers la folie (Paris: Seuil, 1973). [From the English Mary Barnes: *Two Accounts of a Journey Through Madness* (New York: Harcourt Brace Jovanovich, 1972).]

40. Freud, "An Autobiographical Study," *Standard Edition*. (London: Hogarth Press, 1959), 20:28.

41. "Fonction et champ . . . ," *Ecrits* p. 308*n*(111*n*95).

42. I am thinking for example of Dariush Shayegan who wrote on this subject in *Le Matin* in 1979.

43. "La Direction de la cure . . . ," *Ecrits,* p. 640(275).

44. *Ibid.*

45. *Ibid.,* p. 641(275).

46. *Ecrits,* p. 350.

47. *Œuvres complètes du pseudo-Denys l'Aréopagite,* trans. Maurice de Gandillac (Paris: Aubier-Montaigne, n.d.), pp. 182–83.

48. Freud, "The Dissection of the Psychical Personality," in "New Introductory Lectures on Psychoanalysis," *Standard Edition,* vol. 22.

49. Especially in "La Chose freudienne," p. 417(128–29). See also "L'Instance de la lettre": "Where id was, I must come to be." Translation by Marie Bonaparte, revised and annotated by Lacan: "The ego (of the analyst no doubt) must dislodge the id (of the patient of course)." See "Position de l'inconscient," *Ecrits.* See also "La Science et la vérité," *ibid.,* p. 864: "Where it was, I must come to be as subject."

50. *Télévision,* p. 65.

51. *Ibid.,* p. 66.

52. *Ibid.,* pp. 66–67.

4. The Game of Hopscotch and the Four Corners

1. This "affair"—once again—duplicated, to the point of caricature, the exclusion process dear to the essential Lacan. Flacelière notified Lacan of his dismissal. In response a number of outraged members of the seminar, including Philippe Sollers and Jean-Jacques Lebel, occupied the offices of the director of the Ecole normale. There was a disturbance, the police were called in, and much noisy scandal ensued. But Lacan retained his official title and found refuge at the Law Faculty adjacent to the Pantheon, where he continued to teach in peace until the end. The story shows the powerful effect of being cast out only to be immediately resurrected.

2. Althusser's work is summed up in *Pour Marx* and *Lire "Le Capital,"* both published in France by Maspero (Paris, 1965 and 1968). Published in English translation as *For Marx,* tr. Ben Brewster (New York: Pantheon, 1972), and *Reading "Capital"* (London: New Left Books, 1970).

3. See Michel Foucault, *Les Mots et les choses* (Paris: Gallimard, 1966), translated by Alan Sheridan as *The Order of Things* (New York: Pantheon, 1971).

4. A drawing by Maurice Henry, reprinted in *Les Années 60* (Paris: Editions Metailie, 1980).

5. Published in the special issue of *Magazine littéraire* devoted to Jacques Lacan, February 1977.

6. "La Science et la vérité," the last article in *Ecrits,* beginning p. 855.

7. Especially in a still well-known article first published in *La Nouvelle Critique* in 1947. Even the Soviet psychologist Philippe Bassine did not go this far in his work on the unconscious published in Moscow.

8. "La Science et la vérité," *Ecrits*, p. 858.

9. Cf. Paul Ricoeur, *De l'interprétation* (Paris: Seuil, 1965). Translated (by Denis Savage) as *Freud and Philosophy: An Essay on Interpretation* (New Haven: Yale University Press, 1970). Lacan's comment appears in *Ecrits*, p. 867.

10. "La Science et la vérité," *Ecrits*, p. 872.

11. *Ibid.*, p. 874.

12. Unpublished seminar (based on my own notes, taken in 1965).

13. *Ecrits*, p. 197. The problem is the following. Imagine a prison with three prisoners and a warden. The warden tells the prisoners that he must release one of them. "I am going to put a disk on each of your backs. There are five disks in all, three of them white, two black. But you will see only the backs of the other two prisoners. The man who can guess the color of his own disk will be set free." The warden then puts a white disk on each prisoner's back. Neither of the black disks has been used, but the prisoners don't know this. After a while, however, all would have come to the same conclusion, as Lacan explains. They would have reasoned as follows: "My disk must be white. If it were black, the other two could have reasoned as follows: If my disk were also black, the third man would have seen at once that there were two blacks and therefore that his disk was white, and he would have been released. Since nobody was released immediately, it must be that we all have white disks." From this simple exercise Lacan drew sweeping conclusions as to the nature of humanism. A man knows that he is a man. Men recognize one another as men. I assert that I am a man lest I be convicted by other men of not being one. Logically, this is still reasoning by exclusion. Who is excluded? He who does not belong to the same human group. This text appeared in *Les Cahiers d'art* in 1945. On the cover were written the dates 1940–1944.

14. Unpublished seminar, my notes (1965).

15. D. W. Winnicott, *Jeu et realité: l'espace potentiel* (Paris: Gallimard, 1975), p. 59. [From the English *Playing and Reality* (London: Tavistock, 1971).]

16. *Ibid.*, p. 60.

17. *Ibid.*, p. 67.

18. *Ibid.*, p. 143.

19. According to "Une Question préliminaire à tout traitement possible de la psychose," *Ecrits*, pp. 531 ff.

20. *Ibid.*, p. 549(194).

21. *Ibid.*

22. *Ibid.*, p. 551(196).

23. "Réponse au commentaire de Jean Hyppolite," *Ecrits*, p. 388.

24. *Ibid.*

25. Or again, in other contexts, a "misconstruction" (*méconnaître*) essential to "knowing oneself" (*se connaître*).

26. "L'instance de la lettre . . . ," *Ecrits*, p. 507.

27. Freud, *Standard Edition*, 12:16.

28. "Du traitement possible de la psychose," *Ecrits*, p. 583(219).

29. Michel Foucault, ed., *Moi, Pierre Rivière* (Paris: Gallimard, 1973).

30. *Ibid.*, p. 77.

31. "Du traitement possible . . . ," *Ecrits*, p. 583(221).

32. "Subversion du sujet . . . ," *Ecrits*, p. 812(310).

33. With an allusion to Mme Edwarda, *Ecrits*, p. 583. Lacan summarizes Schreber's theodicy in these words: "Dieu est une p . . ." (God is a w(hore)). The passage on the Presence and the Joy is on p. 575. In Lacan's introduction to the French translation of Schreber's *Memoirs* by Paul Duquenne (*Cahiers pour l'analyse*, no. 5), Lacan is even more explicit: "What is involved is in no sense mystical asceticism or an effusive account of the patient's actual experience but a statement to which the only introduction is the logic of treatment."

34. "Subversion du sujet . . . ," *Ecrits*, p. 806(305).

35. See Claude Lévi-Strauss's admirable preface to the work of Marcel Mauss, *Sociologie et anthropologie* (Paris: Presses Universitaires de France, 1950).

36. "Subversion du sujet . . . ," *Ecrits*, p. 808(306).

37. *Ibid.*, p. 822(320).

38. *Ibid.*, p. 825(322).

39. *Ibid.* (323).

40. *Ibid.*, p. 826(322–23).

41. *Ibid.* (323).

42. "Lettre de dissolution," *Ornicar?* (1980), 2(20–21):9–10.

43. *Ibid.*

44. "La Science et la vérité," *Ecrits*, p. 877.

45. As Serge Gainsbourg sang in one of his last songs: "C'est l'hymne à l'amour . . . moi l'noeud . . . Enfin, c'qu'il en reste . . ."

46. See the chapter entitled "Ronds de ficelle," in "Encore," *Seminaire*, book 20.

47. "Lettre de dissolution," *Ornicar?*, 1980, 2(20–21):9.

48. "La Science et la vérité," *Ecrits*, p. 861.

49. "Après la dissolution," *Ornicar?*, 1980, 2(20–21):12.

50. *Cahiers pour l'analyse*, no. 5.

51. "Encore," *Séminaire*, book 20, p. 107.

52. *Scilicet*, 1970, no. 2/3, p. 191. Postscript to an article on "the topology of unconscious formations."

53. "Le facteur de la vérité," in *Carte postale* (Paris: Flammarion, 1980). [Available in partial translation in *Yale French Studies*, 1975, no. 52.] The origins of the idea of "phallogocentrism" are remote, going back to Derrida's earliest works, particularly one of the most important of his books, *Glas* (Paris: Editions Galilee, 1974). Lacan himself rarely used the term "phallocentrism."

54. "Après la dissolution," *Ornicar?* (1980), 2(20–21):12.

55. "Le Seminaire sur la lettre volée," *Ecrits*, p. 15.

56. *Ibid.*, p. 36.

57. "Le Facteur de la vérité," *Carte postale*, p. 467.

58. In "Encore", *Séminaire*, book 20, p. 116, Lacan does homage—the word

is aptly chosen—to his daughter, the only person, he tells us, who understood that for Don Juan woman is "minus one."

59. "Hommage fait à Marguerite Duras du ravissement de Lol. V. Stein," *Cahiers Renaud-Barrault,* 1965, no. 52, p. 11.

60. "Les Quatre Concepts fondamentaux de la psychanalyse, l'Anamorphose," *Seminaire,* book 11, p. 82.

61. "Les Quatre Concepts fondamentaux de la psychanalyse," *Séminaire,* book 11, p. 90.

62. *Ibid.,* p. 89.

63. "Hommage à Marguerite Duras . . . ," *Cahiers Renaud-Barrault,* 1965, no. 52, p. 10.

THE FIREBIRD

1. "Fonction et champ . . . ," *Ecrits,* p. 303.

2. "Variantes de la cure type," *Ecrits,* p. 348.

3. Pierre Bourdieu, "Genèse et structure du champ religieux," *Revue française de sociologie,* 1971, p. 321.

4. "Radiophonie," *Scilicet,* 1970, no. 2/3.

5. "La Séminaire sur 'La Lettre volée,' " *Ecrits,* p. 27.

6. "Radiophonie," *Scilicet,* 1970, no. 2/3.

7. *Ibid.*

8. According to Marie Delcourt, *Hermaphrodite* (Paris: Presses Universitaires de France, 1978), and Jean Hubaux and Maxime Leroy, *Le Mythe du phénix* (Paris: E. Droz, 1939).

9. Hubaux and Leroy point out that the resurrected Christ was interpreted in terms of the phoenix in imperial Rome, where pagan myths encountered early Christian beliefs.

THE WORKS OF JACQUES LACAN

Ecrits. Paris: Les Editions du Seuil, 1966. An anthology of Lacan's essays. A selection of these has been published in a translation by Alan Sheridan, *Ecrits: A Selection* (New York: Norton, 1978). The French edition includes the following essays:

"Au-delà du principe de réalité." Marienbad, 1936
"Le temps logique et l'assertion de certitude anticipée." First published in *Les Cahiers d'Art,* 1945.
★"L'agressivite en psychanalyse." Brussels, 1948.
★"Le stade du miroir comme formateur de la fonction du je." Zurich, 1949.
"Introduction theorique aux fonctions de la psychanalyse en criminologie." With Michel Cenac. 1950.
★"Propos sur la causalité psychique." Bonneval, 1946.
"Intervention sur le transfert." 1952.
★"Fonction et Champ de la parole et du langage en psychanalyse." Rome, 1953. (Also known as the Rome report or Rome discourse.)
"Introduction et réponse au commentaire de Jean Hyppolite sur la "Verneinung" de Freud." Hôpital Sainte-Anne, 1954.
★"Variantes de la cure type." 1955.
"Le séminaire sur la Lettre volée." 1955. Note that Lacan chose, for theoretical rather than chronological reasons, to place this essay at the beginning of *Ecrits*. A partial translation of this essay may be found in "Seminar on 'The Purloined Letter,'" Yale French Studies 48 (1973).
★"La chose freudienne, ou sens du retour a Freud en psychanalyse." Vienna, 1955–1956.
★"Situation de la psychanalyse et formation du psychanalyste en 1956."
"La psychanalyse et son enseignement." 1957.

★ Also included in the English selection.

★"L'instance de la lettre dans l'inconscient ou la raison depuis Freud." 1957.
★"D'une question préliminaire à tout traitement possible de la psychose." 1955–1958.
"Jeunesse de Gide ou la lettre et le désir." *Critique,* 1958.
★"La signification du phallus." Munich, 1958.
★"La direction de la cure et les principes de son pouvoir." Royaumont, 1958.
"Remarque sur le rapport de Daniel Lagache: 'Psychanalyse et structure de la personnalité." Royaumont, 1958–1960.
"A la mémoire d'Ernest Jones: sur sa théorie du symbolisme." Guitrancourt, 1959.
"Propos directifs pour un Congrès sur la sexualité féminine." Amsterdam, 1960.
★"Subversion du sujet et dialectique du désir dans l'inconscient freudien." Royaumont, 1960.
"Position de l'inconscient." Bonneval, 1960.
"Kant avec Sade." *Critique,* 1962–1963.
"Du 'Trieb' de Freud et du désir du psychanalyste." Rome, 1964.
★"La science et la vérité." Paris, Ecole Normale Supérieure, 1965.

Other works of Lacan include:

Television, 1974. Seminars of Jacques Lacan (text compiled by J.-A. Miller):
Book I: *Les écrits techniques de Freud.* 1975.
Book II: *Le moi dans la théorie de Freud et dans la technique de la psychanalyse.* 1978.
Book XI: *Les quatre concepts fondamentaux de la psychanalyse.* 1973. Translated by Alan Sheridan as *The Four Fundamental Concepts of Psycho-Analysis.* New York: Norton, 1978.
Book XX: *Encore.* 1975.

De la psychose paranoïaque dans ses rapports avec la personnalité, followed by *Premiers écrits sur la paranoïa.* 1975. This is Lacan's thesis in medicine, first published by Le François in 1932. Included are three articles: "Ecrits 'inspirés': schizographie," first published in *Annales medico-psychologiques* in 1931; "Le problème du style et la conception psychiatrique des formes

★ Also included in the English selection.

paranoïaques de l'expérience," and "Motifs du crime paranoïaque, le crime des soeurs Papin," first published in *Le Minotaure* in 1933. The whole collection was republished in 1980 by Skira-Flammarion.

In addition to the works cited above there are extant versions of many papers and comments delivered at one time or another by Lacan. A list of these, undoubtedly incomplete, may be found in the special issue of *Magazine littéraire* devoted to Lacan (February 1977). Strictly speaking, this completes the list of items of which Lacan authorized publication (or republication by Les Editions du Seuil in his *Complete Works*). The following additional articles may be of interest, however:

"La famille, le complexe, facteur concret de la pathologie familiale; les complex familiaux en pathologie," *Encyclopédie française.* Paris: Larousse, 1938, vol. 8.

"Le nombre treize et la forme logique de la suspicion," *Cahiers d'Art,* 1945–1946.

"Maurice Merleau-Ponty," *Les Temps modernes* (1961), pp. 184–85.

"Hommage fait à Marguerite Duras du ravissement de Lol. V. Stein," *Cahiers Renaud-Barrault* (1965), vol. 52. Published by Gallimard.

"Réponses à des étudiants en philosophie," *Cahiers pour l'Analyse,* 1966.

Introduction to Paul Duquenne's translation of Schreber's memoirs, published in *Cahiers pour l'Analyse,* 1966.

Seminar "L'étourdi," 1972, published in *Scilicet.* Paris: Seuil, 1973.

Seminar "Ou pire," published in *Scilicet.* Paris: Seuil, 1975.

"Conférences et entretiens dans des universités nord-américaines." Published in *Scilicet.* Paris: Seuil, 1976.

"Radiophonie," transcription of a radio broadcast, published in *Scilicet.* Paris: Seuil, 1976.

Mention should also be made of notes written by Lacan for inclusion in his various publications, especially for the 1966 edition of *Ecrits:* "Ouverture de ce recueil, de nos antecedents, du sujet enfin en question, d'un syllabaire après coup."

It would be possible to extend this list indefinitely by including the innumerable pirate editions of the master's words, stolen from him—and from his publisher. Of these, the best known, occasionally referred to by Lacan himself, is "Le mythe individuel du névrosé," his essay on Goethe. It is available in a version not approved by Lacan, as are certain other texts not sanctioned by the signature of either Lacan or Miller. Beware of "appellations non-controlées"! On the other hand, it is worth pointing out that Voltaire's essay on the Affaire Callas was also circulated surreptitiously in this way.

Finally, three articles on the history of psychoanalysis and Lacan's relationship to it, which were published in *Ornicar?* are worth mentioning:

"La scission de 1953." With a note by Lacan, 1976.
"L'excommunication." 1977.
"Après la dissolution." 1980.

The foregoing list is not intended to be complete. It reflects the author's personal selection of works related to the arguments put forward in this book.

INDEX